Don't Drink Your Own Kool-Aid

Don't Drink Your Own Kool-Aid

USING A SPIRITUAL GURU
TO WIN YOUR ASCENSION

KIM MICHAELS

Copyright © 2015 Kim Michaels. All rights reserved. No part of this book may be used, reproduced, translated, electronically stored or transmitted by any means except by written permission from the publisher. A reviewer may quote brief passages in a review.

MORE TO LIFE PUBLISHING

www.morepublish.com

For foreign and translation rights,

contact info@ morepublish.com

ISBN: 978-87-93297-14-2

The information and insights in this book should not be considered as a form of therapy, advice, direction, diagnosis, and/or treatment of any kind. This information is not a substitute for medical, psychological, or other professional advice, counseling and care. All matters pertaining to your individual health should be supervised by a physician or appropriate health-care practitioner. No guarantee is made by the author or the publisher that the practices described in this book will yield successful results for anyone at any time. They are presented for informational purposes only, as the practice and proof rests with the individual.

For more information:

www.ascendedmasterlight.com

www.transcendencetoolbox.com

CONTENTS

Foreword by Moira Prophet Siskind 9
Foreword by Tatiana Prophet 15
Foreword by Dr. Richard Bartlett 27
Introduction 35
1 | Why Would You Want to Ascend? 37
2 | What It Really Takes to Ascend 49
3 | How to Get Started on the Spiritual Path 61
4 | The Guru Shows You What You Cannot See 75
5 | Why You Decided to Hide from the Guru 93
6 | How to Free Yourself from the Fallen Beings 107
7 | Knowing What Kind of Planet You Are on 121
8 | How to Actually Remove Evil 131
9 | The Imperfect Myth of the Perfect Guru 145
10 | How to Avoid Abusing a Guru 155
11 | Wanting a Guru to Tell You What to Do 169
12 | The Dangers of Blaming Your Guru 185
13 | Taking Yourself and Life too Seriously 195
14 | Turning a True Guru into a False Guru 213
15 | The Conscious You and the I AM Presence 227
16 | Having no Regrets about Life on Earth 243
17| Why Did This Happen to Me? 257
18 | The Determination to Ascend 267

19 | Why Nothing Can Be Predicted with Certainty 279
20 | The Dilemma Facing Spiritual Movements 293
21 | The Last Steps Towards the Ascension 307
22 | What It Feels Like to Ascend 317
23 | Letting Go in Order to Ascend 329
24 | Dare to Live Your Own Life 341
25 | Love Matters More 355
26 | Recognizing Ascended Masters 357
27 | To My Students—Past, Present and Future 361
28 | Invoking the Presence of Guru Ma 375
29 | Decree to Guru Ma 393
Glossary 397

NOTE: *This book may contain terminology that is not familiar to you. For a definition of unfamiliar terms, please see the Glossary in the back of the book.*

If you are not familiar with the expression "Don't drink the Kool-Aid," it is commonly used in the United States to refer to people who become blinded by an illusion, often created by a strong leader, and cannot see beyond it.

FOREWORD BY MOIRA PROPHET SISKIND

NOTE: *Moira Prophet Siskind is the daughter of Elizabeth Clare Prophet and Mark Prophet.*

Friday, 11/13/15: Day of the Divine Feminine

Over the last 25 years of my adult life, my personal journey with my mother has been fueled by a tender love, which seeks understanding beyond all else. Often she wasn't able to communicate with me through speech. First we were separated by distance and then she was diagnosed with Alzheimer's disease in 1997 and passed away in 2009. At regular intervals, I was there bringing my children to visit. And I was there with her when she passed; but that was just the beginning of the journey.

For those of us who have experienced the passing of a loved one, we talk about sensing if they are near or if they are far, or where they "are." Those feelings are real. And that's what's so beautiful about this book. It confirms what I have come to know in my own heart. When somebody passes, you can "know" in a general sense what they are doing. And that comes from the abiding connection of love. The connection is always there, kindled and enlivened through the feelings we have for that person.

So, I've been tracking my mother, first through her illness – 12 years of Alzheimer's – then through her passing from the physical, and now from beyond, all through love. Often I feel her presence over me through songs on the radio speaking to me, inspirations for my work in teaching, shafts of colors around me or just in the language of synchronicity speaking to me in the perpetual flow of life—being in the right place at the right time. A deep gratitude abides with me for the delightful gifts of her loving presence in my life from beyond the veil of time. And I invite everybody to reach beyond their own grasp, to focus your loving attention without restraint on a question or a being, on yourself or a personal issue, and to be open to the flow of love, which brings knowledge, insight and healing.

Yogananda writes about the power of loving devotion in spiritual inquiry, which opens the flow for the wisdom of the heart. This is how he advises us to read scripture so that we can ascertain the intended meanings. Maybe it's a good way to approach this book.

My sister Tatiana and I have each chosen to embrace *Don't Drink Your Own Kool-Aid* and the teachings of the ascended masters coming through Kim Michaels after experiencing deep personal connection with the material. We can feel this way in loving respect and gratitude for the teachings of the ascended masters as brought through our parents in their lifetimes. They are from the same stream and couldn't exist without the other. We embrace the current reality of our time.

Mother loved to say: "God is no respecter of persons." In other words, the law of the spirit will seek to fulfill itself, water seeks its own level, if it can't come through a door it will find a window and so on. These are important messages for our time, which could not have been given 10, 20 and 30 years ago.

Foreword by Moira Prophet Siskind

Mankind is always evolving with the cosmos and the spiritual teachings available worldwide today are vastly accelerated from when my parents were teaching in their time precisely because they and others like them paved the way.

What we can truly know only comes to us from our personal experience. We have to be able to stand on our own two feet and decide truth for ourselves. This is spiritual development. Spiritual development gives us the ability to recognize truth in all its forms. That's what I learned from my mother. You've got to stand for something and you've got to decide what that is for yourself.

Some say that ascension is when you "graduate" from earth's schoolroom and you no longer "have to" return to earth and take a physical body again because you have completely transcended any attachment to doing so. Or what if like me, you are here by your own choosing? What if you came to earth to help? Yes, you may feel homesick or out of place so to speak but now is our time. Our reason for being keeps us Present, bringing ascending and enlightened consciousness into reality now.

So rather than focus on the "what ifs," I like to go into the inner space of my own heart and connect with what IS, the light intelligence and divine blueprint in all life. And it is here that I recognize my mother's eternal nature and her clear voice in this book.

I have a very personal relationship with my mother, and if you are reading this, maybe you do too. Or maybe you were meant to start one or learn something here from her teaching, her continuing story and her presence in your life. Fortunately, I was able to grow with my mother these last many years through being open to doing so. Otherwise this work may not speak to me, and I wouldn't be able to recognize it from within myself.

I do not believe there is only one messenger for an age or even that once a messenger always a messenger. The spiritual world sends many messengers that come to us throughout the ages and our lives in many forms and on different levels. The famous quote of Master Morya is: "If the messenger be an ant, heed him!" We are given nearly infinite opportunities to listen for wisdom and to respond to the call of the heart.

In a sense, we are all walking messengers, some just more prolific and formalized. We are all broadcasting into the collective, making our contribution. Just sit still and listen to all the "radio towers," or "wifi hubs" around you. It's incredibly loud! Everyone is broadcasting their channel so to speak – walking around with the sum of their experiences, opinions, sensory impressions, soul intelligences and complex emotional and physical desires – and putting them out there.

And what I'll say is this: I like the way Kim Michaels thinks. His words are very clean and direct with minimalist lines. Maybe it's because he's from Denmark. The teachings coming through are progressive and freeing. I look forward to absorbing his work for years to come. He builds on the current body of ascended master revelation as could only be done at precisely this time, now. I've only read this book and he has dozens in print while he churns out more all the time.

It could be said that maybe he has an edge because he's trained as an architect and he can design language and reason on a frame efficiently. He very well could have assimilated my mother's lectures and dictations to such a point that he is a perfect mimic of her speech patterns and syntax—directly related to how thoughts are distilled into language. These are all human aspects which potentially contribute to the lens, the instrument that is uniquely Kim. But if you think it's easy to write as profoundly perfect as he has here, give it a try yourself. Go on, let's see your Theory of Everything, your story, your lessons—put it out there to share! My experience is that it's easier said than done.

Foreword by Moira Prophet Siskind

And of course for me *Don't Drink Your Own Kool-Aid* both in audio and print has been so much, much More, truly a gift from Guru Ma thanks to Kim. He has enabled a voice for her to make sense of the past and to share a clear way towards creating the more conscious future that we desire. It's my belief that this beautiful work has come through Kim because he made himself ready and available to receive it. Kim dictated this book into his recorder in little more than a couple weeks. The sheer volume of work which he has put together at *www.transcendencetoolbox.com* is literally overwhelming for even the quickest speed readers among us (which I am not).

I am grateful to be ready and able to accept this gift with open arms. When we ascend, for me it's total Oneness with all of creation and the being that is the pure spirit fire essence of who we are, increased by the sum of all of our lives and deeds distilled into soul/spirit gold. Can you feel this possibility for yourself right now? We can only take with us what is real and abiding and eternal. And here, Guru Ma through Kim shares her amazing experience of that journey.

*With Tender Love,
Moira Prophet Siskind*

FOREWORD BY TATIANA PROPHET

NOTE: *Tatiana Prophet is the daughter of Elizabeth Clare Prophet and Mark Prophet.*

Every child must separate from her parents. And every soul must eventually separate from the creator and think for himself. That is the goal of free will. I had to do both at a relatively young age, leaving my idyllic childhood and the mother I loved so much at the age of 23. She was not only my mother, but she was my spiritual guru. And when I left, my process had only just begun, for I had to make my way in the world for nearly 17 years—observing, digesting, exploring, thinking and ultimately coming full circle back to my spiritual roots.

It was at the point when I was beginning to pursue a more mindful path that my sister Moira (who had her own journey with our mother) first told me about the book *Don't Drink Your Own Kool-Aid*. I laughed aloud at the title. I knew I had to read it. Not only was it by my mother (from the afterlife), but its title encapsulated the cultural clichés of my childhood in a powerful statement—turned on its ear. And the author was my mother, a larger-than-life public figure who made it her life's work to bring us communications from heaven. Now she was apparently speaking to us from heaven through a new messenger.

For a part of me, this idea was hard to accept. The story of my mother was that of a New Age rise and fall. A spiritual leader and New Age guru to tens of thousands, my mother had led me through an exciting yet chaotic childhood. Life was one crisis after another as I watched her ascend to New Age stardom, and as a very small child, I yearned for normalcy. I even fantasized that other parents in the community would be my parents. Indeed, I was surrounded by many people who raised me as if I were their own, and they showered me with love. When my mother found the time, she also showed me true love, affection and pride; life with a New Age guru was not easy, and it would be decades before I could come to forgive her for seldom putting me first.

Then in the 1990s, my mother essentially threw away her credibility by urging her flock to leave their jobs, move to Montana and prepare for an imminent nuclear war. Yet in spite of this mark on her legacy, there was another part of me that was excited about the idea of this book. I knew my mother to be a superstellar spiritual being who was nevertheless flawed like all of us. In fact, I had often wondered if the shelter episode was not a test for all of us to listen to our higher selves on this one, and not to her. Before even reading the book, I suspected that this was what the title was trying to say.

I had heard other claims of communications beyond the grave from my mother. But I had never felt compelled – or ready – to evaluate any of them. My sister Moira had read and told me about some of them, but Kim Michael's book was the first of the messages from my mother that I actually read. I was finally ready.

As a child, I was innately spiritual and disciplined. I wrote esoteric minimalist poetry. At 5 years of age, I insisted on fasting

Foreword by Tatiana Prophet

for 3 days on nothing but apple juice. While I'm sure imitation was at the heart of my vision quest, that three-day apple juice fast was indicative of how far my dedication went—and this did not waver until I was 21 years old.

All of that changed when our group took a doomsday turn, led by my mother and the messages she took from the ascended masters. After years of obsessive preparations, topped off by a couple of prayer-filled nights in underground bomb shelters, I was left shaken and cynical.

A couple years later, spiritually wounded from the doomsday events, I left the community at 23, knowing I needed to make my way in the world. Leaving was the first big independent decision I had made without my mother's help.

What a long journey it was from the center of the idealistic tahini-eating, carrot-juice drinking, yoga-practicing community that I was born into (as the baby of the family, no less), to the community of one – the cynical hard-driving, hard-living journalist and musician I had become – the woman who believed we didn't need ascended masters, progressive revelation, and most certainly not a guru.

Fast-forward 17 years, and I was sick and bored from overwork, and surfeited in various forms of escape from my past and the trauma of my upbringing. I found myself returning to my spiritual roots, propelled by an intense need for help from something bigger than myself. I was struggling to find my way back to essential truths. And I was finally going through the process of forgiving my mother. At this juncture, I was finally ready to take in messages, like the one inspired by Kim Michaels, that were similar to those I had been brought up with. The title of his book intrigued me. I intuited that it held much promise. And yes, I had to find out if the book actually concluded that one's own "Kool-Aid" was the most potent of all.

As I lay in bed, reading the Kindle version of *Don't Drink Your Own Kool-Aid* on my phone, I laughed with pleasure at the musings of a woman who had once instilled in me serenity and fear along with everything in between, including the highest love one could imagine of a daughter for her mother.

No, I'm not suggesting that this book belongs in the humor section of the bookstore, even though I do believe several passages would fit in well there. But I do think it has the makings of a best-seller in the spiritual self-help category and will likely become a classic among serious spiritual seekers.

Even on the printed page, my mother's personality comes through. If it wasn't "her," it surely felt like her. And I should know because, from the age of 14, it was I who sat in her office for hours on end editing the books she was writing. In this book, I could detect the syntax that marked my mother's style of communication, both in its formal and informal modes. And in it, my mother, now the Ascended Master Guru Ma, was the best of her former self.

For one thing, having been funny while on earth, mostly in her private moments, and sometimes in public, in the book, she has an even better sense of humor about many more things. While reading the book, I felt a radiation of love, light, a buoyancy of spirit, and most of all, hope presented in a humble, direct, and practical manner. More importantly, I was pleased and pleasantly surprised that the book does not shy away from topics I really wanted to hear her discuss. For example, how could a supposedly awakened and nearly perfected guru, such as my mother, deliver messages from the ascended masters that contained errors in judgment colored by her own personality? Guru Ma gives honest explanations that clear up a lot of questions I had, including tough ones like: "How could she, using the name of the ascended masters, admonish her entire congregation to leave their careers, run up credit cards and prepare for a nuclear war as if it were going to happen the very next day?" (For those at home wondering about preparedness, in my humble opinion, preparedness is one thing; rushed preparedness is

Foreword by Tatiana Prophet 🌿 19

another). Her explanation in the book laid to rest my disquietude about why she felt compelled to do this.

Another issue I had trouble with was the way that my mother ran her organization. In the community, my mother rarely relinquished control over anything, and she had a hot temper to boot. There are many to this day who do not understand how she could have been a true guru and been so flawed in her management and interpersonal style. There are many who worked closely with her who have expressed to me that they do not believe she is ascended because of these and other issues. Guru Ma addresses these issues in a refreshing way; but not only does she address them, she reveals that she was able to make her ascension specifically because she underwent the illness of Alzheimer's disease in the last 12 years of her life. She explains that she could have changed the course of events with a change in consciousness:

> It was a symbiotic process where I was a reflection of the consciousness of the students and the students were a reflection of my consciousness. We had a potential to spiral higher together and we did spiral higher together, but we could have gone further. I am not saying this to in any way find fault or place blame. As I have explained in great depth – I hope – when you ascend, you go beyond the need to find fault, you go beyond the need to blame anyone. You also go beyond the need to protect anyone and to wear velvet gloves. The gloves come off, as everything else comes off. You do see reality, and I simply state the reality that I, in my embodiment, did not go as high as I could have. Neither did my students transcend themselves as much as they could have. Had we done so, we could have gone higher together. We could have received a higher level of teaching from

the ascended masters. I could have stayed in my position as a messenger longer, my illness could have been postponed and we could have had more years together with more teachings being brought forth. This did not come to pass. There is no blame, there is no regrets. It was what it was, but the question is, for those who were my students while I was in embodiment and who still have years left in a physical body: "Are you willing to perhaps begin transcending yourself as you could have done but have not yet done? Are you willing to catch up?"

The book also reveals why we, here on earth, need a guru or spiritual teacher outside of ourselves versus the teacher that is already within. I was surprised at how simple the answer was: the ego's filter prevents us from seeing our own foibles. So, until we transcend this aspect of our ego, we need a guru. Eventually, however, there comes a time when we must learn how to think for ourselves. That was the conundrum we dealt with in our community. How do you obey the guru unquestioningly, and still obey your Higher Self? What if your Higher Self says something different? During the shelter episode, I remember observing a few people who told my mother: "We love you and respect you, but we will not be moving to Montana." She accepted these decisions. In the book, Guru Ma tells us that for a time, you need a guru. And then for a time after that, you need to make your own decisions. Who knows how many of us were ready to make our own decisions? But how different would the outcome have been if more of us had succeeded in thinking for ourselves?

Guru Ma points out that a true guru is tailored specifically for your personality and spiritual growth. That guru can take the form of someone we would not expect. What matters is whether that guru is getting us to see ourselves as we truly are.

Foreword by Tatiana Prophet

And, she says, what is also important is not so much what the guru says or does; what matters is how you react to your guru. At the end of the day, Guru Ma points out:

> You will not make or break your ascension by drinking my Kool-Aid or not drinking my Kool-Aid. You will only make your ascension when you stop drinking your own Kool-Aid.

And to think that for 17 years I had decided we did not need ascended masters, gurus or even the goal of the ascension. In fact, in my 20s, I had decided that dictations from the ascended masters were an outdated, perhaps never even necessary, mode of spirituality. In my own personal Martin Luther move, I decided that all that mattered was the relationship with yourself. Yet Guru Ma explains why all of that is important in a fresh, new way.

Even during those years in the "wilderness" when all I had was a desire to be self-aware (no desire for a guru or to make my ascension), I still I wondered: how do I see my own blind spots? Gaining the understanding from this book that a true guru does not need to be perfect because what matters is your reaction to the guru, changed everything for me because this was not the way I was brought up.

In life, my mother put forth the idea that, like Mary Poppins, she had to be practically perfect in every way. She addresses this topic in the book, saying that according to most who seek a guru: "any person who makes a claim [to be a guru] had better be perfect." The book even nails the nuance that many of her followers paid lip service to her imperfections, yet could not shake the belief that she should be free of mistakes—especially big ones. Surprisingly, in the book, my mother admits that she welcomed this attitude toward her. She explains that she "thought that the masters were perfect, and in order to be a worthy messenger and worthy representative of the ascended masters, I had to be perfect, or at least I had to strive for perfection." As a newly ascended master, she admits, "this was clearly an unbalanced state."

There are many people to this day who believe that my mother could not have been unbalanced about anything—even when what she said was contrary to their own Higher Self (if they were at the point of being able to discern their Higher Self from their ego). Making your guru perfect, then, means you are drinking your own Kool-Aid, Guru Ma tells us, because you are objectifying the guru and not truly seeing the guru. How could you, when you are focused on your own ideas of what a guru should be? My mind was officially blown when I grasped this concept.

My mother's fall from grace, and the cynicism I as her daughter subsequently descended into, are at the heart of this book and its title—and only half the reason it is so satisfying. The other half has to do with the astounding revelations it makes regarding life on this planet as a spiritual being.

One of my favorite passages in the book deals with the idea of an angry, vindictive God—which has no place in reality. Guru Ma asks:

> How do we gain access to this wonderful kingdom of this wonderful God? We have to live up to some superhuman standard of perfection. If we do, it will be thumbs up and God or Saint Peter will let us in. If not, it will be thumbs down and we will burn forever in hell. Quite a tough situation, I would say. If you do not live up to a superhuman standard of perfection, the only other option is that you burn in hell—forever, and ever and ever. ... If you do not live up to the superhuman standard of perfection, you are not even worthy to ask for God's help...

Foreword by Tatiana Prophet

There is no need for her to elaborate; the preposterousness of the angry God stands on its own. She handles this idea with such grace and humor in the book that I was stunned.

Guru Ma predicts that those who denounce the book will be her staunchest followers. And she has been proven right. It is hard to know what to say to those who believe there is yet no messenger forthcoming to follow in my mother's footsteps, particularly when that is exactly what my parents did. They picked up where Guy and Edna Ballard and Geraldine Innocente left off. In fact, Guru Ma points out that in the Aquarian Age there will be many messengers versus a single messenger, to appeal to the diversity of the masses who resonate with different types of individuals. This book resonates with me not only because I recognize my mother's voice in it, but because it addresses many concepts I have often contemplated.

Guru Ma takes the teaching of karma to a whole new level, and at the same time clears up the apparent callousness of the attitude she had espoused in her last life when misfortune befell her followers—the idea that this was their karma. She freely admits this was a callous attitude, and explains a new wrinkle in the karmic veil. Without giving the book away, I will give you a taste of her explanation. She shows us that before karma becomes physical, it can manifest in higher levels, and never has to reach the physical if our consciousness is raised. Guru Ma explains that:

> There is no ascended master, no member of the Karmic Board and no judgmental God up here in the ascended realm who is looking down upon you and evaluating what you deserve based on you being such a bad person. In the ascended realm there is no judgment, no condemnation, no sense of guilt. What you did in the past was to experiment with your co-creative abilities. This is exactly what God

gave you the right to do and what God wants you to do. ... The purpose is that you generate an impulse that is returned by the cosmic mirror. By experiencing the return, you can evaluate simply: "Do I want more of this, or don't I want more of this?" If you don't want more, you know you have to refine your consciousness so that you do not continue to send out the same kind of impulses. If you want something that is better, something that is higher, then you know you have to raise your consciousness.

Above all, the most important practical piece of spiritual knowledge that I have received from Guru Ma, with the invaluable aid of Kim Michaels, is that we don't have to feel bad – about anything – anymore. With the above explanation, and others, we realize: a) nothing is done that cannot be undone, and b) we need to take ourselves a lot less seriously because it's really not all about us.

This book left me with a wonderful, buoyant sense of comfort—a buoyancy I once felt as a child. I now feel awake and spiritual on the heels of separating out from my physical and spiritual parents. Another little tidbit I discovered was that, according to this book, my mother finally made her ascension on July 4, 2012. It so happens that right around that time was when I was able to connect with the soul of my mother and finally forgive her.

I still have a lot to learn, yet I feel wiser after having come full circle into an understanding of why I choose to help raise up the planet, why I choose to pursue the ascension, and why I choose to help free the planet from control by those who think they know better than God and the miracle of free will.

It is a goal well worth the inconvenience.

Tatiana Prophet
November 2015
Pacific Palisades, California

FOREWORD BY DR. RICHARD BARTLETT

NOTE: *Dr. Richard Bartlett ND, DC was the personal physician of Elizabeth Clare Prophet.*

I have been a student of the ascended masters for over 30 years. My Journey of Discovery began in a very bizarre fashion on the occasion of my marriage to my first wife. After the wedding, I traveled with my new spouse to Phoenix, Arizona to meet her sister. While I was there I happened to wander into a quaint little out of the way bookshop, browsing to see if anything sparked my interest. I was about to leave when an 'inner voice' instructed me to ask if there was something there that I needed to be aware of. Instantly, my eyes fell upon a fake leather binder on the bottom of a slightly dusty shelf.

Trusting that this might be important, I plucked up the large, fake leather, white folder, which bizarrely had swastikas and poorly drawn stick figures scrawled on it in blue ink. Upon opening this somewhat dubious treasure, I was shocked to discover that it contained a number of lessons from a group of beings that were called the Ascended Masters of the Great White Brotherhood! Scanning the pages,

I felt an inexplicable wave of Peace, coupled with a growing excitement that enveloped me. I could hardly wait to get home and explore these well-hidden treasures in detail!

Returning home, I began reading the lessons carefully and with due reverence, absorbed their content. I was introduced to beings with names that were strange, yet somehow comfortingly familiar. El Morya, Saint Germain, Kuthumi and many more. This was so exciting that it was like falling in love for the very first time all over again, yet somehow deeper in a soul-nourishing way that earthly romance could never fulfill! I was beginning to find my way home to the heart of God!

In the back of this book of lessons was an address where you could contact the organization that had published the book for more material. Without hesitation, I ordered the new material and somewhat anxiously awaited its arrival in the mail. When it finally came, I was in for a heart-wrenching shock! As I eagerly started to read the new material, I instantly knew that whatever had breathed life into those old lessons I had so lovingly read, was simply not there in this new material, not at all. This was dead, it had none of the spirit that permeated the old manuscript I had found. To say I was heartbroken doesn't even begin to express what I was feeling. Little did I know at the time, but I had just passed a crucial test of spiritual discernment. There is a saying that God will not leave you comfortless, and also that when the student is ready, the Teacher appears. Several weeks later, she did!

My first wife was a teacher in a School of Metaphysics that was loosely founded on a series of spiritual disciplines and exercises, many of which I later discovered came from the Self-Realization Fellowship founded by Paramahansa Yogananda. Included in the school's curriculum were specific exercises in meditation and concentration. One exercise I faithfully practiced was a candle concentration exercise. In this exercise you were to relax and stare gently at a candle flame. Every time your mind was distracted from contemplation of the flame, you were to make a mark on a piece of paper conveniently situated in front of you. The idea was to, over time, be able to reduce the number of mental distractions recorded over a ten minute (initial) period of candle contemplation.

One day, several weeks after the crushing disappointment centered around realizing that the new lessons I had received in the mail were not of the same quality and vibration, I happened to enter a health food store and spa. While browsing, I spied a back room through a crack in a partially open door. On the wall was a large poster that looked somehow like my candle concentration exercise. I asked the store owner if the poster in the back room was some version of this now familiar exercise. She laughed gently and told me: "That is a chart of your I Am Presence." It is a teaching about the nature of your 'Higher Self' as taught by the ascended masters.

As soon as I heard the words "ascended masters" I simply had to know more! The store owner informed me that her teacher, Elizabeth Clare Prophet, was giving a seminar that weekend right in this city. She handed me a leaflet that included a picture of Elizabeth Clare Prophet and a brief, personal invitation that she signed: "I Am Guru Ma." I must say, somewhat sheepishly now, I was not impressed! I remember huffing under my breath: "I Am Guru Ma! So what! Just who do you think you are, lady?" However, I did buy El Morya's book, *The Chela and the Path*.

The night of the event, which was being held at the convention center in downtown Oklahoma City, I had a lucid dream where I was running barefoot through the streets of downtown frantically asking everyone I met if they could help me find where Guru Ma was speaking!

Nine months later, give or take, I was standing outside in a long line waiting to see the premiere of the Led Zeppelin movie with my wife and my sister, when I heard a deep commanding voice say to me in my mind: "Look at these people, they are like dumb driven cattle! Follow not them, follow thou Me! Excelsior!"

I repeated, word for word, what I had just heard to my wife and sister and we left! The next day, a Sunday, we all drove to the Summit Lighthouse study group in Oklahoma City. Standing at the podium in this little blue house was Dr. Jacque Rowe, who turned out to be a clairvoyant Chiropractor and my first mentor in the Healing Arts! I later became the Vice President of that study group and a dedicated student of the ascended masters.

Fast forward a few years and I am attending chiropractic school in Dallas, Texas. During the first semester of school, my son Nathaniel was born with bronchitis, allergies, and terrible recurring bouts of pneumonia of occasionally life-threatening proportions. After trying all that my chiropractic instructors had to offer, and having exhausted the traditional medical treatment avenues, I concluded that my son was born to me and so it was my responsibility to heal him. In my third year of chiropractic school, I found a technique Master who taught me some very cutting edge techniques that allowed me to do exactly that! Returning home from that seminar, I did what I was shown and in 30 minutes, after three agonizing years of searching for an answer, my son was healed! God does hear and answer our prayers! Little did I know that at the same time I was experiencing the answer to my prayers, Elizabeth Clare Prophet, the very same Guru Ma, was praying for an answer to her health problems! Little did either of us expect at the time how wonderfully the answers to both of our prayers were intricately linked and intertwined!

After I graduated, I moved to Montana expressly to be close to Elizabeth Clare Prophet, and I even had some curious idea that she needed the powerful skill sets I had garnered in the Healing Arts in search of a cure for my son. Listen to your heart when it speaks, heed it whenever you can, and your life will be blessed beyond comprehension! I listened and obeyed. I will not tell you it was easy or without some intense personal trials, but eventually Elizabeth Clare Prophet asked to meet with me. She had reports from her staff and many individuals about this chiropractor with very unusual skills. First she sent Erin Prophet, her oldest daughter, to check me out. Two days after meeting Erin I was summoned to meet Mother, as we all called her, and the rest, as they say, is history.

That first night I treated her, I stayed and worked on her all night long. In fact, Mother and I saw the sun rise together as I was just completing this Herculean endeavor of Healing Love. Mother told me then: "Richard, I have need of you. Will you come join my personal staff?" She meant that same day! I told her I would, although humanly it was not something I really thought would be very much fun. I was wrong! For eight years, sometimes day and night, I was by her side. Elizabeth suffered from debilitating hypoglycemia, fatigue, and even occasional seizures. We had an intense doctor-patient, Guru-chela relationship, and a loving personal friendship. During those eight years, I came to know her better than most people would ever have the opportunity to experience. I saw the glory of her 'Christ Mind' as a true representative and messenger of the ascended masters. I also saw her human personality, with all of the quirks and imperfections that we all, yes even gurus, are prone to within the parameters of the human condition. I am sharing with you how well I knew her so that you can hear what I am about to say, as it might just be one of the most important statements I will ever make.

Elizabeth Clare Prophet died after a bout with a diagnosis of Alzheimer's in 2009. Over the years after her passing I went on with my life, and in many ways I distanced myself from the intense disciplines and rigors of the spiritual path I had willingly subjected myself to under Guru Ma's direction. I moved on with my life and left that intense period with Elizabeth Claire Prophet behind me. However, as I have already stated, when the student is ready, the Master(s) appear; again! You see, God will not leave the earth's children without ongoing guidance and the Spirit of Continuous Revelation. Recently one of Guru Ma's former students left a personal message on my Facebook page that Kim Michaels had written a book that was dictated to him by Guru Ma. That book is this very book that you now are reading. Within the first chapter I knew, beyond any shadow of a doubt, that this book was indeed dictated by my very own Beloved Elizabeth! The tears flowed unrestrictedly down my face as I wept with gratitude. Immediately it all came rushing back: Mother, the ascended masters, the reality and immediacy of the personal spiritual path!

The more I read with loving astonishment, the more I knew that this was her, the living Ascended Master, my beloved friend and Guru! As I write this, tears are flowing again! This was a Guru Ma the world had never seen. She was talking very frankly about the mistakes she had made, the stubbornness of her all too human ego, and the many things she perhaps could have done differently. Here was the very private woman that I had the great pleasure and amazing opportunity to know deeply. Here was the very same being who had spoken frankly and often to me about her emotions, her regrets, her private concerns. Even the language patterns that she used in these powerful dictated pages were identical to the wondrously complex woman I had known so well.

Many in the former activity that I was associated with have clung to the old teachings and dispensations, thinking perhaps that a rote performance of spiritual mantras, coupled with a rigid and somewhat inflexible set of disciplines would save them or help them to win their ascension. But, as Guru Ma explains within these pages, the River of Life flows ever on, always with the drive to be MORE. Kim Michaels is an authentic Messenger of the ascended masters who has been entrusted to bring to the world their ever-transcendent progressive Spirit of Revelation. Please do not cling to an outmoded, though revered, spiritual tradition. The ascended masters have moved on and their message in this dispensation has transcended the limitations of the previous rigid model under Elizabeth Clare Prophet. The Living Ascended Master is speaking right now to you in the pages of this incredible book dictated to her chosen messenger, Kim Michaels! Aren't you curious as to what the living master has to share with you? Read on and prepare for your life to move into a divine, ever-upward spiral of momentum! Jump with both feet into the Living River of Life!

Dr. Richard Bartlett ND, DC
Founder of Matrix Energetics
Grateful student of the ascended masters!

INTRODUCTION

You do not ascend by taking action on earth. You ascend by *reflecting* on the actions you have taken, and the actions you have *not* taken, on earth.

Without taking action there is nothing to reflect upon. Without the reflection there is no self-transcendence. Without self-transcendence there is no ascension.

The ascension comes when you have reflected upon your actions, come to understand the self that was the foundation for those actions and you have then decided: "I AM more than this self. I no longer want to be this self. I will let it die so that I can be reborn as *more*."

I AM the Ascended Master Guru Ma. I am a recently ascended master, having ascended on July 4, 2012. I am giving this and the following teachings precisely because I have ascended so recently. There are people on earth who believe that once you ascend, you have attained some state of perfection. The outer mind, the intellectual mind, wants to believe that if you are perfect, you cannot change. The ascension does not mean a static state of perfection; the ascension means that you rise through a much swifter process of growth and learning than what you can experience on earth.

Truly, it can be said that when you ascend is when the process of growth really begins. As an ascended master, you grow very rapidly. You quickly transcend the state of consciousness you had immediately after your ascension, and in a short period of time – measured with earth years – you have moved very far beyond the state of consciousness, the sense of self, that you had while you were still in embodiment on earth.

When you have been an ascended master for a short period of time, as measured with earth time, you have gone so far beyond the state of consciousness people have on earth that you can barely remember what it was like for yourself to be in embodiment. This makes it somewhat more difficult to speak directly to the people who are still in embodiment. This is precisely why it has been determined by our councils that *I* should be the one to step forward and give this series of discourses on what it means to ascend, what it means to be a newly ascended master, what it means to be in your last embodiment and what you have to go through in order to qualify for your ascension.

I have also been selected to give these discourses because in my last embodiment on earth I was a public figure. My name was Elizabeth Clare Prophet, and I was known as the leader of a New Age spiritual movement, named the Summit Lighthouse or Church Universal and Triumphant. My wonderful "admirers" in the press loved to call it "CUT." CUT was the name they gave us and it was indeed an amusement, although I must say it is far more amusing today than while I was in embodiment. Of course, everything that happened to me on earth is far more amusing today than while I was in embodiment—and so it will be for you after you ascend.

1 | WHY WOULD YOU WANT TO ASCEND?

What does it mean to ascend? It means that you transcend the self you had while you were on earth. It is precisely the self you have right now that makes you take seriously the conditions you encounter on earth. It is the self you have that makes you attached to certain things or conditions on earth. It is the self that makes you feel burdened by what you encounter on earth. The ascension is the process of shedding this self so that none of its cares and attachments mean anything to you anymore.

Non-attachment to what people think

I know this will sound harsh to some people. I know that many of the people who knew me while I was in embodiment will want to maintain the view of me that they had or still have. It does not matter whether they count themselves as my faithful followers and accept me as a genuine spiritual teacher or whether they count themselves as my critics, having adopted a negative view of who I was and what I did. Many people are still attached to the view they had of me.

They will want to maintain that view, and therefore they will not want me, the ascended master that I am now, to come and disturb them in their view of me. I actually have no intention of disturbing anyone's view of me. I am not here to explain, apologize for or make light of anything I did or did not do in my last embodiment. If I had any desire to affect any person on earth or to change their view of me, I would not be an ascended master. You cannot ascend if you are concerned about your public image in your last embodiment. Then you will have to take another incarnation, seeking to overcome your attachment to your public image. You ascend only when you have overcome all of your attachments to anything that happens on earth or to the way human beings in embodiment on earth look at you or anything that you did or did not do.

Attachment is not the same as love

Again, I know that some of those who knew me in my last embodiment will feel that this is harsh. Those who see themselves as my faithful followers will want to feel that I still care about them. They will want me to uphold their image of me. It is not that ascending makes you *not* love people on earth. When you ascend, you transcend all *attachments* to any person on earth. Even those who were your family or close friends and associates in your last embodiment need to be transcended, or at least your *attachment* to them needs to be transcended.

This does not mean that you do not love them, but you do not love them in a human sense. You do not love them as they see themselves. You love them for how *you* see them, now that your consciousness is freed from the mental box – the perception filter, the self – that you have in the unascended state.

Anyone and everyone who is still in a physical body – regardless of their level of attainment – still have a perception filter that must be transcended in the process of the ascension.

There is no one who ever *has* ascended while retaining the slightest portion of the earthly perception filter. No one ever *will* ascend and take any aspect of the human with them into the ascended realm.

The challenge of being an ascended master

It is a fundamental challenge that when you have become an ascended master, you have shed the perception filters that human beings still have on earth. How do you communicate with human beings who are trapped in a variety of different perception filters? How do you communicate to them what it is like *not* to have a perception filter, not to be blinded by this coloring of the human self? How do you make people understand what you would so like them to understand, namely the incredible freedom and joy it is to shed this human self and rise into the clarity, the purity and the ineffable, infinite joy of the ascended state?

Consider that you have a person who has been blind from birth. You take that person to the beach in the evening, and you stand there and you are looking at the beautiful sunset. You are describing to the blind person how the sun turns red and plays hide-and-seek behind the dark clouds. You are attempting to be as poetic as you can be in describing the beautiful scenery, but the person has been blind from birth. How can that person truly relate to what you are describing? How could the person ever, in his or her mind, have an experience similar to the experience you are having by looking at the sunset?

Now imagine that you took this person, who had been blind from birth, and you were able to restore the sight so that the person could now experience the sunset. Then, the person's mind and heart would be opened to a direct experience rather than having to relate to the sunset through your description. Not only is your description based on *your* experience, which is different from the way the other person might experience the sunset, but more importantly, your description is translated into words and words are by nature limited. They are not so well suited for describing a deeper inner experience. For that matter, words are not so suited for describing a sensory experience.

Try describing the taste of your favorite food to someone who has never tasted it. You will immediately begin comparing the taste to something the person *has* tasted, but what if the person had never tasted anything? How would you then describe this taste? If a human being has never had any experience that resembles what you experience in the ascended state, how can you even begin to describe what it is like to be in the ascended state? This is a fundamental difficulty that you do not actually fully acknowledge and appreciate until you have ascended.

Ascended masters are so much more

While I was in embodiment on earth – and while I was in the position of a spiritual teacher that was looked up to by thousands of people in an organization – I was rather convinced that I had a good grip on what it meant to be an ascended master. I felt that I could give a good worded description of who El Morya was and what he was like. I would have claimed with absolute conviction that my perception of El Morya and my description of him was quite accurate. I would not necessarily have claimed that it was the fullness of who El Morya is, but I certainly would have claimed that it was a fairly accurate description.

Now that I have ascended, I have experienced that El Morya is so much more than what I conceived him to be while I was in embodiment that it truly defies description. I now see that I was like the blind person relying on a description of the sunset. Sure, I had direct encounters with the ascended master that I saw as El Morya, but I had only experienced him through the perception filter that I still had while in embodiment. I was not as open as I could have been to acknowledging that he is far more than I could possibly experience while still in embodiment on earth. Why is this so?

How do you truly experience Master MORE? You experience him by coming into oneness with his Presence, and this is something you cannot fully do while you are in physical embodiment. You are still seeing everything through your perception filter. Only when you shed that perception filter, and are free to be who you really are, can you fully come into oneness with Master MORE. Only when you know that *you* are more, will you know how much more he is. You will know this only by experiencing.

I am today an ascended being. I have experienced that Master MORE is so much more than I could ever envision before, but yet I have not experienced the fullness of Master MORE. Every time I come into oneness with him, I experience a new facet of this being, whom I still admire as my greatest teacher, sponsor and example.

I also know that the moment I have been in oneness with him and go back to focusing on my own further growth as an ascended master, then Master MORE has already transcended himself. The next time I focus my attention upon his Presence and come into oneness with him, he is *more*—and that is precisely why he changed his name to Master MORE.

How do you want to relate to ascended masters?

Many will reject this and say that an ascended master could not change his name. Many will reject that I am the real, ascended Guru Ma. Ironically, most of those who will reject this dictation as genuine are those who claim to be my most devout followers. How can you be one of my true followers if you will not recognize that as an ascended master I have transcended not only who I was – who I saw myself as when I was in embodiment – I have also transcended who *you* saw me as and who you still see me as.

Do you want to continue to relate to me through the *images* that you formed in your mind, either based on your direct experiences of me or based on someone else's description that you may have read or heard? I know well that many will want to cling to their mental image for yet another while. I have no attachment to this. I set you free to hold on to your image of me if that is what you desire.

It is not my intention with this series of discourses to reach out only to those who knew me while I was in embodiment. It is my intention to set forth a teaching that can help a broad spectrum of spiritual seekers, both now and in the coming times, who might find this book.

Your motivation for wanting to ascend

What does it truly mean to ascend? Well, it means something that cannot be described in words. How do we of the ascended masters motivate people in embodiment to strive for the ascension?

Without striving for the ascension, it cannot be attained, although it is not the striving that brings about the ascension. No matter how hard you strive, you cannot *force* your ascension, but neither will it be achieved without striving. This is another enigma that words are not so suitable for conveying.

Let us instead consider the question that everything human beings do starts with a motivation, a desire. If you are to put forth an effort directed at attaining something called the ascension, you must have a desire to ascend. It is impossible to convey with words the fullness of what it means to be in the ascended state. It is, however, possible for a human being in embodiment to have some glimpse of an experience of the ascended consciousness. This is what has often been called a spiritual or mystical experience. There is a great variety of them, and I would say that a substantial part of the people who are today involved in spiritual movements or spiritual activities have had such experiences. Many are not necessarily fully aware of the experiences or what they mean, but there has been some direct experience that there is a state of consciousness beyond what is called normal human awareness.

It must, however, be recognized that in this day and age we of the ascended masters have been allowed, by the Karmic Board and cosmic councils, to give forth a teaching that is given in a public forum. The teaching is disseminated through words – in books or on websites – and this means that anyone can find these teachings. It should be recognized that it is quite possible to have an interest in spiritual matters that is primarily based on intellectual reasoning and understanding—not so much on direct experience.

Beyond intellectual curiosity

Many of the spiritual seekers you see out there are driven by curiosity. They want to know, they want to understand. They sense that there must be more to know about life than what they were told as they were growing up, be it from church, state or the educational system. They sense that there are answers to the questions about life and they are willing to look beyond traditional sources to find such answers. Virtually all spiritual seekers have this intellectual curiosity, this intellectual interest in understanding the spiritual side of life.

It should be noted that if you are to ascend, you are going through a process that takes you more and more away from *understanding* spiritual topics and more and more towards *experiencing* a higher state of consciousness. If you look at my parable about the blind person hearing a description of the sunset, you will see that this person is relating to the sunset through words. It is relating to something that is external to its inner experience. The words may trigger a certain inner experience, but it is also possible that the person continues to relate to the phenomenon only as an external, remote phenomenon that it knows only through a description given with words.

Teachings that will not help you ascend

There are many spiritual and religious teachings on earth that are meant to give people only a *description* of the spiritual side of life. Such teachings do *not* come from the ascended masters. The teachings that do not seek to take you beyond words are given from a lower level than the ascended level. It may be from the lower levels of the etheric or identity octave, it may be from the mental realm, it may be from the emotional realm, also called the astral realm, or it may be from the level of human beings in embodiment.

These teachings are given by beings who have not yet ascended, and that means they have not transcended the consciousness where you relate to something from a distance, where you relate to everything through a perception filter. These teachings do not have the goal to set you free from all human perception filters. They actually have as their goal to imprison you in a certain perception filter. They give you the belief that either this is the absolutely highest possible perception filter or it is the one that will guarantee your salvation after this lifetime. The effect is that you give your energies to the very beings who produced the outer teaching. You become the ones who feed them with energy, the energy that they cannot obtain from within themselves because they have not been willing to transcend their separate selves.

We of the ascended masters have been willing to transcend our separate selves, and therefore we have no desire to have you relate to us, to God or to the spiritual reality through a description given by words. It has never been our goal to give an outer teaching that becomes a substitute for direct inner experience. This is a point that it can be very difficult for people in embodiment to fully grasp and accept.

How you make your own Kool-Aid

In all honesty, I never fully grasped and accepted this while I was in embodiment myself. This is due to the fact that while I was in embodiment, I had spent a very large amount of time, energy and attention on not only pursuing the spiritual path for my own growth but on teaching that path. I served for decades as a messenger for the ascended masters, as the head of a sizable spiritual organization and as a spiritual teacher who brought forth many teachings.

Throughout all of that time, I was motivated by my true desire to help people ascend. I was focused on bringing forth a teaching that had the highest possible ability to bring people to the ascension. It was my hope to bring forth a teaching, an organization and a set of practices that could take almost any student and bring that student to the point of having qualified for his or her ascension.

All of my time, attention and energy for over forty years were fed into this goal. What happens when you feed so much energy and attention into a particular goal is that you build a certain sense of self. This self can have many components, but if your goal is to bring forth a teaching, an organization and a set of practices that can take people to the ascension, then you are building a sense of self as a teacher who is accomplishing or has accomplished this goal.

You want to believe that your outer structure can fulfill your desire. You look at the vastness of the teaching that has been brought forth. You look at the profundity of the teachings. You look at the efficiency of the decrees that were given by so many people for so many hours at so many services. You begin to – if I may use a popular expression – drink you own Kool-Aid. You begin to feel convinced that this actually *does* work, that your teaching *is* bringing people closer to their ascension.

This is both true and untrue, and this is a point that all sincere spiritual seekers can benefit greatly from pondering. I know very well that a substantial part of the people who might read this teaching will not be able to grasp it at first. I also know that if you are willing to contemplate this, along with the teachings I will give later and other teachings we have given, then you *will* eventually grasp it.

What did I say in my introduction? It is not the actions you take that will qualify you for your ascension, but neither will you qualify without making an effort. This is the enigma faced by all spiritual students. Just as I – as a leader and teacher – drank my own Kool-Aid and wanted to believe that all students who followed my teachings would qualify for their ascension, so were there many among my followers, my students, who drank that Kool-Aid.

They wanted to believe that having found this organization, having found this teaching – having practiced the decrees for so many years and hours, having been on staff, having taken courses at Summit University, having gone to conferences, having done all of these other activities – they had surely qualified for their ascension. The reality is that for some people the activities they had done had indeed brought them closer to their ascension. Yet, the activities themselves could not bring them through the gateway to the ascended state.

The gap between the unascended and ascended state

The gap between the ascended and the unascended state of consciousness is huge. It is so huge that there is absolutely no way you can fathom this when you first find the spiritual path. You could say that even we of the ascended masters are engaging in a certain form of deception when we give teachings to unascended students. If we were to tell you how big the difference is between the unascended and the ascended state, most students would become discouraged and feel it was hopeless. Why even bother trying when the gap is so huge that it seems almost impossible to cross?

This is a mechanism that is built into the human ego and which the false teachers are very skilled at taking advantage of. It is not for nothing that it has been said that discouragement is the sharpest tool in the devil's toolkit. We must therefore give you a somewhat optimistic view of what it requires to make your ascension. Certainly, the organization that I was the leader of for so many years did give an optimistic view of what it takes to qualify for the ascension. This does not mean that it was an erroneous view, but it does mean that it was a view that could be read by *anyone* but that did not apply to *everyone*.

There were some people who could find the organization and the outer teachings – who could study the teachings, follow the practices, engage in the organization – and through those outer practices they would balance so much karma and consume so much misqualified energy in their four lower bodies that they would rise much higher in consciousness and therefore come close to the ascended state. There were also some people who could find the outer teachings – who could study them diligently, who could give decrees for hours upon hours, who could take active part in the activities of the organization, often serve on staff for years or decades – and yet they did not actually come closer to qualifying for their ascension. At least they did not come to that stage where they had fulfilled the outer requirements for the ascension.

The reason was that these students kept engaging in the path through the outer, intellectual perception filter. They kept looking at the path as an *external* process that required them to do outer things, but it did not require them to do the one thing that Jesus – 2,000 years ago – said was the key, namely to look at the beam in your own eye.

A spiritual teaching cannot help everyone

I would have been reluctant to admit this while I was still in embodiment, for I so wanted to be able to help everyone. The fact is that a substantial portion of the people who found the teachings – who joined the organization, who did all of the outer things right – did not make decisive progress towards their ascension despite all of their efforts. The reason was that they still looked at the path of the ascended masters as an *outer* path. They thought that by doing the outer things, they would *automatically* shift their consciousness without having to directly look at themselves.

There were also a substantial part of the students who *did* understand the need to look at themselves and who did so all along, as they were engaging in the outer practices and studying the teaching. These were the students who made progress, and many of them have already qualified for their ascensions in an outer sense. Many of them can do so in this embodiment even by following the teachings given and engaging in the organization as it is today.

2 | WHAT IT REALLY TAKES TO ASCEND

Regardless of the outer practices, there is a requirement for the ascension which was not sufficiently documented, explained, understood or accepted in the organizational culture. This was due to the fact that I, myself, had not sufficiently understood this point.

As long as you are still in embodiment, you are looking at everything through a perception filter. There are only two relevant questions here. Number one: "How dense is your perception filter?" Number two: "How attached to it are you, how willing are you to look beyond your perception filter?"

The danger of being in a position of leadership, of being in a position as a teacher, is that you so want to believe that your teaching really can help people that you can become attached to your own perception filter. You believe what you want to believe, namely that the outer teaching, the outer structure, is enough for people to qualify for the ascension.

The subtlety is that the outer teaching, brought forth by Mark and myself, *is* sufficient for many people to fulfill the outer requirements for the ascension. The decrees given through us by the ascended masters are sufficient for many people to balance enough karma that they qualify for their ascension. Engaging in the other practices and organizational activities was sufficient for certain people to qualify by fulfilling the outer requirements. *Yet the ascension is not a mechanical process.* You cannot define a set of outer teachings and practices that will automatically guarantee that anyone who applies them will ascend.

There *is* a set of outer requirements that were described accurately through the organization and the teachings: You must balance at least 51 percent of your karma. You must fulfill a certain portion of your divine plan, your sacred labor. Nevertheless, these outer requirements are not enough to bring you through the shift in consciousness from the unascended to the ascended state. Why is this so? Because the transition from the unascended to the ascended state is a shift *in consciousness.*

It is not a matter of fulfilling outer requirements. It is a matter of you going within, looking at the beam in your own eye, looking at the sense of self you have and coming to the recognition that you are more than this self and that you no longer want to be limited by this self and its perception filter. Do you understand, at least intellectually, what I am seeking to convey here? *Do you begin to understand this?*

Your personal requirements for the ascension

Take my own example: I learned about the ascension at a fairly early age by meeting Mark Prophet. I learned about the requirements. I had a somewhat somber assessment given to me by El Morya of what it would take for me to personally balance the karma I had made in past lives and qualify for my ascension. I knew at a fairly early age that this would require a substantial effort from me. It would require studying and understanding certain teachings. It would require me to give a certain amount of decrees, both violet flame and others. It would also require me to give a certain amount of service to other people whom I had wronged in past lives.

I knew that qualifying for my ascension was an all-consuming process that would require total dedication and substantial amounts of effort. There is no question that this was a requirement. I needed to do those things, to give that service, in order to qualify for my personal ascension. What I did not fully understand – through those decades of being so focused on this service – was that by giving this service I was actually building and reinforcing a certain "self." I built a self not only as a spiritual leader and teacher but also as a person who was eagerly following the spiritual path and applying myself with a certain intensity.

The intensity that I put into my path also translated into creating the intensity of the self that I built as I was walking that path. Now, understand the subtlety. I could *not* have walked my personal path, I could not have fulfilled the outer requirements for my ascension, without having had that self. If you want a metaphor, then consider, as has so often been said in Buddhic teachings, that the human condition is like the Sea of Samsara.

You are here on one shore. In front of you is the Sea of Samsara and you need to cross to the other shore in order to make your ascension. In order to navigate this turbulent Sea of Samsara without being "driven by the wind and tossed," without drowning in the ocean of the astral sea, you need to have a vessel, a vehicle, a boat. That boat needs to be strong enough so that it can take you – given who you are and where you are at in consciousness – safely across the Sea of Samsara.

It is *absolutely* necessary that you have such a boat. You see many people who find the spiritual path in some form and who make an effort to make progress, but who are derailed by various things in their psychology. They simply do not have a strong enough vessel that they can navigate their own personal

Sea of Samsara. They cannot withstand the waves and the winds sent by the fallen beings and the false teachers, and they cannot navigate the sea sent by the mass consciousness. The reason being that a lot of the turbulence you experience on your path is created by your own subconscious mind, by your past momentums, your psychology, your *unresolved* psychology.

How to resolve your psychology

One could ask: "Can't you stay on this side of the sea and resolve your psychology before you start to cross the sea?" This is not the way to cross the sea. In order to cross the Sea of Samsara, you cannot simply stand on the shore, for in reality there is no shore. You are already in the sea so you must sink or swim. If you do not have a strong enough sense of self to carry you through the turbulence, you will not make it. You will be pulled down by a maelstrom of your own unresolved substance or the external opposition created by the mass consciousness and the false hierarchy, the dark forces that seek to derail the progress of anyone on this earth.

Spiritual growth is a two-fold process of building a sense of self that will carry you through, but at the same time resolving some of the unresolved psychology that is like an anchor that prevents your boat from making progress towards the farther shore. This is why I said that there are some people who find an outer teaching, even a genuine ascended master teaching, and they use it to build a boat. The boat is safe; it can bob up and down safely on the waves without being overturned or shipwrecked. Because they look at the path as an outer path, they are not going within and looking at their own psychology, and therefore they have an anchor that keeps the boat in the same place. Maybe the boat is moving forward very slowly, but in many cases it is just in the same place. Because the boat is still going up and down with the waves, these people think they are making progress.

The people who do make genuine progress are those who have used the outer teaching and the tools to build a boat that can sustain them in the waves, but at the same time they are going within and looking at their own psychology. They discover a certain rope that is tied to an anchor that is holding back their boat, and then they cut that rope. Now, the boat can make progress until another anchor catches on a rock deep below, and then they look at that, cut that rope and make progress again.

Dismantling the boat that carried you across the sea

How do you make it to the farther shore of the Sea of Samsara? You must gradually cut all of the ropes that are holding back your boat. At the same time, you must navigate the waves that are sent at you from the outside, from the mass consciousness and the dark forces. Then you may make it to the farther shore. In the process, you may have felt that you had to greatly reinforce your boat, and now you have built this very strong, sometimes very sophisticated and elaborate, boat. Here you are. You can look out to the sea and see that you have gone through the biggest waves. You are now in the shallow water near the shore; the shore is right there.

Will you not reason at that point that you have been successful, that you did a good job of building your boat? After all, it took you across the Sea of Samsara. Yet my beloved, while the boat could take you safely across the Sea of Samsara, the boat cannot sail up on the farther shore. You will not land on the farther shore until you jump out of your boat. What will it take for you to jump out of your boat? You will have to be willing to *leave your boat behind!*

How can you do this unless you are willing to look at your boat, or rather the self, that brought you through the Sea of Samsara? How can you leave that self behind? You can do so only through a choice, an act of free will. You will have to stand back and look at the self that brought you through the Sea of Samsara, that brought you to the point where you have fulfilled the outer requirements for your ascension. Then you will have to honestly and openly recognize that regardless of what qualities are embedded in this self, it was still only a self that was built from the unascended state of consciousness. It will *not* bring you into the ascended state, for did not Jesus say to Nicodemus: "No man has ascended back to heaven save he that descended from heaven."

The self that you have built on your road towards the ascended state is *not* the self that descended from heaven. It is a self you have built in order to navigate the Sea of Samsara, the unascended realm. It has been valuable for you, it has served its purpose of bringing you across the Sea of Samsara, but it cannot take you into the ascended realm and you cannot take it with you into the ascended realm.

This means you must now systematically – plank by plank, rivet by rivet – dismantle your boat, dismantle your self. This is how you will fully qualify for your ascension. Only after you have dismantled the separate self, will you be an ascended master.

I am today an ascended master because I spent twelve years suffering from Alzheimer's while I was working at inner levels on dismantling the self that I had built over many lifetimes. I had reinforced this self in my last embodiment in order to fulfill the service that I had vowed to fulfill as a spiritual leader and teacher. It was not wrong to build this self, but it was built only for a purpose and it could take me only so far.

My beloved, you also have built a self. It has taken you to where you are right now. You will need this self to make it through the rest of this embodiment, but in order to ascend, you will have to dismantle this self. I know very well how the self will react to these statements. Your separate self will react exactly as mine did when I was still in embodiment.

Unmasking the separate self

What I am talking about here is a self that is more than the ego. The self is a useful vehicle; the ego is attachment to the self. The Dweller on the Threshold, as we called it in the Church, is like the anchors that are holding you to the bottom of the Sea of Samsara. For each decisive step you take upwards on the path, you must face the old decision that caused you to descend to that stage, to that step. You must face the momentum you have created from that sense of Self.

This is the dweller that you must face and slay, or rather transcend, before you can take the next step up the spiral staircase. The ego is more like the attachment to the dweller and the attachment to the outer self. You, therefore, come to the point where you have slain the elements of the dweller, you have cut the anchor ropes, your boat is now nearing the farther shore. Your ego is not an anchor being dragged behind the boat like the dweller; your ego is *inside* the boat with you.

In order for you to jump out of the boat, you must face that last element, which could be called the last element of the dweller, depending on how you want to use words. This is attachment to the self that brought you across the Sea of Samsara. You must see that you are more than the self and you must decide to jump out of the boat. When you have jumped out of the boat, you can begin to dismantle it.

In my case, I had taken a vow that I would not leave my physical body until I had qualified for my ascension. In the end, I could not fulfill that vow. The reason I had to go through a period of being in a virtual coma due to Alzheimer's was that I needed to do work at inner levels to dismantle the self that had brought me to that point of having met the outer requirements. It took me so many years to dismantle that self, but then I still had to let go of the physical body and wait some years before I fully qualified for my ascension. I was then able to ascend with one hundred percent of my karma balanced, therefore becoming an ascended master from the beginning—although still going through a certain process of adjusting to the ascended state, as we all need to do.

A great opportunity for dismantling the self

Why am I giving you this teaching? Because those who are at a certain level of the spiritual path will be able to grasp and accept this teaching. They will be able to use it to start dismantling the self and the attachment to self before they leave the physical body. This will be a great advantage for you because I assure you that the self you have built, in order to navigate the Sea of Samsara, will have certain aspects that actually prevent you from balancing certain parts of your karma and resolving certain aspects of your psychology.

You see, my beloved, the Sea of Samara is a treacherous place. The false teachers, the fallen beings, the dark forces have done everything they can to put as many traps and as many roadblocks in your way as at all possible. In order to make it past some of these roadblocks, you must close your mind and your aura to these influences.

While you are facing a certain challenge, it is necessary for you to be focused, to be one-pointed and to ignore anything that detracts you from making it through. If you have ever been in a small boat on the open water, as I was blessed to experience in my childhood, there will be certain times where you can see the harbor up ahead, but between you and the harbor is an area of very turbulent, very choppy, waves. What you need to do in order to make it through that is to "batten down the hatches," as they say, and head straight for the opening of the harbor without veering right or left.

There is no opportunity here to balance your karma, to look at your psychology. You need to be focused on making it through this turbulent area. Once you are through it, then you have an opportunity to say: "Do I now need to carry this self that brought me through that phase? If I dismantle this self, can I then take a better look at my psychology? When I see a certain psychological hang-up, I can then dissolve it. I do not need to carry it with me."

"When I have dissolved a certain hang-up, I can now see, openly and honestly, what I have done to other people in this life or in past lives that has caused me to make karma. I may then have an opportunity to still interact with some of the people with whom I have karma. From my state of resolved psychology, I can dissolve that karma much more quickly. Even if *they* do not respond positively to my changed state, *I* can at least free myself from that karma."

This is a growth opportunity you do not have when you are either out of the body or when your body has been incapacitated, as mine was. This means it is much more difficult for you to balance the karma and resolve the psychology. Believe me, I know from experience.

My body may have seemed to be relatively inactive, my mind might have seemed to be *very* inactive during those years. I can assure you that my mind at inner levels was extremely active, doing all of the things that I had never had the time or the attention to do while I was in embodiment and so focused on what I saw as my outer mission. Surely, I had an outer mission, but my greater mission was to qualify for my ascension and set an example of how *you* qualify for *your* ascension. This task I had sometimes neglected due to the demands of running an outer organization.

Why this teaching is given

I am giving you this teaching with the blessing of the Karmic Board, the Darjeeling Council and other ascended councils. We of the ascended masters have a desire to use my example to help you avoid having to go through the same arduous process. It would be easier for you if you understood this teaching before you leave the physical body and if you apply it and make use of it while you still have time in the body.

I am grateful for this messenger being willing to be the open door. He has been somewhat hesitant to take dictations from me, even though he has for some time recognized that I am an ascended master. This reluctance is understandable, for as a messenger for the ascended masters, you are concerned about being the purest possible vessel. You know that if you have any kind of knowledge or opinion about a topic, you may not be neutral enough to be able to be a completely open door.

Given that this messenger was a part of the organization that I was running, he has been concerned about whether he would be able to be neutral enough. He has come to recognize that while he may never be able to be completely neutral while he is in embodiment, he can be *neutral enough* that my Presence and my Being can still shine through these dictations for those who have eyes to see and ears to hear.

No messenger can do more. No message, no matter how pure, can penetrate the perception filters of those who still want to relate to the ascended masters from a distance, through a mental image, through a perception filter based on the outer teachings or even the outer person of the guru who was in embodiment. Most students of the ascended masters have a perception filter of the ascended masters, but when you have met a physical person who was the guru or the messenger, it is so much easier to build a perception filter. After all, you have directly perceived this person.

The challenge I hurl at all students at the end of this discourse is this: I AM the Ascended Master Guru Ma. Do you want to relate to me as I AM, or do you want to continue to relate to me through your present perception filter of me?

The choice, my beloved, is entirely yours. Understand that I do have a right from the ascended state to give forth a teaching that can challenge your perception filter *if you are willing to have it challenged.*

I am who I AM and I know who I AM. If you want to know who I AM, you need to come to know who *you* are. It is for this purpose that I have given this and will give the following teachings. Guru Ma I AM.

3 | HOW TO GET STARTED ON THE SPIRITUAL PATH

I AM the Ascended Master Guru Ma. It still gives me great joy to say this through a human messenger in the physical octave on earth. I am an *ascended* master; I am not an embodied human being. Neither am I an *unascended* master—or not master. I am an *ascended* master.

The decisiveness of the step that brings you into the ascended octave cannot be fathomed until you experience it. There is no experience that you could ever have on earth that is quite as decisive as actually taking that last step into the ascended realm. The only thing that somewhat compares is the death of the physical body where your lifestream, your soul, experiences the decisiveness that the physical body it has been wearing for decades is gone—completely gone. You also experience that the life you have had for decades – the family, the friends, the outer situations, the possessions, the creature comforts – is *all* gone. It will never come back in that exact form. You know you will have other lifetimes, but the lifetime you have just left will never come back.

You have lost any control over what you had, any control over what you had in that lifetime. While you were still alive and conscious, you had a position in the eyes of other people. Through that position you could command a certain respect, a certain obedience. You had, through that position, control over your circumstances. Once the heart stops beating and the body draws its last breath, you lose all control over that lifetime. What is left then? When we speak of control, there is only one form of control that you can take with you after the body dies. *It is self-control.*

Most lifestreams on earth have not begun to understand that the only form of control they really have on earth is self-control. They have not begun to understand what this truly means. Instead, even when the body dies, the soul in many cases is still so identified with the ego and with the self it has created that it thinks the ego can exert control.

The lifestream, the Conscious You, is identified with the soul vehicle, the boat that it has created in order to cross the Sea of Samsara, or at least navigate the Sea of Samsara. It believes that even though one physical body has died, the self will still carry over. In its next lifetime, it will be able to get greater control by building on to that self. This is the central challenge on earth; this is the central challenge for those who truly want to make their ascension. This is something we need to talk about.

For whom am I teaching?

It has been said by the ascended masters that: "When the student is ready, the teacher appears." This means that there is no teacher on earth who is attempting to teach all people on earth. You can have a broad teaching that reaches out to a large number of people, like Jesus taught the multitudes in parables. You can have a more inner, a more advanced, teaching for those who are ready for it, as Jesus expounded all things to his disciples. Nevertheless, no matter who you are as a teacher, you can only teach a certain range of the people on earth.

Let us therefore clarify for whom I am giving the teachings in this book. They are primarily given for those who have the potential to qualify for their ascension in this lifetime or the next. They will also be of value to those who are at the more mature stages of the spiritual path where they are very sincere about making spiritual progress, even it is not in their divine plan that they ascend in this lifetime.

Overcoming the "us versus them" mentality

While I was in embodiment as a spiritual teacher, the organization that I was heading had a certain organizational culture. This culture was in large part dominated by Mark and myself, but it was not exclusively created by us. It was indeed a product of all of the people who were part of the organization. Depending on their role in the organization, they would have a greater or smaller impact on the organizational culture, perhaps even what we might call the collective consciousness of the organization.

This organizational culture did contain certain elements of value judgment. Our organization was directly and openly geared towards teaching the path to the ascension. We taught a very strict path of discipline with certain outer rules for behavior. We taught that it was an arduous path of surrendering to the will of God and the will of the ascended masters. We had a very low tolerance for those who would not submit to this path. Underneath was a certain value judgment that many people on earth simply were not ready for the path that we were following, those of us who were on the inside.

There was a certain "us versus them" mentality where we clearly saw that "us" – we who were on the inside – were the most advanced students. That is why we were able to recognize and follow "the most advanced spiritual teaching on the planet," as we believed we had been given. It was implicitly said – and in some cases by some people openly said – that those who would not accept our teachings or our disciplines simply were not ready for it. They were not advanced enough, they were not mature enough.

Regardless of the fact that I had a certain element of this attitude while I was in embodiment, I wish to state from the ascended realm – with absolutely no doubt – that this attitude and any aspect of value judgment can come only from ego. It has no reality whatsoever in God. It has no reality whatsoever in the ascended realm.

This is not to say that it is not understandable that people build this attitude. Those who are serious about making their ascension, or making decisive progress on the spiritual path, will have to navigate their own personal Sea of Samsara. They will have to create a vessel, a boat, that can withstand the raging waves and the torrents that are sent at them by the dark forces (who oppose the spiritual progress of all people on earth), by the mass consciousness (that does not want anyone to rise above the norm) and by their own subconscious momentums.

When you look at spiritual and religious movements, and for that matter any kind of organized movement on earth, you see in virtually all of them a tendency to have this "us versus them" mentality. "We are the ones who are on the inside, and we are in a certain sense superior to those who are on the outside." Many Christian fundamentalist churches in the United States have members who believe this every Sunday when they come together. They sit there in their little church, which may only have a few hundred members, and they believe that because they have the only literal interpretation of the Bible, they are the only ones who will be saved when Jesus comes back to roll up the world as a scroll.

We in the Summit had an aspect of that mentality, and if you look honestly at most spiritual and religious movements, you will see exactly the same. What I wish to convey here is that we of the ascended masters have completely and utterly transcended this mentality. The reason I am telling you this is twofold. One is to let you know that in order for you to become an ascended master, you need to transcend it as well. The other reason is because I want you to know that we of the ascended masters do not look at the spiritual people on earth and judge them based on a value judgment.

No student is more valuable than any other

Here is how the ascended masters look at people on earth. We look beyond the outer person, the physical body, the outer personality and we see deeper. We see deeper into the lifestream itself, which is even beyond the soul vehicle, the boat that you use to navigate the Sea of Samsara. At the deepest level, we see that all people who are in embodiment on earth are expressions of God's Being, and they are on the path of expanding the self, expanding their self-awareness. All human beings – regardless of their outer characteristics or the inner characteristics of the psychology of the soul vehicle – are on this path. We also know, and we see, that you cannot actually create any form of value judgment or scale that says that a lifestream is more advanced than another.

Be careful to consider the subtlety here. I have said that as a spiritual teacher you can only teach a certain range of students. We of the ascended masters are looking at the people in embodiment on earth, and we have a certain criteria for determining where people are at in consciousness. We evaluate, first of all: Is that person teachable for our level of teaching? There are many, many people on earth, in fact the vast majority of people on earth, who are not teachable for any teaching given directly by the ascended masters. There is no point in us giving dictations or other teachings that are aimed directly at these people for they are not ready for it. They will have to learn from the School of Hard Knocks by seeing the Ma-ter Light outpicture their state of consciousness in physical circumstances. They will have to attend this school for some time – in many cases for many lifetimes – before they will be ready for our teachings.

When we look at those who *are* ready for our teachings, we must also evaluate which level of teaching they are ready for. There *is* a certain scale, which says that there is a range of consciousness, as we have given you teachings that there are 144 levels of consciousness possible on earth. We can evaluate which level of consciousness a student is at. If a student is below the 48th level of consciousness, then we cannot reach that student with a direct teaching and the student must be left to the School of Hard Knocks.

When a student goes above this level, it enters the seven levels of initiations of the First Ray [These initiations are described in the books in *The Path to Self-Mastery* series.] When it rises above that, it enters the seven levels of the Second Ray and so on until it passes the 96th level and now reaches an entirely higher level of initiation.

We do look at where a student is at and we seek to give that student a level of teaching suited to its level of consciousness. What I wish to convey here is that there is no value judgment associated with this. It is true that some students are at a higher level of consciousness, but this does not mean that we consider them more valuable.

We see that any student, regardless of its level of consciousness, still has the potential to progress with quantum leaps. It is not common that a person on earth progresses many levels of consciousness in one lifetime, but it is *possible*. Therefore, we know that we cannot impose any kind of judgment upon a student and that student's capacity to rise. On the other hand, we also know that each student is at a certain level of consciousness, has a certain history and therefore has a certain potential to grow in a given lifetime.

The complexity of your divine plan for this lifetime

What I wish to convey to you is that before any human being on earth takes embodiment, that person is offered counsel by the ascended masters. It is not all people on earth who are willing to take advantage of this. Many of the people below the 48th level will actually reject this counsel between embodiments. Nevertheless, there are still ascended masters who are assigned to guide those people and who therefore make up – even without the participation of the soul – a divine plan for the coming embodiment.

Let me talk about those who *are* willing to accept the counsel of the ascended masters in between embodiments. Before such a person re-embodies, it has meetings with its ascended teachers. In these meetings we look at the complexity of the lifestream, its past history, not only what we call its karma but also its psychology, its momentums, its habit patterns and its desires. We look at the desires that brought it into embodiment, the desires that it has developed over time. What does it desire to *experience,* what does it desire to *do* on earth?

As I said in my first discourse, we of the ascended masters give a somewhat optimistic view of what it means to ascend. The same thing, in a sense, takes place when the lifestream defines its divine plan. In reality, the picture is exceptionally complex. What you have created in terms of the soul vehicle over many lifetimes – for most people thousands of lifetimes on this and other planets – is an extremely complex, interwoven web of beliefs, attitudes, energies, spirits, momentums and this and that. It is so complex that hardly anyone could fathom it with their conscious minds. In fact, *no one* can fathom the complexity with their conscious minds.

In between embodiments, you are not limited to the conscious mind so you can fathom – depending upon your level of consciousness – a great part of the complexity of your individual situation. You are therefore able to understand much more about yourself and the complexity of your situation than you can with your conscious awareness. It is based on this that you create your divine plan.

Here is what I wish to convey. When you are in between embodiments and when you are in direct council with your ascended teachers, you also have no value judgment. You are looking at yourself neutrally. You are looking at some of the complexities of what you face. Then, you are making decisions based on a higher vision than you have right now when you are looking at life through the perception filter of the physical body and the outer mind.

Between embodiments you do not judge yourself

This is important because when you are formulating your divine plan, there is a very clear division of labor. Your ascended teachers are showing you the complexities of what you face with your psychology, your karma, all of the things you need to go through in order to make progress up the spiral staircase. They are showing you the conditions, and they are showing you various paths that you can follow. For most people, there are various paths that they can take in a lifetime. Your responsibility is to look at this and then make a choice: "This is the path I want to follow in my next lifetime. These are the circumstances in which I want to be born. These are the people I want to meet. These are the situations I wish to experience. These are the desires I wish to pursue." And so forth and so on.

The ascended masters have no value judgment of you or what you should do. Neither do we have any desire to tell you what to do. This is something that it is almost impossible for people in embodiment to fathom. When I look back at myself and my own growth in my last embodiment, I can see that if you had told me what I just told you, I would not have been ready to accept it. I would not have been able to fathom exactly how completely free of judgment the ascended masters are. The reasons I would not have been able to fathom this are complex, but part of it was that I did not free myself from the image of the angry and judgmental God in the sky that has so dominated humankind for thousands of years, including in the Age of Pisces.

You have embodied on a difficult planet

It also relates to the fact that I looked at the conditions on planet earth, being born just before the Second World War. I was very much aware, at an early age, of the horrors of war. I was only five and six years old when we learned about the Holocaust. Although we were certainly given a very black-and-white, exaggerated image of this, it was clear to my young mind that there was evil in the world. It was also clear that with human power it would be impossible to eradicate evil. In my mind, I formulated a desire to have some ultimate divine power who could take control of earth and eradicate evil, a desire, a mentality, I did not fully let go of while I was still conscious in my physical body.

The stark reality, the *brutal* reality, is that there is no such God who has ultimate control over what happens on earth. Yes, there is a God who has defined certain parameters and conditions. Yes, there is a council of ascended masters, called the Great Karmic Board, who are in charge of releasing or holding back humankind's karma. But there is not the God in the sky who is ready to step in at any moment and take away evil because people pray to that God.

The reason is that planet earth is a particular kind of cosmic schoolroom. There are many, many, many planets in the material universe with intelligent life, with self-aware beings.

Many of them are very different from earth, and the physical bodies worn by these self-aware beings are very different from your bodies. There are many planets, and earth is one of these planets, where the inhabitants have been allowed to outplay the lower aspects of the duality consciousness, the consciousness of separation.

This is why you see so many examples of man's inhumanity to man; the Holocaust certainly being the extreme example that opened my eyes as a child. Many other worse atrocities have taken place and are still taking place on this planet. This is allowed by cosmic law. Earth is one of these kinds of planets, and therefore the only realistic way to look at earth is that this is a sort of way-station for those who still deserve an opportunity to be in physical embodiment but who do not merit the incarnation on a higher planet. They have not overcome the tendency to use violence and force against others. Most lifestreams on earth have ended up here because they could not maintain embodiment on one of the other planets that have risen beyond this level of consciousness.

When I say that the earth is a low planet, I say this without value judgment. It is simply an evaluation of how far lifestreams have gone into the duality consciousness, how separated they see themselves from God and each other.

Letting go of unrealistic expectations

Once you realize that earth is a low planet, then you can let go of certain expectations. You can let go of the expectation that God will someday enter human affairs and in miraculous ways set everything right. What did Jesus demonstrate by taking physical embodiment? What did he demonstrate by displaying that he did not have or did not use the power to destroy evil but that he allowed evil to destroy his physical body? He demonstrated precisely that God has given control of this planet to the free will of the inhabitants of the planet. Free will reigns supreme on earth, which means that God will not come in and set things right. It is the beings in embodiment who must set things right by embodying the Christ consciousness rather than the consciousness of anti-christ. This is a special challenge for most people on earth.

It was a very difficult challenge for me in my last embodiment, a challenge that I did not fully pass, a test I did not fully pass, while still conscious in the body. The reason it is so difficult is that those of us who are spiritual people are spiritual because we have had some experience, some direct experience, that there is a higher reality beyond the material world. Many of us have subconscious memories, sometimes glimpses of conscious memories, of a reality, a state of consciousness, a state of life, beyond the material world.

I had this as a very young child. Many, many people have had the same. Some have forgotten, but many spiritual people are re-remembering their early childhood glimpses of a different state of consciousness. Because of this, we have a clear inner sense that what we see around us on earth is not the highest potential, is not the only possible state of affairs.

A serious detour on the path to the ascension

Allow yourself to step back and think about this for a moment. If it was true, as psychologists proclaim, that you are the exclusive product of your genetic inheritance and your environmental influences, then all people on earth should grow up with a complete acceptance that the way things are on earth, right now, is the only way they *can* be. If all people had grown up with this sense that the way things are is the only way they *can* be, then how would society ever have progressed from the cave man stage to the present level of civilization? Progress is only possible because there are some people who have an inner sense that the way things are right now is not the only way they could be. Improvement is possible, something higher than what they see around them is possible. All of the people who have been instrumental in bringing forth the ideas that brought humankind forward have had this sense, whether they have been openly spiritual or not.

We can say that this is the basic sense of spirituality: The unwillingness to accept what you see around you as the only possible reality, and the willingness to open your mind to ideas that could raise the current conditions that you see around you.

Most spiritual people have this inner sense that there is a higher world where beings do not do to each other what human beings do to each other. It is built into our spiritual striving that we look at conditions on earth and say: "This is not right, this should not be so. This is not the way things ought to be. There is a higher potential; there is a higher reality. Things should be better."

I know well that you can look at people on this planet who do not have this sense. They accept conditions for what they are. They live their entire lifetime accepting the conditions they have been given and never really seek to raise themselves beyond it. You will also see millions and millions of people who have this sense that improvement *is* possible, that certain things should not be taking place on this planet.

You see that we are facing a difficult task. We are here to improve things on earth. We are here *not* to accept status quo, but to raise our own consciousness beyond the collective consciousness and to do something to improve conditions on earth. I was driven by this from my very early childhood, being only three years old when I experienced my own father taken away during the war on suspicion of being a German spy.

I came into embodiment with this desire. Most of the people that I ever came in contact with during my past lifetime, and certainly most of the members of my church, had this inner desire to improve earth. There is nothing wrong with this. It is part of your reason for coming into embodiment on this planet, but what I am seeking to convey to you is that this attitude can become a very serious detour on the spiritual path. There are, in fact, many people who have missed their ascensions because they were so preoccupied with fighting some battle on earth that they thought had some ultimate or epic importance.

Your situation is a result of your own choices

What you need to consider is free will. When you meet with your ascended teachers before you come into embodiment, you are the one who looks at the conditions created by your own past choices. You sit there and you see what your ascended teachers are presenting to you. You see that the conditions you are facing today are the results of choices you made in past lifetimes.

Surely, you made those choices by responding to conditions on earth, to the actions of other people, but *you* made the choice. There was never a situation where you had no choice, where you had only one option. You see clearly that the statement so often heard on earth: 'I had no other choice' is never accurate. You always have at least one other choice than the one you made.

You know that your personal situation is the result of choices you have made. You also know that when you go into your next embodiment, the conditions you face are conditions you have chosen. There were other options, but you chose to come into embodiment in your present body and situation. You also know that all other conditions on earth are the result of choices made by other people. You have this awareness that everything is a product of choice. *Everything is a product of choice,* which means what? It means there is no condition that you face on earth that you cannot change through your own choosing. This is a statement that requires some contemplation. It can be understood at various levels, and I will talk about them later. For now, what I wish you to see is that your personal situation is a result of choices you have made. The collective situation that you currently see on earth is the result of choices made by humankind as a whole.

This means that free will is the supreme law for earth. Everything on earth is subject to the free-will choices of human beings embodying on earth. God will not step in and solve a particular problem or all problems, neither will God end the world and throw the bad people in hell and raise the good people to heaven. You are stuck here, and all human beings are stuck here, until your own choices qualify you to ascend from earth.

4 | THE GURU SHOWS YOU WHAT YOU CANNOT SEE

I said earlier that when you give a teaching, you must choose the audience. I have chosen as my audience those who have the potential to ascend after this or the next lifetime and those who are so mature on the spiritual path that they can benefit from these instructions. The core of the instruction I am giving is that if you are to make your ascension, there is only one way to do so and that is to take full, absolute and final responsibility for yourself, for your own lifestream. You must accept that there is no power on earth and no power in heaven that *can* or *will* override, take away or neutralize your free will. *You* have the capacity to determine whether you ascend or do not ascend. It is *your* choices that will determine whether you ascend or do not ascend—nothing else.

Even this is a statement that can be understood at different levels. It is the choices of your *total consciousness* that will determine whether you ascend or not, but not all choices in your total consciousness are necessarily made by you consciously, by the Conscious You that is the core of your being, the being that descended from heaven.

In many cases, you have allowed the outer self, the soul vehicle, the ego, the various spirits in your being to make certain choices for you. It can be said that, strictly speaking, the choices made by your ego, are not *your* choices because your ego is not you. As long as you are allowing the ego to make choices for you, then they are still *your* choices in the sense that they are part of your consciousness. They will have a direct impact on whether you can free yourself from the earth plane and the soul vehicle.

Consumer spirituality

Why am I starting out with this instruction? When you look at the spiritual people on earth, you can see certain patterns. I first met Mark Prophet in the 1960s and we started running the Summit Lighthouse together. I saw what happened to the spiritual landscape on earth during the 1960s, the 1970s, the 80s and the 90s. There was a tremendous growth in the number of people who were open to spiritual teachings, and this was the result of a general raising of the collective consciousness.

Many, many people suddenly became aware of an interest in the spiritual side of life, yet they were not ready to truly engage in the spiritual path in its true, inner aspect. You will see today that there are many people who are interested in spiritual topics and read books, go to seminars or lectures and participate in various courses or classes. For them, spirituality is either a form of entertainment, that simply distracts them from the dullness of their everyday lives, or it is even a form of consumption.

There are people who are constantly buying and reading the latest book that is talked about, but when they read a book they do not actually absorb it. They do not actually let it change their fundamental outlook on life. For them, it is just something they consume. It gives them temporary nurturance, as when they consume a meal or a granola bar. They buy it, they eat it, they enjoy it while they are chewing on it, but once it is swallowed, it is out of their minds. So it is with many people who consume spiritual books and spiritual teachings.

Again, there is no value judgment from the ascended realm for this. We simply observe that such people have not crossed the threshold where they are ready to begin to take responsibility for themselves. They are still hoping for the outer path, the automatic salvation, where if you read the book – if you follow the outer rules, if you go to church on Sunday, if you confess your sins, if you don't eat this and you don't eat that – then God will have to save you in the end. In the meantime, you can live any way you want here on earth, and you do not have to look at the beam in your own eye. It is the willingness to look at yourself – and to see something that your ego resists that you see – that is the decisive factor on the spiritual path.

Why self-observation causes pain

Let me give you an insight that will help you. The driving force on the spiritual path is that you come to see something in yourself that is created out of the consciousness of separation, duality, anti-christ. It is an element of unreality that you cannot take with you into heaven. It is a certain state of consciousness, what we have called a perception filter because it colors the way you look at a specific aspect of life. The driving force is that you come to see this; you come to see that you have it in your consciousness.

It is possible that you can see this by having the Conscious You detach itself from your normal consciousness. You can therefore come to see it as neutrally in the body as you see it before you take embodiment. This is possible; it is an ability you can cultivate as you mature on the path. When you first become aware of the path, it is inevitable that you do not see something in yourself as if you were detached from it. You see it while you are still very much colored by it. What does this mean? It means that what you see in yourself will be unpleasant for you.

For example, if you have pride, if you have a tendency to judge others, you need to see this in yourself. Your ego will resist that you see it, but when you finally see it, seeing it in yourself will cause you pain. You will now judge yourself the way you have been used to judging others. You will judge yourself for having judged others because now you see that you are judging others. You also see that this is not right, and you will judge yourself for having done what was not right.

Those who are ready to step on to the more serious levels of the spiritual path are the ones who are willing to endure this discomfort, this embarrassment, this pain. Those are the ones who are ready for the later initiations of the ascension spiral. After you have gone through a period where you have been willing to look at yourself regardless of the pain it causes, you can come to a point where you can now do this without feeling the pain. You have dis-identified yourself so much from the ego that you can look at yourself and your psychology neutrally. This will take some work. Those of us who have ascended have had to go through that period where we saw things in ourselves and it was painful to see them.

The basic dynamic on the spiritual path

While I was a spiritual leader of a fairly large organization, I interacted with thousands of people. I was often in the position of being the outside force that caused people to confront something in themselves that they had not been willing to confront on their own. I was often in the role of the guru who put up a mirror in front of people and said: "Now see, you *do* have this tendency. You do have this element of ego. You do have this Dweller on the Threshold that is acting out." Do you know how many people got angry with me because I was the one who made them see what they did not want to see? Do you begin to see how toxic this tendency can be? Do you begin to see the basic dynamic on the spiritual path?

There are levels of the spiritual path. There is an outer level, and I saw this very well in my church, where people need a somewhat simple teaching, a somewhat simplified teaching, for what it means to make progress on the path. We fulfilled this through our decrees and our decree sessions. These were people who needed to have certain basic spiritual teachings, which we gave them, about your I AM Presence, about your Christ self, about your aura, your chakras. You need to purify your chakras, you need to balance your karma. You have the ability to do this by invoking the violet flame and other spiritual energies.

There were many people who came and this is exactly what they needed. For a time, sometimes for years, all they needed to do was really to sit at home on their own and give the decrees. Or they would come to services and once in a while to conferences where they would decree with others and therefore experience the uplifting power of the decree momentum of a large group of people. This was all they needed, this was all they could handle, but this was an *outer* path.

The true *inner* path to the ascension is precisely the phase where you begin to confront your own momentums. You begin to see something in yourself that your ego does not want you to see. It is both possible and impossible to go through this period on your own.

It is possible that you can be willing to look at things in yourself, that you can detach the Conscious You sufficiently from the soul vehicle that you can look at yourself neutrally. This is a later stage on the path. It is impossible to get to that stage without having a guru, a teacher, who is outside your mental box, outside your perception filter. The entire effect of having built a soul vehicle that can take you across the Sea of Samsara is that the soul vehicle acts as a filter that blinds you to certain things so that you are not pulled into a negative spiral by the false teachers.

The first stage of the path

Did you hear what I actually said? In my first discourse I said that the conditions on the Sea of Samsara are treacherous. There are many traps, and in order to create a soul vehicle that can take you across, you must create a vehicle that does not have any openings for the temptations of the false teachers. You close off certain things that you do not see, and therefore you can make it across the most turbulent area of the Sea of Samsara. In order to make it to the ascension, you need to recognize that the only reason you were vulnerable to the temptations of the false teachers in the first place is that you had elements of the duality consciousness in your own being.

Do you understand how this works? There is the Sea of Samsara. Most people on this earth are completely submerged in it. The majority of human beings are simply overwhelmed by the mass consciousness, the Sea of Samsara. They are flowing with the currents in the mass consciousness, as you saw the fish flowing with the Gulf Stream up along the East Coast of North America. They do not even know that they are in this current and that they are being moved along with the current. They actually think – as the fish might think if they could think – that they are free to swim in any direction they want—and they *are*. You can go back and forth any way you want, but you are still being moved along by the greater current that you do not even see.

Your first task on the spiritual path is to pull yourself out of the Sea of Samsara. We may say that you pull yourself up on some shore. You are standing now on this side of the sea, and you know that your goal is to get to the other side. You cannot get to the farther shore by swimming in the sea, the waves are too rough, the current too strong. You need to build a boat, a vehicle, that will carry you across so that you are floating on the sea without being pulled down by it. What do you need to do? You need to build a boat that has a strong hull so that it can float. The hull needs to be closed so that the water cannot come in and weigh down the boat until it sinks.

You build this soul vehicle by closing off certain things. For example, you might build a vehicle by looking at the teachings of Jesus about turning the other cheek and not resisting evil. You may decide with a firm outer will that you will never use violence against anyone. This is a decision that many spiritual people have made with the outer will. This becomes part of the hull of your boat, and it keeps out the waves from the mass consciousness and the false teachers. They would gladly see you, as so many people on earth are, trapped in a spiral of violence and revenge and more violence—and they never get out of it, like so many people in the Middle East and elsewhere.

How can you make progress when you are constantly making more karma by taking revenge for something you do not even know what was about? You do not even know what the conflict between Arabs and Jews is really about. No one can remember when it started, yet they are still trapped in this cycle of revenge for revenge and revenge for the sake of revenge, thinking that their God requires blood sacrifices and the spilling of blood to compensate for the past spilling of blood.

Why your perception filter blinds you

In order to avoid being pulled into these spirals in the mass consciousness, you need to build a boat. You will know from the ocean that it is possible that you can be caught in a wave and actually sucked down. It is possible that you can rotate around with the wave without ever coming to the surface, and that is the situation of many people on earth.

You build a boat that can float and takes you out of these currents and these downward pulls. You do this by making a firm decision: "*This* I will not do!" This creates a secure hull in your boat. Why was it possible that you could have been pulled into such a downward spiral? Because you had an element of that consciousness in your own being already.

You *do* need to build the boat that can carry you across the rough waves, but then – when you have passed through those waves – you need to look at the fact that you still have an element of the duality consciousness in your own being. You need to see it, see it for what it is and consciously throw it out of your being.

As you throw that element out, you also need to dismantle the part of your boat's hull that was meant to shut out the external influences that correspond to that particular element of ego and duality. If you only threw out what is in your consciousness – but did not dismantle the defense against the outer forces that you have built – then you are not free from that consciousness. There are actually people who have, over time, freed themselves from a certain element deep within their beings, but they still have an outer personality, an outer habit pattern, that is constructed to shut out that external influence. That means you are still carrying some element of it with you in your consciousness; you are not free of it.

The guru helps you see what you cannot see

How do you become free of these elements in your own being that are meant to shut out certain influences? Consider that you have created an element of your soul vehicle, your boat, that is meant to shut out the temptation to engage in violence. This means that when you are successful in building this, you are actually building a filter. There are certain things you simply cannot see; they are blocked from your vision. The devil comes to tempt you, but you do not even see the temptation because your perception filter is so strong that it blocks out the devil's temptation.

This is perfectly valid and valuable for a time. You need this blocking in order to make it through the turbulent part of the Sea of Samsara. The blocking also prevents you from seeing the elements in your own being that are still there and that are the reason you needed the defense from outer forces. The perception filter not only blocks what is coming from the outside, it also blocks your vision and your ability to see what is inside.

How do you step out of this perception filter? You need a teacher, you need the guru. You need some outside force that can demonstrate to you that the way you look at life is not the *only* possible way to look at life. You need someone who will challenge your perception filter and say: "Maybe your filter has outlived its purpose and it is no longer helping you navigate the rough waves. It is actually like an anchor dragging behind your boat and preventing you from making progress. It is certainly preventing you from stepping onto the farther shore."

There is a period of the spiritual path where you *do* need a teacher in one form or another. Many people are not ready to have an outer teacher in the form of a physical guru that they can recognize and interact with. Some people have passed through the stage where they need such an outer guru, but there is no one who cannot benefit from an outer guru. Even if you don't strictly need it, you still make faster progress by having the outer guru.

How do you respond to the guru?

We now come to the simple concern of how you respond to an outer guru. This is an extremely important topic to consider. I have told you that before you come into embodiment, you are in council with your ascended teachers. You look at your life, you look at your psychology, and you see: "Here is a particular part of my perception filter that has outlived its purpose. It protected me during certain rough embodiments I had in the past, where I was exposed to certain outside forces, and I needed that protection to get me through it. Now it is actually holding me back, and I need to transcend it in this lifetime."

You then say: "Which situation do I need to be in, in order to transcend this particular limitation?" Then you make the choice to put yourself in a particular outer circumstance that forces you to confront the initiation that you need to pass in order to make progress.

You know, while you are out of the body, that once you get into the body there will be a resistance from the ego and your past momentums to you seeing what you need to see. You are often choosing to deliberately go into a situation where you are forcing yourself to face conditions that make it difficult to ignore what you need to see. It makes it difficult for you to ignore the initiation.

When you come into the physical body, into the outer mind, you will be blinded by the very condition that you need to see and see through. You will be colored by the very condition that you need to free yourself from in this lifetime. This means that your ego and your past momentums will resist that you see what you need to see and that you make the choice to transcend it.

What you often choose to do, especially when you are nearing the higher levels of the path where you have a readiness to ascend, is that you force yourself to have a guru, an outer teacher, who can help you see what you need to see. This is especially true for those who know that they have the potential to ascend in this or the next lifetime.

You are deliberately choosing to expose yourself to a particular guru who has the capacity to force you to see what your ego does not want you to see. The question therefore becomes: "How do you respond to the guru? Do you even recognize the guru?" As El Morya, or Master MORE, says: "If the guru be an ant, heed him." We might also add: "If the guru be *not* an ant, heed him anyway—or heed *her*." Whatever situation, whatever initiation, you face there will always be a guru who can help you overcome that initiation. This is embodied in the statement: "When the student is ready, the teacher appears." It is a cosmic law that when you are facing a certain initiation there will be a guru who can help you see what you need to see. That guru may not necessarily appear as what we normally call a guru. The guru might take on a humble disguise as another person, perhaps a person you think is below you. "It is from children and fools that you shall hear the truth."

There is always a guru who can help you see, but the question is: "Can *you* see the guru?" Will you even consider that this is a guru who is here to show you something, and will you then heed the guru?

Because this is a subtle initiation, many of the people who are most eager to make progress will choose – before coming into embodiment – to put themselves in contact with a person who appears as an actual guru. Their reasoning is sound: "If I meet a person that I recognize as being a teacher, as being a guru, then it is more likely that I will listen to the guru." It is not an unsound reasoning, but there is no guarantee that you will recognize a person as a guru and still be able to extract the lesson that the guru is meant to teach you.

The fundamental challenge with gurus

The difficulty is that when you are in embodiment and looking through your own perception filter, you are also looking at the guru and the guru's teaching through that perception filter. You are deliberately shutting out what the guru tells you about the consciousness behind your perception filter. You may be willing and able to hear much of what the guru teaches, but there is a part of you that will try to shut out the one lesson that you are meant to learn from this guru.

The excuse that most people come up with on the spiritual path is that they are meant to learn something with the outer mind, something that can be grasped with the outer mind. They are meant to learn something about the spiritual realm, about their auras, their chakras, their this and their that. They are meant to learn all kinds of things about what is outside themselves but not about the beam in their own eye. So many people get caught up in this culture of thinking that: "If I follow the guru's directions – if I live my life the way the guru tells me to do, if I come on staff, if I don't eat this and I don't eat that, if I don't wear black clothes and I don't wear orange clothes, if I don't drive a red car – *then* I am making progress."

You are not actually making progress until you see the element of duality that is standing in your way in this lifetime, the element that is your greatest test and initiation in this lifetime. You will not learn this lesson by listening to the outer teachings, to the words of the guru. How will you then learn the lesson? You may learn it by looking at your *reaction* to the guru. "What is it that the guru brings up in me? How do I respond, not only to what the guru says but to the guru's presence?" This is the one lesson that most students, including most students who came to me in my church, do not understand, do not grasp, do not acknowledge.

The lesson you are meant to learn is not obvious. As a guru, I may see the lesson you are meant to learn, but I cannot express in words exactly what you are meant to learn. What needs to happen inside of you is that you have a direct perception, a direct experience, where you look at your perception filter from outside your perception filter. Words alone will not trigger this experience. You must have that direct experience of stepping outside your perception filter, seeing that you are more than this and then seeing how the filter is limiting you.

That is when you see an element of ego, that is when you see the dweller. You look it straight in the face and say: "Oh, but I see now that *you are not me!* So why am I attached to you? I am no longer attached to you. You can go, I have no more need of you in my life experience." You are not fighting the dweller, you are not afraid of the dweller, you just see it for what it is, see its unreality, see that it is not you. Then you look up and say: "Oh, I am *that* I AM up there, not this little 'I am' down here that I thought I was for so long."

A deeper aspect of the guru-chela relationship

What I am telling you here is that there is a deeper aspect of the guru-chela relationship that was not clearly explained in my church, or for that matter in any outer teaching that you might find on earth. I am attempting to explain this. Perhaps this is not even possible to explain in words, but nevertheless this has never stopped us, who are the ascended masters, from trying to express in words what cannot be expressed in words. At least there is *something* that the students can grasp and use to have the shift in consciousness. The words will not produce the shift, but they can start the spiral that eventually produces the shift.

What I am saying is this: I was in my last embodiment in the position of being a guru. Tens of thousands of people found the teachings, found the church, came to a conference, came to a lecture, saw me on TV, read the books, saw videos and tapes. Tens of thousands of people encountered my Presence as a true, living guru, which I was. Yet I was not the kind of guru that the people who encountered me saw me as. Neither was I the kind of guru that I saw myself as while I was still in the body. I was not the kind of guru that I portrayed myself as being while I was in the body.

If you really want to know what kind of guru I was and what kind of guru I am, you must be willing to do two things.

You must be willing to look beyond the outer form that I had while I was in the body. The way to do this is to realize that the importance for you of encountering my Presence had nothing to do with the outer form and how I was portrayed as a guru. It had everything to do with one thing only: your *reaction* to my outer form. If you are not willing to look at your reaction to my outer form, then you have not even begun to make use of me as a guru. Of course, the same applies to any other guru that you might have encountered on your spiritual path.

It is not the outer form that matters; it is your *reaction* to the guru that can show you something about the state of consciousness that you need to transcend. This is the one thing that I would like all people who encountered my outer form to know and to grasp. It is the one thing that could help them make the progress that they themselves chose, that they wanted to make, by encountering me as a physical guru.

Everyone who came in contact with me chose to do so before they came into this embodiment. You chose to do this for a specific reason. You knew that I was the one who had the potential to force you to see in yourself what you had not been able to see—and what your ego and your dweller does not want you to see.

It is not a matter of obeying my outer teachings and rules. It is a matter of seeing your *reaction* to me. Follow that reaction until you see the underlying consciousness that is your reaction to the guru as a concept. This is the guru as Maitreya or as whichever other ascended master was the one that you chose to walk away from in your own Edenic environment, your own first mystery school.

Why so many reject the guru

So many students came to my church and encountered me – in some cases personally, in others they never encountered me personally but they still encountered me – and they thought it was the outer form that was important. Every single person who encountered me had chosen that encounter because they wanted to force themselves to learn a certain lesson. So many people came to me, focused all of their attention on the outer form, and used my outer form as a justification for not looking at their own reaction and therefore not being able to learn the lesson.

You cannot learn the lesson from any guru unless you look at your *reaction* to that guru. It is impossible. *It is impossible!*

If there was one thing I would like to convey to all people who encountered my physical form, it is precisely this: There are two reactions that will prevent you from learning the lesson you could have learned from your encounter with me. One is that you focus on my outer form and find some perceived imperfection that you use as an excuse for rejecting me, rejecting my message or at least rejecting specific aspects of my message.

This is the outer rejection of the guru, but everything has an Alpha and an Omega aspect. The other way to prevent yourself from learning the lesson is to look at my outer form and my outer teaching and elevate it to some status of superhuman perfection. You think that everything I did or said was superhumanly perfect, and you decide you will blindly follow my teachings and my outer rules and directions. You will do everything I told people to do, and then you think you will automatically qualify for your ascension—for have you not obeyed all the directions of a true guru?

There is the *rejection* of the guru, the outer rejection based on form, and there is the *acceptance* of the guru, but it is an outer acceptance based on form. *Both* serve as an excuse for not looking at yourself, not looking at your own *reaction* to the guru, not looking at what that says about the unresolved substance in your psychology. Both of these reactions serve as an excuse for *not* learning the lesson that you chose, that you wanted to learn from encountering my Presence. *I did not choose it for you. The ascended masters did not choose it for you.* I did not force you to come into my Presence; I am not seeking to force you to learn the lesson that you have the potential to learn. I am simply seeking to point out to you that *you* chose to encounter my Presence in this lifetime.

It is never too late to learn your lesson

Regardless of how you reacted while I was still in a physical body, you have the potential to learn the lesson that you wanted to learn. *It is never too late. I* am no longer in the body, but this does not mean that *you* cannot learn the lesson you were meant to learn from me. You still have your reaction to me. If you are willing to think back to when you encountered me – if you are willing to look at your reaction and follow it all the way to the core consciousness, the core choice, behind it – you can still learn the lesson.

What was the lesson you wanted to learn? Well, it could be many things, it could be at many different levels. Certainly, at the very basic level is a very important lesson. If you are to have any chance of making your ascension in this lifetime, you will have to look at the decision that caused you to turn away from a true guru the very first time you did this. Whether it was Maitreya in the Garden of Eden or another ascended master in another planetary system, perhaps in a previous sphere, it matters not.

There was a point in your past where you decided to turn away from a true guru and go into the Sea of Samsara and follow the false gurus. If you are to make your ascension, you must uncover that decision and transcend it. You can uncover that decision if you are willing to look at your reaction to me or to another physical guru, or even to the concept of a guru, and honestly examine that reaction.

This is the true lesson you are meant to learn from any guru. If you are one of the people who has the potential to ascend after this or the next lifetime, you chose to encounter whichever guru you have encountered, whether it was me or some other guru. You made this choice because you wanted to force yourself to confront your reaction to a guru, a person that you recognize as having the authority and the position of a guru, a person that you recognize as being more advanced spiritually than yourself.

You wanted to force yourself to examine your reaction to this situation where you are confronting a person, or a being, that you perceive as having the position of guru—with whatever that means to you. When you look at whatever that means to you, you will see precisely the false image of the guru that you have created and that you projected upon the true guru. It was not actually the true guru that you turned away from. It was your false image of the guru that you turned away from.

This means that your turning away from the guru was turning away from an illusion. It was an illusion that caused you to turn away from the true guru. How will you ever come back into oneness with the true guru? Only by dismissing that illusion. There is no other way. *There is no other way.*

This is the one message that I would like to give to all those who encountered my physical form, and it is my hope that this book can find its way to these people. It is an important, an essential, a make-or-break-it kind of lesson. I will speak more about it, but certainly one must recognize the conditions of time and space and give one dictation at a time. Even though I am an ascended master who could speak indefinitely, we must recognize that your ability to absorb must follow the cycles of space and time.

5 | WHY YOU DECIDED TO HIDE FROM THE GURU

Guru Ma I AM. And an ascended master I am. How do you become an ascended master? You become an ascended master by letting go of *everything on earth*.

There is literally *nothing* on earth that you can take with you into the ascended realm. What you *can* take with you is what is stored in your causal body, but what is stored in your causal body is very different from the memories stored in your soul vehicle. What enters your causal body is impressions, lessons, memories, but they are not filtered through the perception filter of the soul vehicle. They are seen through the neutrality and the clarity of your I AM Presence and the Conscious You in its pure state.

Seeing life without a perception filter

What do I mean when I say the Conscious You in its pure state? I mean in the state it was in when it originally descended, not necessarily to earth, but when it for the first time descended from the spiritual realm into an unascended sphere. You descended in innocence. This means that you had no perception filter. There was nothing to color your view. There was nothing to give you a sense of value judgment.

What would happen if you could look at life on earth as you experience it right now without any perception filter? What would it be like to look at life on earth through that pure innocence of the person that first descended from heaven? What would you actually see?

Why am I talking about this? Because I wish to give you an impression of how the ascended masters see the earth. This is something that is difficult to express in words and it is difficult to fathom for most people, but there is still value in bringing forth a statement in words so that people might contemplate it and therefore stretch the mind.

I do not expect that by reading my words, you will instantly snap out of your perception filter. You will have a certain coloring with you as long as you are in embodiment on earth because there are certain aspects of this perception filter that are inconsequential to your ascension.

Gurus who claim to be fully evolved

I know that if you survey the situation on earth, you will see that there is today, and there has been in the past, any number of spiritual leaders or gurus who have made the claim about themselves, or whose followers have made the claim about them, that they had reached some ultimate state of consciousness—whether you call it enlightenment, cosmic consciousness or being an *unascended* ascended master.

I certainly made certain statements about myself that were embellished upon by my followers, and a myth was created that Elizabeth Clare Prophet had reached some ultimate state of consciousness. Let me point out to you from my own experience that it *is* possible to raise your consciousness to a high level while you are still in embodiment. It is *not* possible to reach some state of consciousness where you have absolutely no perception filter, where you have absolutely no element of the human consciousness.

When you see a guru who claims that he is God incarnate or has reached some ultimate state of enlightenment while still being in a physical body, you should ask yourself a simple question: "If you are so highly evolved, why are you still in a physical body?" The answer, in many cases, will be that the person is still in a physical body in order to do something for the unenlightened people, in order to do God's work. This may be what the person truly believes. I certainly believed, as long as I was conscious in my physical body, that I had a mission, a purpose, that I was here to do something for God and that I was doing something for other people.

Why are the ascended masters still with earth?

The brutal fact – that you only see from the ascended realm – is that this claim of doing something for God or doing something for other people is still a perception filter. If you claim that you are here to do something for God or do something for others, you are implicitly making the claim that you are here to change something on earth.

This will be a startling statement, surely. Even when he is speaking these words, my messenger senses the reaction from the collective consciousness to these words being spoken in the physical. Surely, many of my own students – and many other spiritual and religious people around the world – will say that this cannot be true. Surely, many ascended master students – whether they followed my church or another – will say that it cannot be true that the ascended masters *do not* want to change things on earth. But *it is actually true.*

Why then, you might ask, are the ascended masters with earth? Why have they not simply moved on, as indeed some people on earth claim they should have? There are some people who deny the existence of ascended masters. There are some people who do not deny that ascended masters exist, but claim that they remain with earth only because there is something they have not resolved and therefore they cannot move on—thereby claiming that even an ascended master has unresolved issues.

Strange as it might seem, these people are actually making their claim in good faith. They are even right. Only, they are not talking about ascended masters. They are talking about impostors of ascended masters who live in the lower etheric or the mental realm and claim to be ascended masters. These beings have not moved on. They do have unresolved issues, and this is proven by the fact that they are seeking to change people on earth.

How do you become an ascended master? By leaving behind *everything* on earth, including the desire to change anything on earth. This was one of the hardest lessons for me to get before I could qualify for my ascension. Oh yes, they tried to help me. Lanello tried to help me, Master MORE, or as I saw him, El Morya, tried to help me. Jesus tried to help me, Saint Germain tried to help me, Mother Mary tried to help me.

I kept reasoning with them, saying that, surely, this could not be true. If it was true, would it not invalidate everything that I had done from my early childhood of sensing I was on a mission to help God bring peace to earth and improve things on this planet?

All of my service during my teenage years, my youth, during my work with Mark, doing my work with the church; all of this would seem to have been for nothing if the ascended masters did not want to change something on earth.

Ah, but you see, the ascended masters do not want to change anything on earth; they want *human beings* to change conditions on earth. They only want human beings to do this out of their completely free will. This is what is so difficult to understand, to grasp, to accept while you are still in embodiment. Let me attempt to explain why it is so difficult to get this.

The contrast between innocence and evil

Let me speak about my own example. If you have read anything about my childhood, you will know that I grew up with an alcoholic father who, almost on a daily basis throughout my entire childhood, would be drunk at night and would be verbally abusive towards my mother. I had, of course, chosen to come into embodiment in this situation, and I did this because by choosing a father who had such an extreme issue, I was hoping to force myself to learn the lesson I needed to learn. I did not learn that lesson while I was still living at home with my father. I did not even learn it while I was conscious in my body. I only learned it afterwards, and that is why I wish to pass it on so that there is a record of my unlearned lesson—and others might learn it.

The effects of being a young child and witnessing this abusive behavior of my father was that I formed a deep desire to not only change my father but to change conditions on earth so that no child would have to grow up in such a situation. What also happened during my childhood is that I was born right around the time of the outbreak of the Second World War. When I was only three years old, my father was taken away under suspicion of being a German spy. I experienced firsthand what a war situation can be like, even though we had no direct fighting where I lived. After the war, I was exposed to the newsreels and all of the news coverage of the Holocaust, and I was deeply and profoundly shocked that such inhumanity could take place on the same planet where I was living.

Do you understand – perhaps through your own experience – what was the issue that was so dominant in my childhood? I know that for many people these issues have not been so extreme in their childhood, but I also know that many spiritual people have had childhoods that were fully as difficult or even more difficult than my own. I have, over my many years as a spiritual leader, had so many students come to me who were even more deeply scarred by their childhood than I was myself. And here I was, the halt, seeking to help the lame.

What is the issue here? The issue is very simply the contrast between innocence and evil, pure unadulterated, unmasked evil. Consider my own situation. From a certain outer standpoint, you could say that I had an idyllic childhood. I grew up in a beautiful and peaceful small town. My parents were still living together. They were not lacking for money. We had a beautiful house that we were constantly upgrading and remodeling and making more beautiful. We had a beautiful garden. When I think back at my childhood, I can see that there was a part of me that had what any child should have: the innocence of growing up in a beautiful garden in an idyllic environment.

There were times where I sensed this, yet there was always a shadow hanging over my home and my childhood. It was that I never knew when my father would come home and what state he would be in. How severe was his abuse? How drunk was he? What was he going to say or do? I had on one side the idyllic environment of the beautiful garden, my wonderful dog, my friends and the flowers and the birds and the bees and all of this beauty. But always, as a looming shadow, was this evil that came through my father and for which I felt I had no protection, I had no escape, I had no recourse.

This is a situation that all children on earth have to deal with. We all have to deal with it in varying degrees. We all have to find a way to deal with the fact that we are on a planet where on the one hand there is such beauty and idyllic conditions, and on the other hand there is the threat that some evil can come in at any moment and overturn the beauty and the idyllic scenario. Who has not dealt with this?

If you as an adult say: "Oh I don't remember dealing with this in my childhood," then the key words are that you don't remember because you *did* have to deal with it. You may have suppressed what you did. You may have suppressed how you dealt with it, but you had to deal with it because you cannot grow up on this planet without dealing with it at some point or another. Your parents might have shielded you for some time, but it is inevitable that at some point, you will be confronted with the existence of evil in some form.

We deal with evil by creating internal spirits

How, then, do we deal with this? We deal with it by creating at least two spirits, as the Maha Chohan has explained through this messenger. If you take my father's case, he himself was not necessarily what you could call an evil person. When I say this, I say it guardedly. His behavior, his attitude towards life and his behavior towards my mother and me were evil. There was no question about it. His actions were evil, his words were evil, but if I had told him that he was an evil man, he would have been shocked and surprised.

In a sense, I understand the reaction. He was not deliberately seeking to hurt my mother or myself. He was simply insensitive to how his actions and words affected us. The real question is: What makes it possible that human beings can become so insensitive to the suffering of others that they do not see how they are hurting those others?

The answer is spirits, the creation of spirits. My father had a core of his being that was not evil. Once in a rare while, this would shine through. On a more regular basis, he behaved like a normal, kind person. It was mostly when the alcohol entered his system that he lost control and was taken over by the two spirits that dominated his life. There was one spirit that was quite aware that you cannot mess with God and God's law and get away with it. He would often tell me that everything you do comes back to you. What I did not perceive as a child was that behind this statement was a deep, almost absolute, resentment of this fact. He actually hated God for having created a cosmic law that returned to him what he sent out. This was a spirit that he had created over thousands of lifetimes, not even on earth but way beyond in previous spheres, for he had indeed fallen in a higher sphere. It had become so strong that he had no way of seeing beyond it.

On the one hand, there was a spirit who completely understood God's law but rebelled against it. Of course, this spirit could not exist on its own. When you recognize that there is a law that you do not have the power to change or avoid, what is the point of rebelling against that which cannot be changed? The spirit of rebellion must have an evil twin, which feels powerless and resents the fact that it is powerless. His other spirit felt completely powerless towards God and was therefore looking for some way here on earth to capture a sense of power. This was what he had attained in capturing my mother, who had her own spirits and therefore was essentially looking for someone to abuse her so that she did not have to take responsibility for herself.

The type of lifestreams that cannot be helped

My point here is to describe the basic mechanism that applies to all people on earth, including all who are spiritual students. What you have on earth is a dynamic that is not well known at all outside ascended master teachings. It is only through the grace of the ascended masters that we have been given at least a hint of the real dynamic on this planet.

The dynamic is that you have two different kinds of lifestreams on this planet. You have, as Jesus himself attempted to explain, the tares among the wheat. These are the lifestreams that have deliberately, consciously and willfully rebelled against God and God's design of the universe. Most of these lifestreams did not rebel here on earth or even in the current material universe, the current sphere, as Maitreya has explained through this messenger. This, by the way, is a teaching that goes far beyond what was given in my own church, for it could not be given in the old dispensation.

Most of these lifestreams rebelled against God in a higher sphere. They have fallen through several spheres, and their rebellion has only grown stronger to the point that in some of these people the rebellion is absolute. When I say "absolute," I do not mean that it could not be changed, but that the likelihood of them being willing to change it is, for all practical purposes, zero.

I can look back today, as an ascended master, and I can see that even if I could appear to my father as an ascended master, I still do not know what I could have said to him that would have helped him turn his life around. I have, in the process leading up to my ascension and even since, looked back several times upon my childhood and considered what could possibly have helped my father. I still do not have a clear answer. I can see things that I could have said, that I was not able to say as a child or as a young adult or even later in life. I still cannot say that I am convinced that saying any of these things would have actually made a difference for my father.

This is the one group of lifestreams that you have on earth. There are those who are so entrenched in their rebellion against God that no force outside themselves could possibly change them. This is a sobering realization when you first come to it.

When you are not one of the lifestreams that rebelled against God, you have a deep desire to believe that change is possible. In a sense, you are right: Change *is* possible. It is always possible that a lifestream could turn around, yet the realization you come to is that there is nothing that any *outside* force could do that could turn around one of these lifestreams. *You* cannot help them. There is absolutely nothing you could do to help these lifestreams, to change them, to turn them around, to awaken them. *There is nothing you could do.*

This is the one group of lifestreams that you have embodying on earth. My father was one of these fallen lifestreams who had in a very distant past rebelled against God. What he was today was only a shadow of who he was as a being when he first rebelled. He was far more powerful, but through his continued abuse of power, he had reduced his powers to do evil to the point where he was only able to control one other human being, namely my mother.

The type of lifestreams who want to help others

You also have the other group of lifestreams. These are those of us who did not rebel against God. We did not leave the Garden of Eden out of rebellion against God and God's design for the universe. What we all need to recognize and come to terms with is that we *did* leave the garden, and we did so because we turned our backs upon the teacher.

If you take the story of the Garden of Eden, as it is given in Genesis, you can see the symbolism. There was the serpent in the Garden who was trying to tell Eve that what God had said, what the teacher had said, was wrong. This demonstrates the kind of lifestream that rebels against God.

Eve was tempted by this. She made a mistake, but her real mistake was that after she saw that she was naked, she did not want to come back to the teacher. Adam and Eve decided to hide from the teacher.

You now have the two groups of lifestreams: Those who deliberately and willfully rebelled against the teacher and those who are merely hiding from the teacher. If you are a lifestream that has rebelled against the teacher, it is very, very difficult for you to come back into the circle of oneness of the teacher. If you are one of the lifestreams that is merely hiding from the teacher, it is possible for you to come back, but you can come back in only one way: by looking at the reason you decided that you had to hide from the teacher.

Why did you decide that you had to hide from the teacher? Because you had created a mental image of the teacher, you had projected that image upon the teacher and you believed that this is how the teacher was. Based on this image, you believed that when the teacher found out that you had eaten the forbidden fruit against his instruction, he would react in a certain way. In order to avoid that reaction, you decided to hide from the teacher. If you were to come to see that your mental image of the teacher was completely out of touch with the reality of who the teacher is – if you were to really acknowledge that your mental image was an illusion – then you could come back to the teacher.

You need to acknowledge that all of this time – all of these long millennia, possibly millions of years and thousands upon thousands of embodiments – you have not been really hiding from the teacher, you have been hiding from a mental image. This mental image is a complete illusion, a fabrication that has nothing to do with reality.

You have been hiding from a mirage whereas the real teacher is still there. He is ready to start your relationship with him anew at any moment. You must be willing to come back to him without relating to him through the image that you had created.

Why did you eat the forbidden fruit?

What will it take for you to come to this realization? First, you must recognize that you created your mental image based on your own self, your limited self. This self is not who you really are. It was simply a self you had taken on in order to experience and do certain things in the world of form. It was out of this self that you created the mental image of the teacher, for you projected the elements of your self upon the teacher.

You thought that the teacher would react to you the same way that you would have reacted if you were in the teacher's position. In reality, you were not relating to the teacher based on who you really are and who the teacher really is. You were relating to yourself through this self, and you were relating to the teacher through the mental image of him that you had created by projecting the qualities of your own self upon the teacher.

You can go even deeper and ask: "Why did I eat the forbidden fruit?" There was for you personally some temptation, some curiosity, some question of wondering what it would be like to experience life through a separate self, a self that was not seeing itself as an extension of God and as part of a greater whole. This separate self could believe that it was better than others, that it could do whatever it wanted without considering how it affected others or any number of other temptations of experiences that you cannot have while you are connected to the teacher and in the circle of oneness of the teacher.

You began to wonder: "What would it be like if I was outside the circle of oneness and could behave in this particular way? What would that be like?" It was your curiosity that caused you to first taste the forbidden fruit. When you had tasted the fruit – and when you realized that you could not actually hide this from the teacher – then the very experience that you desired to have now became the perception filter through which you were looking at the teacher. If you had desired a certain experience, such as feeling better than other people, then you would think that the teacher would feel better than you because you made the mistake of going into the duality consciousness. You thought that the teacher would be as judgmental towards you as you had been towards others through your separate self.

It goes with the territory, my beloved. If you have entered a separate self that is judging others, the most unpleasant thing you can experience through that separate self is that you are judged by someone else. The very fact that you are judging others means that you are projecting upon the teacher that he will be judging you. You are then thinking that the worst thing that could ever happen to you was that you had to go back to the teacher and endure his judgment. *That* is why you would rather run away and hide so you did not have to endure from the teacher what you projected would come.

In reality, you are the one who has entered into duality and separation. The teacher has stayed in oneness. You are judging everybody else, but the teacher is not judging everybody else, including *you*. The teacher is not the one who will judge you. You will, as Jesus explained, judge yourself.

When you take on the consciousness, the perception filter, that judges, you will judge everything, including you. Of course, you will not admit this. You *cannot* admit this while you are in the perception filter. By the very fact that you are judging others, you must project that there is some external authority who is judging you and who is the ultimate judge. There is the teacher, but behind that is God and so we have the image of the judgmental God.

We did not create the perception filter we took on

When you begin to see this, then you can begin to consciously say to yourself: "Listen, I have had enough of this. I want to see what this perception filter is, I want to see its unreality and I want to transcend it. I want to go beyond it for I know I am more than this." In order to get to that point of being free of your perception filter, you have to do one more thing. You have to realize that the perception filter of the separate self, the separate self itself, the consciousness behind it, was not actually created by you. It was created by the beings who rebelled against God.

Why did I say that it is almost impossible for the fallen beings, the rebellious beings, to get out of their rebellion? Because if they were to admit that this is a perception filter, then they would actually have to admit that it was created by themselves. You are not one of the rebellious beings. You have not actually created the perception filter. You took it on. You made the choice to take it on, yes, and you are responsible for that choice. You must undo that choice in order to be free of it, but you did not actually rebel against God. You took on an element of the separate self that was created by those beings who rebelled against God. This is why it is easier for the lifestreams who are *hiding* from the teacher to come back than it is for those who are *rebelling* against the teacher.

6 | HOW TO FREE YOURSELF FROM THE FALLEN BEINGS

How do you, truly, come back to the teacher? By recognizing that an ascended master has never taken on the perception filter of the fallen beings. When I say "never," this is a statement that must be qualified. If the ascended master ascended from earth or another unascended sphere, then that lifestream did take on the perception filter in the past, but it has risen above it by ascending. Nevertheless, if you were one of the lifestreams that were with Lord Maitreya in the mystery school called the Garden of Eden, then in all of the time since Maitreya became the head of that mystery school, he has never taken on the fallen consciousness.

Regardless of how deep that you might have gone into that fallen consciousness after you left Maitreya, he has been completely unaffected and has never taken on the fallen consciousness. He does not look at you and does not judge you as you judge yourself or judge him. Maitreya is an ascended master who has no perception filter affected by the fallen consciousness. Maitreya has not followed you in your detour into the fallen consciousness, has never looked at you the way you have looked at yourself or looked at the world. Neither has Maitreya looked at himself the way you look at him. This means that Maitreya today is completely neutral and non-judgmental towards you or any choice you have made in separation.

The ascended masters do not judge you

Whatever you may have done on earth, whatever consciousness and separate self you may have created, Maitreya – and any ascended master – stands ready today to help you, exactly where you are, start the path that leads you to the ascension. Maitreya does not say: "Oh you have done this, you have done that, you should feel bad." Maitreya simply says: "Are you ready to move on, for I am ready to help you move on? Have you had enough of the separate self? Then let us move on together."

There is no other reaction here. There is no judgment from an ascended master. There is no consciousness in the ascended masters that you have to acknowledge your mistake and feel shame or guilt. This is all a projection of the fallen consciousness and its perception filter. All of the images of the angry and judgmental God – that have been floating around in the collective consciousness on earth for millennia – all of these images came exclusively from the fallen consciousness. They did not come from God. They did not come from the ascended masters. This is one of the shocking realizations you come to.

I, myself, had to acknowledge that as long as I was conscious in the body, I was affected by this image of a God who was looking down on earth and having condemnation of the evil that was going on here on earth. I had the image that before a lifestream could truly engage in the spiritual path, it had to come to that point of humility, of admitting its mistakes and therefore feeling bad about those mistakes. I had the sense that a student had to submit to the teacher, had to be willing to admit its mistake or its inadequacy, and accept whatever the teacher said out of the recognition that it had sinned and that it needed the teacher in order to be redeemed.

It was shocking to me to realize that this was a mental image that I had taken over – partly from my father, partly from the collective consciousness – and that I had projected upon the ascended masters. It was shocking to me to realize that I had projected qualities upon El Morya that El Morya does not have. I still remember, at inner levels, coming to this realization, suddenly seeing it. It was like one of the greatest shocks that I have ever experienced. While my body was incapacitated, I experienced in my finer being this complete shift where the scales fell from my eyes and I saw that El Morya was not the strict, blue-ray master that I had projected upon him for so many years.

In my finer bodies I rushed to Darjeeling. I rushed to Morya and I fell on my knees and I looked up at him and I said: "Master, I apologize. I am so sorry that I projected this image upon you." What was his reaction, my beloved? Well, his reaction shocked me even more. He looked me straight in the eye and said: "Why do you feel you need to apologize to me? Get up and get out of your self-pity and stop looking at me as a being who needs an apology from you. I only need you to free yourself from your self-created illusion so that you can be who you are and therefore can relate to me as I am."

I got up and, again, I felt as if my entire world had been turned upside down, inside out. I was shocked, and then, suddenly, I was not standing in front of Morya, looking at him. I was one with Morya looking at me, looking at my own lifestream, my own self. I suddenly saw this self that was the overlay over my real, innocent inner being. I saw how Morya saw it, without any judgment from him, simply a recognition of its unreality and the deeper reality that I am. Then, I switched back, and I looked at the self from the inside and I said: "Poof," and it was gone.

The joy of being liberated from your separate self

Then, I looked at Morya, who was grinning from ear to ear. No words could possibly be said. No words were necessary, for we were one in the deepest joy possible, the joy that you experience when as a student you have come back to oneness with the teacher. This is the greatest joy you can experience as a being who is transcending the separate self: coming back into oneness with the teacher. After you ascend, there are other joys, but for a being who has been trapped in separation there is no greater joy than coming back to oneness with the teacher.

Ah, how I wish all of you, who are spiritual students on earth, could experience even a glimpse of this oneness with whomever ascended being is your personal teacher. Even a glimpse, a split second, would change you forever, change your identification with this outer self that seems so all-important to us while we are in embodiment. Why does it seem so all-important? Because *we have drunk our own Kool-Aid!*

Surviving the abuse of the rebellious lifestreams

We have become convinced that we are here on earth to solve a problem, to affect a change. This is the next phase in freeing yourself from the outer self. What have I said happened in my father's case? He was trapped between two spirits, but what happened to me as a child growing up in that environment? What had happened to me in past lifetimes that caused me to choose that environment?

Here is the simple reality on earth. Ever since the fallen lifestreams were allowed to embody on this planet, they have dominated life here. They have dominated the collective consciousness, the very view of life that has been floating around in the collective consciousness in this and past civilizations. Those of us who are not the rebellious lifestreams, have embodied on earth because we turned our backs to the teacher. As a result of embodying on earth, we have been forced to react to the rebellious lifestreams and their schemes. The rebellious lifestreams have been trapped by their own spirits that kept them trapped in the rebellious state of consciousness. They have perpetrated all manner of atrocities. They have done the most evil, insensitive acts, often for no other purpose than stealing the spiritual light that other people misqualified.

They have also enacted all kinds of schemes aimed at sabotaging the spiritual progress and the ascension of the non-rebellious lifestreams, keeping them trapped in the fallen consciousness for as long as possible, possibly even to the point where they could not make their ascension. The fallen beings have done this because they wanted to prove God wrong. They wanted to prove that it was wrong that God gave all lifestreams, including themselves, free will.

They were trying to use the free will given to them by God to prove that God was wrong for giving beings free will and that free will was a mistake. If you think there is any logic to this, then you are blinded by the fallen consciousness. Only through that perception filter can it seem logical that you can use your free will to override the free will of others and that this can prove the fallacy of free will. The other side of the coin is that people can also use their free will *not* to follow the rebellious lifestreams, and this is the way to make your ascension. Therefore, the fallen beings can never prove free will wrong, for it is the only way that you can grow as a self-aware being.

The point is that those of you who are not the rebellious lifestreams have been forced, over many lifetimes, to react to the abuses, to the evil, of the fallen, rebellious lifestreams. What have you done in this process? What have we all done in this process? Well, we have created our own spirits in order to react to the abuse of the rebellious lifestreams. In my case, as a child with an abusive father, I also created two spirits. One was the spirit that accepted that I could not get away from this father. I was a relatively powerless child and it never seriously occurred to me to run away from home. It simply did not occur to me to run away even though I could have done so. It never occurred to me to object, to seek help, to tell my father and mother that I did not want to live with them but wanted to move somewhere else. I accepted that I had to be in that situation, and this meant I created a spirit that felt powerless: powerless to get away, powerless to change the situation.

Why we believe in superheroes

Such a spirit cannot exist alone for it would be unbearable. It had to have a twin, and that twin was the dream that it was possible to not only change my situation and change my father, but to change the greater situation of earth that I saw in the Holocaust and the war. It was the dream that it was possible to bring change, to bring peace, and that there was some kind of superhero that could come in and set things right on earth.

I understand full well why there are psychologists who say that our belief in God, and even my adult belief in ascended masters, is simply due to our feeling powerless in childhood and therefore dreaming of a superhero, a magic helper, who can come in and protect us from the abuses and the powerlessness and set things right. I understand this. What the psychologists do not understand is that this is not actually a condition of the lifestream itself, of the Conscious You. It is a spirit.

There *is* a spirit that feels powerless and there *is* a spirit that, as a compensation for the sense of powerlessness, creates the image of a superhero. I had over many lifetimes been deeply distraught and disturbed by the evil I saw on earth. I had even had lifetimes in the past where I had been in leadership positions. I had the opportunity to change society, but still felt that I had not been able to affect the change I wanted to see. I had not been able to get rid of evil on earth. This had deepened my sense of powerlessness, it had intensified the spirit that wanted some superhero to come in and bring a solution.

As I grew up, I came into contact with the Christian Science belief system and other Christian belief systems. I came to believe that God and Jesus are the ultimate solution. When I learned about the ascended masters, I transferred this to them and believed that they could bring the solution. They were the superheroes who could and would come in if only I did my part, if only I strove to raise my consciousness, to give the calls and the prayers and the decrees, to teach the teachings, to become a messenger, to become an open door.

As I have explained, beginning with my first discourse, there is a phase on our personal path where we have to go through a very turbulent period. During this period, we are very easily pulled down by the forces in the collective consciousness. We are very easily tempted by the dark forces to go into a negative spiral. We need a vessel that is closed off so that there is no inroad for these external forces. It was indeed in my divine plan that I would become a messenger for the ascended masters, a spiritual teacher and a leader of a spiritual organization. It was perfectly right for me to pursue this goal.

The intensity of the attacks from dark forces

During my youth and my earlier years as leader of the church, I was very vulnerable to the attacks of dark forces. These attacks were extremely intense. My beloved, I do not wish to in any way make it seem like what I experienced was worse than what so many other people have experienced. But I can assure you that as a messenger for the ascended masters, you are probably seen by the fallen beings, who think they rule this planet, as the greatest possible threat. Therefore, they will throw everything at you, including the kitchen sink. They will do everything they can to derail you. The same holds true for any person who has the potential to ascend in this lifetime. The dark forces are there and they will do everything they can to block your ascension.

This means that there was a period in my life where I absolutely needed a vehicle that could pull me through this turbulence and this resistance. The vehicle became my firm belief that it was possible to change things on earth. The ascended masters were the superheroes who would do this if I did my part here below. This was the only way that I, given who I was and given the position I was in, could have pulled through and survived. I am not only talking physical survival – but my physical survival *was* threatened in those earlier years – I am also talking my psychological and spiritual survival.

The intensity of the dark forces is something that will only be believed when you experience it, and I know that many spiritual people have experienced this intensity. Why do you think you have had difficult situations in your childhood and life? Why do you think you have been submitted to these attacks and humiliations from other people? It is the intensity of the dark forces working through these people in their attempts to derail you from fulfilling your divine plan and qualifying for your ascension. All of this is real, in the sense that it has a temporary reality on earth. Those psychologists, and other skeptics, who will deny this are simply out of touch with reality.

They may not have experienced this attack, for the simple reason that they are not a threat to the dark forces. It is those who do attempt to rise beyond the mass consciousness who become a threat and therefore become the target of these attacks. As long as you are floating along with the currents of the mass consciousness, you may never feel an attack from dark forces. It doesn't mean it isn't there. Those who are trapped in the collective consciousness are indeed controlled by the dark forces, but they do not realize it. They have become so used to it, so numb to it, that they do not see it, just as my father did not see how he was controlled by alcohol, by his own spirits and by the demons that came in with the alcohol.

What did I do? I was in a difficult situation as a child. I faced a very difficult challenge as an adult being a woman, being alone, running a spiritual organization, being a messenger for the ascended masters. I simply did what I had to do to survive and to make it through that situation. I did what I had to do, given the outer situation I was in and given the inner situation of my own psychological landscape. I did the best I could, given the circumstances, and I am not saying this to justify myself. I am saying this to make you take a look at your life and see that whatever you have done up to this point was the best you could do, given your *external* and *internal* circumstances.

How we can and cannot remove evil from earth

You have done the best you could do. The question is: By shifting your attitude a little bit, by becoming aware of certain information, could you do better? Are you willing to let me help you shift your attitude so that you can do better?

I have a desire to see you do better in the rest of your lifetime than I did in mine. That is why I give these teachings. What was the case for me? I needed the belief that change was possible on earth, that it was possible for God to relinquish evil and that I could play an important part in God's plan for relinquishing evil from the earth.

Here is where, again, we face one of these subtleties. It is perfectly true that when you stand back from the earth, you see that the ascended masters, the Karmic Board, have a plan for removing evil from the earth. There are people who have reached, in past lives, a certain level of spiritual attainment and who are therefore suited to playing an active part in that plan. I was one of those people and you are too, or you probably would not be reading this. We have the potential to play a part in removing evil from earth, we took embodiment for this reason. This is perfectly correct; it is perfectly valid.

The problem is that the way we remove evil from the earth is by freeing ourselves completely from any influence from the consciousness of evil. That means, as I gave my own example, that I had to free myself from both of the spirits I had created in response to my father and that I had even carried with me from past lives. In order to fulfill our highest potential to help remove evil from the earth, we have to free ourselves from the spirits that we have created in response to the rebellious beings and their evil. It is not a matter of fighting evil and destroying it; it is not even a matter of fighting evil with spiritual means and destroying it.

Freeing ourselves from any influence of evil

We have to free ourselves from it so that we can actually be in embodiment and the presence of evil on this planet is irrelevant to us. This does not mean that we deny the presence of evil. It does not mean that we ignore the presence of evil, but it means that the prince of this world has nothing in us whereby he can force us to react to evil. We have learned the ultimate meaning of Jesus' call to turn the other cheek, instead of reacting to evil through one of the two spirits that evil always seeks to force us to create.

In my childhood, I was dominated by the one spirit that felt powerless. I was constantly longing for the other spirit. When I became an adult – when I met Mark and we started the church and I learned the teachings of the ascended masters – I switched. I gradually pulled my attention away from the powerless spirit, and I started feeling more and more empowered. I *was* in a certain sense much more empowered because I did have a true teaching from the ascended masters and I did have a valid spiritual practice in the decrees.

What I am saying here is this: Even though I was doing the right thing, I still did it with an overlay of the spirit that now felt empowered to fight evil. This spirit was created out of the consciousness of separation. Even though it was a spirit that recognized the reality of ascended masters and the potential to destroy evil, it was not helping me free myself from the consciousness of evil.

Again, there is a subtlety. This does not mean that everything I did was wrong or that it was wasted. I am not here trying to say that all of our decree sessions against dark forces were illusions or that they were a waste of time. They were not. They had an effect, but they did not have the effect that I believed that they had while I was in embodiment.

This is what you need to see if you truly want to be free from evil. You need to see that what the fallen beings, the false hierarchy impostors, have done on earth is that they have created a situation where there is so much evil that it is impossible to embody on this planet without having to deal with evil. What they have then done is that they have created a collective consciousness that makes you think that you have only two ways to react to evil.

If you are one of the beings who did not rebel against God, you will become subject to the belief that evil should not be here, that it is possible to do something to remove evil or destroy evil and that you are here to help in this process. You must do so the only way you can see how to do it based on your individual spirits. There is one spirit that makes you feel powerless towards evil. There is another spirit that makes you feel that you can combat or neutralize evil in this particular way.

Seeking to remove evil through a spirit that is created out of the consciousness that fuels evil, will not remove evil. What will truly bring about the banishment of evil from earth is that a critical mass of people free themselves from *both* spirits, from any influence from the consciousness of evil. They can face the temptations that Jesus faced when he encountered the devil after his stay in the wilderness and many other temptations that he faced. The prince of this world comes and has nothing in you, he has no spirit whereby he can force you to react. This is what I did not fathom while I was conscious in my body.

There are many good reasons I did not get this. My physical illness was one, my upbringing was another. My entire involvement with the ascended masters actually seemed to justify and validate the one spirit, the so-called empowered spirit. I was convinced that it was good that I was no longer feeling disempowered but was feeling empowered. All of this created a perception filter so strong that I could not see beyond it. *I* could not free myself from it while I was still in embodiment, but *you* don't have to wait until you leave the body to begin to see through this.

The many people who were part of my church in one way or another – and who were therefore affected by my perception filter – you don't have to live the rest of this embodiment being affected by this. You can begin to question it, to look beyond it, and to see that this does not mean that you have to jump into the other extreme. The fact that you recognize that there were some aspects of my ministry that were not the highest possible, does not mean that you have to go in and reject me, everything I stand for, reject the ascended masters, reject your own involvement with the ascended masters' teachings. You do not have to feel that it was all a waste, it was all an illusion, it was all wrong, I was a false prophet and this and that and the next thing.

Whether you follow me blindly or whether you reject me, you are responding to me through a dualistic spirit that is exactly what the dark forces and the false teachers want. *Can you not begin to see this?*

Following me blindly, rejecting me blindly—it is a dualistic polarity between the two. What is the right way, the higher way? It is Gautama's way, the *Middle* Way, the straight and narrow way of Christ and the Buddha. I wish I had been able to be more on the Middle Way while I was still in embodiment, but my wish is in a sense futile. I look back at my time in embodiment, and I see that – given who I was, given what the situation was – there is nothing anybody could have said to me that would have changed my perspective. I see this clearly.

Some will understand

If anyone had come up to me and attempted to give me these teachings that I have just given you, I would have rejected them outright. I would have immediately started citing all kinds of dictations from ascended masters as a proof of how wrong what you are saying is. I would have used the teachings of the ascended masters to argue against a higher teaching from the ascended masters.

I can look at the lifestreams of many of the people who were my students, and I can see that they are also in a situation – due to their outer circumstances and their inner circumstances – where the words I am bringing forth in this book are not likely to have any impact on them—even if they ever read them. If they were to read them, they would probably take my own teachings, given while I was embodiment, and use them to reject and argue against the teachings I am now giving as an ascended master. Based on this, you could say that bringing forth this book is an exercise in futility. But as Gautama realized, *some* will understand.

If even one person understands, who would not otherwise have understood, then the effort was worthwhile. This is the principle that Sanat Kumara employed when he came to earth in its darkest hour. He had two beings respond; the ones who later became Gautama the Buddha and Maitreya the Buddha. Because they responded, others were able to respond and such is the chain of hierarchy, the progress of hierarchy. Progress on earth must start with one individual who decides to raise its consciousness beyond the reaction to the rebellious beings. Some - will - *under* - stand - and - *over* - come.

7 | KNOWING WHAT KIND OF PLANET YOU ARE ON

I AM the Ascended Master Guru Ma. If you know anything about my last embodiment, you will know that one of my greatest concerns was education. I gave many lectures or talks about the need for a better form of education, even the deplorable state of modern-day education in the United States. However, the greatest lack in modern education is the lack of awareness of the presence of the fallen beings on this planet.

When you look at my life, you will see that my thinking was very much affected by my awareness that there are fallen beings both in and out of embodiment. There are those beings out of embodiment who are seeking to control humankind from the astral realm, the emotional realm, even from the mental and the lower etheric realm. They have set themselves up as the false teachers, as the false hierarchy, and they are seeking to force or fool humankind into following their schemes.

The primary tool that these disembodied beings use is the fallen beings in embodiment, or the people who are either deceived or overwhelmed by, identified with, the fallen consciousness or a certain aspect of it. It is possible for a lifestream not to have directly, personally rebelled against God but to still have stepped into a self, a role, defined by the fallen beings who did rebel against God. The reason this is possible is partly free will and partly the fact that the presence of the fallen beings on earth forces all human beings to react to this fact.

It is impossible to take physical embodiment on earth without being affected by the fallen beings and the fallen consciousness. It is virtually impossible to take embodiment on earth without reacting in some way to the fallen beings and the fallen consciousness. Furthermore, any way that you react to the fallen beings and the fallen consciousness, will trap you in one of the spirals, the downward spirals, created by the fallen beings to suck you down under the surface of the Sea of Samsara.

The basic facts about life

These are the basic facts about life on earth:

- There are fallen beings in and out of embodiment.

- They have aggressively and deceptively created any number of schemes aimed at forcing you to react to them.

- Any way that you do react to them will tie you to them and to their schemes. It will suck you down into a downward spiral that can quickly cause you to lose control over your life, your free will, your vision, your relationship to God.

If people knew this, would you not say that they have a much better chance of avoiding being sucked into one of the schemes created by the fallen beings? You may have seen on movies that people come to an area and there is a sign that says "Minefield." You may also have seen that there are soldiers who walk into a minefield without knowing that it is a minefield. Surely, it is never a good thing to have to walk through a minefield. But if you *do* have to walk through a minefield, wouldn't you say that it was at least an advantage to know that it is a minefield. Especially if you also knew that there are certain signs you can look for that will tell you where the mines are buried so that you can actually avoid them if you exercise due caution and use your powers of observation.

Would it not be at least reasonable that people would know what kind of planet they are embodied on, what kind of conditions they face, so that they would have a free choice as to whether they would react to the fallen beings or whether they would try to find a way to not react to the fallen beings? If you said: "Yes, this would be reasonable," then it is likely that you are not a fallen being and neither are you identified fully with one of the selves, the roles, defined by the fallen beings. You have started to pull yourself away from identification with the mortal self, the ego, the dweller, the carnal mind, the human mind.

The belief that God gave earth to the devil

There are beings, in and out of embodiment, who would not agree with this statement. They feel that it is perfectly right that human beings do not know what kind of planet they are on. They believe this because they actually have come to believe that God himself has given planet earth, and even the material universe, to the fallen beings as their playground.

These are beings who have created a very peculiar line of reasoning. They have said, long ago in a different sphere: "God has given all beings free will. We think this was a mistake, we resent free will. We want to prove that God was wrong for giving all beings free will. God should have given us, who are clearly the superior beings, free will, and then he should have put all those other beings under our command so that they would have to follow our directions, they would be saved by following our directions. Since God is not willing to do this, we are going to prove to God that his decision to give all beings free will was wrong. How are we going to do this? We are going to do this by taking advantage of the Law of Free Will."

"We are going to take the Law of Free Will to its absolutely most extreme extent. We are going to use our free will to demand of God that we be given an entire realm with self-aware beings embodying and that God leaves that realm and its future to us. God steps out of that realm and lets us do what we want without interfering with it. This is our right according to the Law of Free Will, and we are demanding that God does this, that God gives us an entire world and says: 'I will not interfere, this is *your* world.'"

My beloved, as a human being in embodiment on earth, you have never encountered one of this class of fallen beings for they are no longer allowed to embody on earth. If you could remember very distant past lives, you might remember them from past civilizations where they had set themselves up as the leaders and caused the downfall of those civilizations without ever being willing to acknowledge that it was their doing. In recent times, such beings have not been allowed to take embodiment.

When you walk the path towards the ascension, you will come to a point where you are confronted with this state of consciousness and these beings at inner levels. I actually had almost physical confrontations with such beings while I was still in embodiment and functioning as a messenger. They came to me, not in the physical but certainly in the astral plane and in the mental and lower etheric.

They sent their representatives to me and they tried to either scare me, to persuade me or to deceive me into accepting that

God had given them the earth and that I had no right to accept the mantle of "Messenger of the Great White Brotherhood." I had no right to bring forth messages from the ascended masters for it would interfere with the gift that God had given them. They would say that the ascended masters were violating God's law by seeking to enlighten humankind, for God himself had given them the right to force and deceive human beings without interfering with them.

A very subtle fallen argument

This can be a surprisingly persuasive argument. Would it not seem logical that if you take the Law of Free Will to its ultimate extent, then certain beings should be allowed to say: "We want the opportunity to have an entire planet, or an entire realm, where we can see if we can prove God wrong, if we can prove that nobody will be saved through free will." If you look at this argument through a certain perception filter, it can seem almost airtight. After all, would not that be just the extreme interpretation of the Law of Free Will?

While you are in embodiment, this can be difficult to sort out. I, myself, must confess that I had certain doubts after being presented with this argument. It took me some time to sort this out. In fact, I did not sort it out completely until I had withdrawn from the physical body while my body was still alive.

The deeper reality is that the Law of Free Will does not put any restrictions on your free will. You have been given free will by the Creator of this world of form. There is no limit to how far you can take that free will, how far into an extreme you can go with your own choices. It is literally possible that you can take your free will so far to an extreme that you deny everything that the Creator stands for, that you believe you know better than the Creator, that you are a god, that you are the supreme being and that you know best.

It is possible that a group of fallen beings can take an entire planet and create a downward spiral on this planet that causes lifestreams to become so trapped in the fallen consciousness that they cannot free themselves from this downward spiral and end up going to the second death. It is also possible that the fallen beings can create a downward spiral that will literally destroy the physical planet. This has happened to many planets, even one in this solar system, which is now the asteroid belt. It was close to happening to the earth before Sanat Kumara came here.

In a certain sense, the Law of Free Will sets no limits to how far self-aware beings can go with their free will. There are certain mechanics that the fallen beings simply are not intelligent enough to acknowledge. While I was in embodiment, I would have said that they were not *willing* to acknowledge these facts about the Law of Free Will. I would have said that in their rebelliousness, they knew how the Law of Free Will works and they simply rebelled against it. They were taking advantage of certain aspects of the Law of Free Will and refusing to acknowledge others.

However, in my ascended state I have seen that it really is not *unwillingness* but it is *inability*. These extreme fallen beings are not actually willfully denying certain aspects of free will, they are simply not able to see them, not because they are not intelligent enough as such but because they have not realized that they too have drunk their own Kool-Aid.

They are as trapped by their denial of free will as any of the people who have been trapped by the schemes they have created. "Oh, what tangled webs we weave, when we set out to deceive," as Shakespeare put it. We become the first beings trapped by our own nets, as the spider, although having created the net and being physically capable of moving beyond it, is nevertheless tied to the net it has created. How could it even survive without the net, or so it thinks.

The intricate workings of free will

The fallen beings are so blinded that they cannot see two simple facts. The first is that the universe is a mirror so whatever you do with your free will creates an energy impulse that will cycle through the four levels of the material universe and come back to you at some point in the future. This is not the angry and punishing God; it is simply the mechanics of how free will works.

Free will is very much based on you having creative abilities. If you were in a dark room and had total sensory deprivation, what good would it do you to have free will? There was nothing you could do with it. God has given you free will and has given you a sandbox in which you can build any sandcastle you want. You will, of course, experience the sandcastles you are building. Whatever you send out, will come back to you as a physical circumstance. If it was not so, you would not be able to do anything with your free will.

The other aspect of the Law of Free Will is that free will is *free*. It can never become *unfree*. A third aspect that is also important to keep in mind is that free will is individual. Yes, the fallen beings do have free will, but so does everyone else.

You have a situation on earth where there is a certain group of fallen beings who believe that they own this planet and that God has given it to them. They believe that the ascended masters, who are no longer in embodiment, have no right to interfere with what the fallen beings are doing to people in embodiment. This is both true and untrue. We of the ascended masters have no right to force any human being in embodiment in any way whatsoever. If there is no human being in embodiment who ever asks us for assistance, then we must, by the Law of Free Will, stand by and watch as the fallen beings take this planet into a downward spiral that leads to its physical destruction and disintegration.

The people who are in embodiment still have free will. It is perfectly true that right now most people have a very limited range in which they can exercise their free will. We might say that their free will is no longer free because there are so many options people cannot see. They have such a limited range where they can make choices, and this is the doing of the fallen beings who have deceived human beings into limiting their vision. What the fallen beings will not acknowledge is that even though people's free will has been severely limited, they still have *free* will. God has not actually given planet earth to the fallen beings and said: "Here it is, you can do whatever you want with it." What has been done by the Karmic Board is that planet earth has been designated as one of the planets where fallen beings, and those who have chosen to enter into the fallen consciousness, can take physical embodiment.

God did not give earth to the fallen beings

This has, in a certain sense, given the fallen beings an opportunity to prove whether they can take over and destroy an entire planet, but this is not mandated by God. It is not God who has forced human beings to submit or take in the fallen consciousness. It has happened through their own free-will choosing. In many cases, lifestreams chose to partake of the fallen consciousness on another planet or even in another realm. Nevertheless, it is the choosing of the people who are embodying on this planet that has given earth to the fallen beings, not God and not the Law of God. This means that people in embodiment still have the free will so that if they can see it, if they can see the option, they can cry out for help and then the ascended masters are allowed to answer that cry.

This is why the planet has not already disintegrated long ago. This is why there is today an upward spiral on this planet that made it possible for the ascended masters to reveal their presence publicly in the late 1800s. This was the first time since the time of Atlantis where this had been allowed by the Law of Free Will.

It was a product of the fact that a critical mass of people in embodiment had raised their consciousness, had reached out, had looked at the destructive spirals created by the fallen beings and had said: "There must be more to life than this!" The Law of Free Will does mandate that the inhabitants of a planet can create a self-destructive spiral. However, this self-destructive spiral cannot be created by or fulfilled by a small group of fallen beings. It can only be created by a majority of the original inhabitants of that planet. The fallen beings were not the original inhabitants of earth, they came from the outside. They did not come in space ships, as even I tended to believe while I was in embodiment. They came on the astral plane (in the emotional belt), in the mental, in the lower identity realm and they embodied in those realms and in the physical.

If you are to make your ascension after this lifetime or in your very next embodiment, I – as an ascended master who has newly ascended – cannot see how you can do this without having an awareness of the existence of fallen beings and the challenge they pose to you. There are people who have ascended from earth without having a direct conscious awareness of the existence of fallen beings. They have still developed the discernment that they knew that something was not right, something was evil, something was of the devil, something was false, something was deceitful.

A force seeking to take away your free will

You may call it different things, and you may say that what I am choosing to call it is just another name. So be it. The fact is this: On planet earth there is a force that is seeking to force you away from making the free-will choice to qualify for your ascension, your permanent exit from the earth. If you are to make that ascension, you must find a way to neutralize that force or rather neutralize its influence upon you.

There is no other way to ascend from earth than to neutralize the force exerted by what I call the fallen beings. You can call it other names, but you must find a way to neutralize it or you cannot ascend. You must, as Jesus said, become wise as serpents and harmless as doves. How do you become wise as a serpent unless you acknowledge that the serpents exist and that they have a serpentine logic, which they are seeking to use to deceive you into giving away your free will?

What is it that the fallen ones are seeking to do to you? When you first begin to walk the spiritual path that leads towards the ascension, it is almost like you are walking on a razor's edge. On one side of the edge is deep mud that will suck you down, on the other side is molten lava. Whether you step down on one side or the other of the knife's edge, you are damned if you do, damned if you don't. It seems like it is impossible to walk that knife edge, that straight and narrow path, that Middle Way. Indeed, the fallen beings will do everything they can to either make it impossible or make you think it is impossible.

The key is the words of Jesus: "With men this is impossible, but not with God for with God, all things are possible." "With men" means that with the dualistic consciousness of the fallen beings, the consciousness of separation, it is impossible to avoid reacting to the fallen beings and their schemes. The goal of the fallen beings is to cause you to get off from the knife's edge and step down to one side or the other.

They throw at you something that is aimed at forcing you to react in one of two ways. You either rebel or you submit, rebel or submit, rebel or submit. These are the only options they want you to see.

8 | HOW TO ACTUALLY REMOVE EVIL

There is, of course, a third option and that is to do nothing. If you neither rebel nor actively submit to the fallen beings, they will actually leave you alone. But even if you do not actively rebel or actively submit, you have put yourself in suspended animation. You are paralyzed, you are in a spiritual coma, you are getting nowhere.

This is what you see in much of the New Age movement. I was a spiritual teacher for decades and I was known as a New Age teacher. Oh yes, I saw them come to my church by the thousands, the tens of thousands. I saw how many of them were quickly turned away when they realized that my church did not follow the prevailing New Age doctrine, which is based on the statement: "It's all good."

Look at how many people claim to be spiritual, going around to take all these courses, and they meditate, and they do yoga, and they sing hymns and chants and this and that. They play with crystals and they do all kinds of things that they think are spiritual, but their basic approach to life is that it's all good. There is nothing evil. There is nothing wrong. There is nothing bad on this planet. They don't have to discern. They don't have to consider any difficult questions. They just have to be loving and kind and flow along in their self-created wonderful universe.

"It's all good," they say. If you come and say: "It's *not* all good. There are fallen beings. There is this problem, there is that problem," then they are immediately closing their minds to you. "Oh, you are too extreme. You sound like a fundamentalist preacher. You sound like a doomsday prophet and your name is Prophet. Ha-ha-ha! Who do you think you are? It's all good."

I saw them come, take one look and turn away, never to look again. While I was in embodiment, I was deeply distraught by this. I knew that these people were so close to acknowledging the path. They were the spiritual people, they were open to the spiritual side of life, they were open to something beyond the straightjacket of traditional Christianity. "They *should* be open to the teachings of the ascended masters," I said to myself many times.

Why are they not? Because they have chosen that they will not try to discern. They will not try to sort it out. It was not until I neared my ascension that I was able to let go and say: "Well, these people must be allowed to outplay their free-will choices and see where it gets them."

What saddened me while I was in embodiment was that I could see that if these people had just been awakened, it could have made a real difference on this planet. They could have made a difference for the ascended masters. I saw how many of them had in their divine plans vowed to make that difference. They had become trapped by this movement that "Its all good. We don't need to discern, we don't need to look at any problems, we don't need to look at anything dark or evil for dark forces don't exist." I saw how painful it would be for these wonderful lifestreams when, after wasting an entire embodiment, they would leave the body, face their life review and see how they had thrown away an opportunity that they themselves had chosen before coming into embodiment.

8 | How to Actually Remove Evil

The delicate challenge of removing evil

The cure for this malady that "It's all good" would be to take a little trip to a place in Poland, called "Auschwitz." When you stand in one of these rooms and see the shower heads in the ceiling, you can attune to the fact that thousands of naked men, women and children were herded into these rooms and then exposed to Zyklon B gas until they, after screaming for minutes, died standing up after turning completely blue. *Then* you might have opportunity to reconsider your belief that "It's all good" on this planet.

You *will not,* you *cannot,* remove evil from this planet without looking at it and acknowledging its presence on this planet. Why can't you do this? Because evil must be removed the same way it was allowed to come to this planet, namely through the free-will choices of those in embodiment. The difference is that you can invite evil to this planet without fully recognizing what you are doing. You can invite evil out of ignorance, but you cannot remove evil from this planet without acknowledging what it took to invite it here and what is the consciousness you must transcend in order to withdraw that invitation.

You cannot remove evil in ignorance. You can invite it in ignorance, but you cannot remove it in ignorance. You can remove it only in awareness, and you can gain that awareness only if you are willing to start walking what seems like an impossibly thin razor's edge. It seems like you are damned if you do and damned if you don't—and you *are!* But you still have to *do.* You still have to walk because until you start walking, the ascended masters cannot direct you.

The central challenge posed by the presence of fallen beings on this planet is discernment; the discernment between what is real and unreal. Oh yes, I have recently been in embodiment on earth. I know full well how excruciatingly difficult it is to discern between reality and unreality. As I grew up and experienced the evils in the world – from my father's drunkenness to the Holocaust and many other atrocities that I witnessed – I longed for a sure way to know what was right and wrong. When I met Mark, heard about the ascended masters and started working in the church, I thought: "Now, I have made it. Now, I have found it. Here is my sure guideline in the teachings of the ascended masters and my contact with the ascended masters. This is it; I now know what is right and wrong, what is good and evil."

Not so fast, Betty Clare!" It's never that simple. Remember what I said: The fallen ones present you with a challenge where it seems like the only option is to rebel or to submit. I knew very well that I was not going to submit to the fallen beings, the power elite, and their schemes. I was not going to submit to evil. I was going to stand apart from their power structures and their false teachings and their this and their that. For many years, I thought that I was on the right path by standing away, by denouncing it, by giving decrees for the binding of the fallen beings and this and that.

You are brainwashed to accept fallen ideas

What I did not realize was that in rebelling against the fallen beings and their schemes, I had left the razor's edge. I had become unbalanced. Again, this is a subtlety.

This planet has for a very long time been dominated by the fallen beings and the fallen mindset. No matter where you grow up on planet earth today, you will grow up in a society that is dominated by the consciousness of anti-christ, the mindset of the fallen beings. You may think that you have grown up in a free democratic nation, and certainly it was better to grow up in a free, Western, democratic nation than to grow up in the Soviet Union or some totalitarian society.

You still did not grow up in a truly free society because there are ideas that spring from the fallen consciousness that are so subtle that most people are not even able to question them. They have become so ingrained that people think this is normal, this is true, this is the only way to look at life. You cannot even question some of these subtle ideas. As you grow up on this planet, you are programmed, you are *brainwashed,* into submitting to the fallen beings and their ideas.

How do you then start the path that leads to the ascension? How do you start the path of freeing yourself from this submission to the fallen beings? Well, you must come to see at least some of the lies, some of the illusions. Then you must, as the Bible says: "Come apart and be a separate and chosen people, elect unto God." You cannot free yourself from the fallen beings without rebelling against them. The thing is, rebelling against the fallen beings will free yourself from some of the illusions created by the fallen beings, but it will trap you in other illusions that they have created.

For example, take the statement: "Become a separate and chosen people, elect unto God." Yes, you *can* separate yourself from the false gods of the fallen beings and their schemes. You can think you are becoming elect unto God, but you can only become elect unto the God that you can see and that God was created by the fallen beings as well. The fallen beings have created both the devil seen by human beings and the God seen by most human beings. They have defined both polarities. For those who are beginning to wake up and realize there must be more, they have defined a false path which says that you have to separate yourself from the schemes of the devil and accept the teachings of God. But those teachings of God are also created by or influenced by the fallen beings and the fallen mindset.

The fallen beings have created a false god

You think you are coming apart from the devil and his schemes, being elect unto God, but you are being elect unto a false god.

When I was a child I had a serious accident of hurting my leg, and I reasoned that this was because I had not obeyed my mother and God was punishing me for not obeying my mother. I could not, for the life of me, figure out why disobeying my mother and not hanging the laundry would cause my leg to be hurt in such a way that I almost died and why God would punish me so harshly for such a little infraction. But I had no other way of reasoning about this because, as a child, I still believed in the image of God as the judge in heaven who punishes those who do not obey him.

I could not see that this was an image of God created entirely by the fallen beings. God is not sitting up here in the ascended realm, looking down upon you, evaluating every action you take, every feeling you have, every thought you have and punishing you when you do not do what he wants you to do.

My beloved, I am today an ascended master. I can see everything that goes on in the ascended realm. I have looked, and I could find no such God up here, but I do see a God like that in the astral plane. It is a figure that has been created over eons by the inhabitants on this planet and other planets. It has assumed the appearance and likeness of the angry sky God worshiped by the main monotheistic religions on this planet.

Why is God not the angry and punishing God? Because your Creator has given you free will. God is not punishing you. If you are being punished, you are punishing yourself. What you experience is not the result of God deliberately and willfully punishing you; it is the result of your own past choices simply being reflected to you by the Cosmic Mirror. You have chosen what is coming back to you. You have also chosen to see that this is God punishing you, and you will never ascend until you free yourself completely from that image of God. Why not? Because the ascension is a process of coming into oneness with something higher than yourself. How could you ever come into oneness with the angry and punishing God in the sky? Why would you ever want to come into oneness with that God? It cannot happen.

The ascension can seem to be an impossible task

There are many, many devout religious people on this planet who are sincerely striving for salvation by following their outer religion, but they do not realize that they are facing an impossible task. In holding on to the image of an angry and punishing God, they are making it impossible for themselves to enter the kingdom of God. How do you enter the kingdom of God? By coming into oneness with the God who resides in the kingdom of God that is within you. How can you come into oneness with a God that you see as being external to yourself and see as being an angry and punishing tyrant in the sky?

How could you choose to come into oneness with a God who seemingly wants to control your free will? The real God has given you free will. You can exit the unascended realm only through free-will choices; there is no other way. You descended from the ascended realm through a free-will choice. You will ascend back to it only through a free-will choice. The trick is that in order to make that final free-will choice to enter the ascended realm, you must have freed your mind completely from the illusions of the fallen consciousness.

You must make that last choice to cross the threshold to the ascended realm by making a choice that, for the first time since you descended, is completely and absolutely free because you see all and you see through all of the illusions of the fallen consciousness. How will you ever walk that path when you look at the state of consciousness that most people have been brought up to see as normal, and when you look at the gap between that state of consciousness and the ascended state? You will say: "How could I ever cross that gap?" Again, with men this is impossible. With the human consciousness, with the duality consciousness, you cannot cross the chasm. The challenge you face is created by the fallen consciousness. You cannot use the fallen consciousness to out-maneuver the fallen consciousness. This is what the hard-core fallen beings do not realize. They think they are right and that God is wrong. They do not realize that it is their own consciousness that makes them think that way. They think that what they believe is not a belief but reality. It only *seems like* reality because they are seeing it through the perception filter of their own consciousness. That consciousness filters out reality so all they see is illusion.

Their self-deception is so complete that they think the illusion is absolute reality. You can never out-reason, you can never reason your way out of, this consciousness. There will always be an argument that can convince you and thereby keep you trapped in the house of mirrors. There is no way out through the fallen consciousness. The only way out is to recognize that the Conscious You can never be fully identified with the fallen consciousness, the separate self.

How a true teacher can help you

You have the ability to momentarily step outside yourself and experience a glimpse of a higher reality. This is the value of a true teacher. You will never escape the fallen consciousness without having a guru who gives you a direct experience that there is something beyond the fallen consciousness. There is something beyond the maze, the smokescreen, the veil of illusion.

The difficulty you face is that when you have your first glimpse of contact with a true guru and experience that there is something beyond, your mind is still colored by the fallen consciousness. As soon as the direct experience is over, your mind immediately begins to interpret your experience, to interpret your encounter with the guru, seeking to fit it into its world view and belief system. You are projecting a mental image that comes from the fallen consciousness upon the guru. Walking the spiritual path is not what most people envision it to be. I know that even while I was in embodiment, I created the impression that what you needed was to find a true teaching and a true guru. Then, you needed to follow that teaching, practice the teaching, study the teaching and follow the guru, obey the guru. It was my hope, it was my desire, to create an organization, an environment, where the majority of the people who came there – and diligently applied the teachings and the tools and diligently followed my directives – would qualify for their ascension. That was both an illusion and not an illusion.

It was possible that people could have come to the church, study the teachings, listen to the dictations by the ascended masters and listen to my directions—if they had the opportunity to get personal directions from me. Thereby, they could have qualified for their ascension if it was in their divine plan and they were in their last embodiment.

It was *not* possible because of them blindly following me as an outer guru. It would have been possible only if they had fulfilled the central requirement of a chela on the path to the ascension. *That* requirement is that you do not simply obey the guru blindly, but that you are willing to look at your reaction to the guru. You must ponder what that says about your state of consciousness and about why you left your ascended guru in the past when you first fell into the duality consciousness. *That* was possible, and there were people who came to the church, who interacted with me (perhaps only once), who followed the teachings, listened to the dictations and they were able to look at their own reactions and qualify for their ascensions by doing so.

I did not fully recognize this while I was still in the body and aware and conscious in the body. This is the way it is and always has been for any mystery school, any true spiritual guru. There have been many of them throughout the ages, for the

Cosmic Law is simple: When the student is ready, the guru must appear—in whatever form is possible given the outer circumstance.

You cannot blindly follow a guru

What I am saying here is an extremely important point for those who are willing and have the potential to make their ascension. On the one hand, you cannot make it without a guru, but on the other hand, you cannot make it by blindly following that guru. It is not what the guru teaches you, or what the guru might or might not do for you, that will qualify you for your ascension. Your ascension is *your* ascension. *You* are the one who is ascending. You do not ascend by following anyone or anything outside yourself. You ascend by becoming completely self-sufficient, you ascend as an individual based on your own individual merits.

I wish I could have given this teaching while I was still in embodiment, yet I also see why I could not give that teaching. It was simply because of the law: When the student is ready, the teacher appears. I was the exact kind of teacher that the students I encountered were ready for. I could not have gone higher, and if I had gone higher, my students could not have recognized it. It was a symbiotic process where I was a reflection of the consciousness of the students and the students were a reflection of my consciousness. We had a potential to spiral higher together and we did spiral higher together, but we could have gone further.

I am not saying this to in any way find fault or place blame. As I have explained in great depth – I hope – when you ascend, you go beyond the need to find fault, you go beyond the need to blame anyone. You also go beyond the need to protect anyone and to wear velvet gloves. The gloves come off, as everything else comes off. You do see reality, and I simply state the reality that I, in my embodiment, did not go as high as I could have. Neither did my students transcend themselves as much as they could have.

An opportunity to receive inner guidance

Had we done so, we could have gone higher together. We could have received a higher level of teaching from the ascended masters. I could have stayed in my position as a messenger longer, my illness could have been postponed and we could have had more years together with more teachings being brought forth. This did not come to pass. There is no blame, there is no regrets. It was what it was, but the question is, for those who were my students while I was in embodiment and who still have years left in a physical body: "Are you willing to perhaps begin transcending yourself as you *could* have done but have not yet done? Are you willing to catch up?"

If so, I am willing to tutor you at inner levels if you will tune in to me. I know that there are some who are attuned to me already and I applaud that, I honor it. I also know there are many who have not been able to free themselves from their own images of me, or of the guru in general. They have lost that attunement and cannot attune to me as an ascended master. This is part of the reason that I am giving this book. If you will ponder what I am telling you here, you have the opportunity to go beyond the words and attune directly to me within.

It is not my intention with this book that you should now come and submit yourself to this messenger as you submitted yourself to me. The messenger has no desire for this. It is my desire for this book that you will use it as a tool by attuning directly to my Presence as an ascended master, receiving my guidance from within, the guidance that you could potentially have received from me while I was still in the body, if we had all been able to spiral higher together.

The spiral is still there in the etheric realm. It has even descended into the mental, but it has not yet been pulled into the emotional, through the emotional and into the physical. Are you willing to make your personal contribution to bringing this spiral into the physical? If so, you must confront your own view of the guru and your own reaction to *me* as your guru, as the guru you met physically. To this end, I will give further teachings that will also be of value to all spiritual seekers whether they met me or not, whether they ever come in contact with my organization or teachings.

They are universal for they relate to the relationship between any unascended being and a true guru. As I said, you cannot ascend without having a true guru, in fact, *many* true gurus. You must often meet a physical guru that you can see and hear with your senses, with your outer mind. Then gradually, by following such gurus, you can rise to the point where you can make contact with your inner guru, your ascended guru.

Don't judge the guru that appears to you

Without the guru, you cannot pull yourself beyond the quagmire of the fallen consciousness. No one has ever done it. If you think you can be the first, I submit to you that you are trapped in a very subtle and deceptive form of spiritual pride and arrogance, and it will get you absolutely nowhere. I have seen it, I have seen it in the people who came to my church. Oh yes, they came, and supposedly they submitted themselves to me as the guru, but in their own minds they always thought they knew better.

They judged me in subtle ways. They talked about me behind my back, even though – given my level of awareness – it was very difficult to talk about me behind my back. They thought they could talk about me without being heard. They talked and they talked, and they had theories and they had judgments of how I did this and why I didn't do that, and what I was wearing, and what I was eating, and the rings, and this and that and the next thing.

Oh how they came. Oh how they knew better. Oh how many of them left quickly. Oh how many of them never engaged me in the church, but they came as the representatives of the media, of governments and of these wonderful so-called anti-cult organizations. Oh how they thought they knew better.

Oh my beloved, if you could see the arrogance that I have seen – and if you could see the contrast between the reality of the ascended masters and the arrogance of the fallen consciousness – you would look at this, and you would instantly snap out of any influence of this arrogance.

You would fall to your knees in absolute humbleness before God and the reality of God, the reality of the ascended masters. You would simply say: "Oh God, deliver me from all illusions. Show me the way, and I will follow it for I have had enough of thinking that I know better than the guru. I want the true guru, I want the true guru who can show me the way beyond my self-created illusions and the illusions created by the fallen beings. I have had enough, I have simply had enough of seeing my own self-created illusions being reflected to me by the cosmic mirror. It is enough, I have had my fill of this, I want no more."

"Ah, I want to rise above it, and I acknowledge that I cannot pull myself up by my own bootstraps. I acknowledge that I need a true guru. Give me a true guru and I will recognize that this guru will not be the perfect guru but will be a reflection of my state of consciousness. Therefore, I must not expect, and I *will* not expect, that the guru will give me an absolute truth or will do the work for me. I will acknowledge that it is my responsibility to observe my reaction to the guru and how my mind will come up with these subtle arguments for why I should not follow the guru – or why I *should* follow the guru – or how I should interpret what the guru says. I will look at it, and I will look beyond it until I see why I left the true guru in the first place, why I thought I knew better, why I thought my mental image of the guru was accurate, why I thought my mental image of you, God, was accurate."

"I am willing to free myself from the graven images I have accepted, the graven images that come from the fallen consciousness. I am willing, my God, to have no other Gods before you. I would know you as you are, not as I think you are, not as the fallen beings think you are. I just want to know you as you are!"

9 | THE IMPERFECT MYTH OF THE PERFECT GURU

I AM the Ascended Master Guru Ma, and I come to give you more information, more details, about the guru-chela relationship. As I have explained, there was a point before you descended into physical embodiment for the very first time where you were in a protected environment. This may not have been here on earth, but it was before the first time your lifestream descended into the density of what corresponds to the physical body you are wearing here on earth. You were in this protected environment along with a spiritual being who served as your personal guru, your personal teacher.

The only reason you left that environment, and now find yourself in the unascended state here on earth, is that you chose to turn away, to walk away, from the teacher. Before you can ascend, you must overcome the decision that caused you to turn away and come back into oneness, either with your original teacher or with another ascended teacher. There is no way that any being can ascend without coming into oneness with a guru, a genuine ascended guru.

Because of what I have explained about the fallen beings and their desire to prove God wrong for giving free will, it should be clear that the fallen beings, the false hierarchy impostors, have done everything they can to sabotage the guru-chela relationship. When you look upon earth, you will see many, many schemes that are deliberately created by the fallen beings, by the false hierarchy, in order to make it impossible for people to find a guru or follow a guru. This is what I wish to give you more teachings about so that you at least know what you are dealing with on this planet. You can make choices based on knowledge rather than ignorance.

The challenge of finding a valid guru

The first line of defense, so to speak, for the fallen beings is that they try to make it impossible for you to find a true guru. In the Western world the primary tool they have used, now for almost 2,000 years, has been the Christian religion. As Jesus has explained himself in his magnificent book [*What Would Jesus Say about Christianity?*], the biggest tragedy about Christianity is that it destroyed both the lower and the higher path, the outer and the inner path, that Jesus attempted to give to humankind.

Christianity portrayed Jesus as a savior, not as a guru. Therefore, Christianity has destroyed the guru-chela relationship that people could have had with Jesus. They have even destroyed the concept of a guru-chela relationship, the concept of a spiritual guru. You will see that before the emergence of Christianity, there were, even in the Western world, many religious or spiritual movements that had the concept of a guru or a path of initiation in some form. This was all squashed by the Catholic Church, and therefore it has virtually been eradicated. Scientific materialism has carried this even further by denying that there is a spiritual side to life.

Most people who have grown up in the Western world have grown up without the concept of a spiritual guru who can help you pass a set of initiations before you pass the final initiation

9 | The Imperfect Myth of the Perfect Guru

and ascend from earth. In the East, especially in India, the situation has been slightly different. India has a long tradition of having gurus, and there have been many gurus in India who have been true gurus. What do the fallen beings do in a country where there is a tradition for having spiritual gurus who take on chelas, or students? The fallen beings send their own representatives to set themselves up as gurus. You now have a mixture of true gurus and false gurus, as opposed to the Western situation of no gurus.

The vast majority of the gurus who have appeared in India, and who still today appear in India, are false gurus. They are not sponsored by the ascended masters, they do not recognize the ascended masters, they do not have a mantle from the ascended masters. A mantle is a shield of energy extended by the ascended masters in order to seal the guru, to seal the messenger, from the lower energies in the material realm, making it easier for the messenger to tune in to the ascended realm and receive accurate directions or messages. A true guru has some form of mantle of guru, or mantle of messenger, from the ascended masters.

There are always at least two ways whereby the fallen beings can sabotage any endeavor. One is that you do not even know about gurus or there are no gurus available. The other is that there is a mixture, with the majority of the gurus being false. Your chances of picking a true guru are therefore much smaller.

There is indeed an Indian Black Brotherhood of false gurus who have a very tight grip on the collective consciousness of the Indian people, sending false guru after false guru. In recent decades, where you have seen a growing awareness of the spiritual side of life in the West, many of the false gurus of India have come to the West to parade their wares to those who are unawares of the potential that gurus can be false. You have also seen a few genuine gurus come to the West.

This is, so to speak, their first line of defense – or their first line of attack – to stop you from finding any kind of guru, any kind of path or to stop you from finding a true guru, preferably even getting you to blindly follow a false guru. You will see that many of the gurus in India want their students, want their chelas, to follow them blindly. This is a very old tradition. Now, again there is some validity to this, which I will talk more about later.

The myth of the perfect guru

What is their second line of defense-attack, their second attempt to sabotage you following a guru? The second line of defense very much springs from the way that the fallen beings have portrayed God. There is the graven image that God is the angry, judgmental being in the sky. Implicit in this image is that God is judgmental because God is perfect and we human beings down here in embodiment are imperfect.

How do we gain access to this wonderful kingdom of this wonderful God? We have to live up to some superhuman standard of perfection. If we do, it will be thumbs up and God or Saint Peter will let us in. If not, it will be thumbs down and we will burn forever in hell. Quite a tough situation, I would say. If you do not live up to a superhuman standard of perfection, the only other option is that you burn in hell—forever, and ever and ever.

Based on this image that God has to be perfect, there has been created another mental image that is very much floating around in the collective consciousness. It says that anyone who claims to be a spiritual teacher – a guru, a messenger from God, a prophet or having any kind of spiritual office or mission – any person who makes a claim like that had better be perfect. My goodness, how I experienced this when I was an embodied messenger and guru.

It was absolutely fair that I experienced this. As I was growing up, I did have the image of the judgmental God, the punishing God. I believed that nothing bad would happen to me except God would allow it to happen. God would only allow it to happen if I deserved punishment for having done something wrong. I believed in the image that in order to be acceptable to God, I had to somehow be perfect. When I heard about ascended masters, I believed that ascended masters are perfect.

Here, again, we have one of these subtleties. The ascended masters *are* perfect, but they are not perfect according to any standard defined on earth because any and all standards you find on earth are defined by the fallen consciousness. This is one of the ways whereby the fallen beings have attempted to prevent the people on earth from reaching out and asking for assistance from God or the ascended masters. They want you to believe that unless you live up to this superhuman standard of perfection, you are not worthy to even ask for God's help. The superhuman standard of perfection is defined by the fallen beings, and it is defined in such a way that no one could ever live up to it.

This is what I did not grasp, even when I became an adult. I transferred the image of the judgmental God to the ascended masters, including to my beloved El Morya. I thought that the masters were perfect, and in order to be a worthy messenger, a worthy representative of the ascended masters, I had to be perfect—or at least I had to strive for perfection.

This was clearly an unbalanced state. I see this so clearly now. Could you have made me see this while I was still in embodiment? Not in my early years. I may have been more open to it after we went through the so-called shelter cycle and I received so much negative press that I realized that my public image was beyond salvation. Thus, I needed to actually surrender my attachment to my public image.

Before that happened, I very much had created my own mental image that I did live up to some standard of perfection.

That is why I had been chosen as a messenger, and that is why I had been anointed as a messenger and had received my mantles and was continuing to live up to those mantles. I would not have been open to hearing otherwise because it would have been detrimental to my ability to carry out my mission.

Here you, again, have the consideration I have given earlier that there is a period where you are navigating the turbulent area of the Sea of Samsara, and you need a boat that is closed off so it does not take in the water from the raging waves. I needed this image in order to carry me through. This does not mean that this was the only way a guru or a messenger could have navigated his or her personal Sea of Samsara. It does mean it was the way that *I* could do it, and this was perfectly acceptable because this means that I then became the guru that represented that state of consciousness. I attracted the kind of students who were ready for the kind of guru that I was.

When the student is ready, the teacher appears, and the teacher that appears to you is the teacher that corresponds to your state of consciousness. I did and said certain things that portrayed the image that I had reached a high state of spiritual development and therefore deserved to be a messenger and deserved my mantles. Many of the students who came to me needed and wanted that kind of a guru, and they not only accepted what I had said, what the masters had said, but they embellished upon it and created their own mental images of me.

What I was unaware of in my conscious mind was that the image of a perfect guru is a complete fallacy that you need to overcome before you can ascend. This means that I, in my position as a guru, needed to overcome the image that I had to be perfect. It also means that my students needed to overcome the image that I had to be perfect.

There were some of my students who thought that I could not possibly fail my ascension because I was an anointed messenger. I had all these embodiments, I had balanced my karma, I had done this, I had done that. I *could* fail my ascension because I was no exception to the rule; God is no respecter of persons. It does not matter how high of a position you have here on earth. It does not matter how many people revere you as the perfect human being. You are still subject to the Law of God, and you cannot ascend as long as you have one single illusion left in your being.

Overcoming the illusion of the perfect guru

Certainly, the illusion that God requires you to be perfect – according to the standard of those who have rebelled against God – is an illusion that you need to shed. How do you shed the illusion of the perfect guru? There are two ways that a guru can help you. One is to give you teachings that help you, so to speak, voluntarily question your illusions, to see beyond them and to transcend them. If you will go back and look at the teachings that were given through me, you will find that these teachings were given.

There were hints, there were teachings, and if they had been taken and applied, it could have helped people overcome the illusion of the perfect guru and the perfect chela. There are people who found these teachings and applied them and raised themselves above the illusion. There are also many people who did not heed these teachings and who could not have accepted them even if they were presented in a very direct form.

How, then, do you help students get beyond this illusion? Well, the guru does the second thing. The guru actually lives out, outpictures, acts out, demonstrates the consciousness. You take a certain state of consciousness, you outpicture it to such an extreme that it becomes easier to see. In terms of the illusion of the perfect guru, I did and said certain things that made it easy for students to embellish upon what was said and create their own illusions of the perfect guru. Then, what I did – which was even more important – was that I allowed myself to fall from grace in front of the eyes of my own students and the world.

This was a very difficult thing to do for my outer mind, but it was what I had chosen to do before I came into embodiment. I was not fully aware of this with my outer mind, but I was aware that it was not an inevitability. There were times, critical junctures, where I faced a situation very similar to the situation faced by Jesus in the garden of Gethsemane. You will recall that Jesus had some awareness that he was about to face a very unpleasant situation. He was distraught and then he prayed to God: "God, if it be thy will, take this cup away from me." I had similar situations where I could have asked God not to experience the humiliation that I sensed was coming.

The only way that this could have come about in my case was that I would have been taken out of embodiment. That was not in accordance with my own higher will and my divine plan. I did sense that it was not God's will that I be taken out of embodiment. I did go through the humiliation even though I was not fully aware of why I had chosen this. Therefore, I felt quite distraught about literally, as the Book of Revelations says, having my naked body lie in the streets for all to see.

I don't know if you can begin to imagine what it is like that you have this desire to be the best possible messenger and the best possible teacher you can be. You think that in order to fulfill this, you need to live up to some standard of perfection. Then you are forced to see how your public standing, your public reputation, is suddenly dragged into the mud, and you are portrayed to be the worst possible cult leader ever to walk the face of the earth. It is certainly not a pleasant experience. There is absolutely no question about it.

My comfort was that I knew very well that it was not pleasant for Jesus to be put on trial, to have to drag his cross through the streets of Jerusalem with the people jeering at him, and it certainly was not comfortable for him to be crucified. In retrospect, it is clear that I allowed this to happen because I wanted to do whatever could be done to help my students overcome this illusion of the perfect guru.

Can you put together what I have said here and see why it is so important to overcome this illusion? The fallen beings who form the false hierarchy of earth have set themselves up as the gods on earth, the gods who know good and evil, the gods who define what is good and what is evil, what is real, what is unreal, what is of God and what is not of God. They have defined the god for earth and they have defined the devil for earth. They have defined the illusion that you must choose between one or the other. They have defined what it takes for a human being on earth to enter the kingdom of God, and it takes that you attain some standard of perfection defined by the fallen beings.

In reality, the god that they have defined – the kingdom they have defined and the standard of perfection they have defined as the entry point – is a complete illusion. It has nothing to do with the reality of what God is like, what the ascended masters are like, what the spiritual realm is like and what it takes to walk the path of the ascension and qualify for the ascension.

10 | HOW TO AVOID ABUSING A GURU

You are not required to live up to any standard of perfection defined on earth. "What are you required to do then? There *must* be some standard that you can live up to," cries the ego. You are required to free your mind from any and all of the standards created on earth. There is no external standard that you have to live up to. What you have to do is to stop projecting any *external* standard and any *internal* standard upon yourself.

Remember, I said, quoting Jesus, that only the man who descended from heaven will ascend back to heaven? Only the pure awareness of the Conscious You that originally descended can ascend back. You have taken on a self in the material realm in order to express yourself in the material realm, in order to experience the material realm a certain way. This is all well and good; this is all allowed according to the Law of Free Will. You cannot take that self with you into the ascended realm. In order to qualify for your ascension, you must dis-identify yourself, disentangle yourself, from any and all aspects of this self.

What is the standard that you, personally, must live up to in order to qualify for your ascension? What is the path you must follow? Who has defined the path? Who has defined the standard? Was it defined by God the Almighty in heaven? Was it defined by the ascended masters or the Karmic Board? Was it defined by the devil? Was it defined by the fallen beings, the false hierarchy? Nay, *it was defined by you!*

How you defined the path to your ascension

From the moment you left your first teacher, you have created an elaborate separate self that has innumerable beliefs, mental images, illusions. It is a very complex structure you have created. This, again, has been in order. It has given you certain experiences that have risen to your causal body and therefore can help you in your continued growth. In order to ascend, you must dismantle your boat and rid yourself of all elements of this separate self.

The separate self was created out of your own choices. The path that *you* must follow to *your* ascension is to undo all of your choices. It is like the popular Star Wars movie where Luke Skywalker is initiated by Yoda, and Yoda says: "Luke, you must *unlearn* what you have learned." You must *unchoose* what you have chosen. *You* chose; only *you* can unchoose. That is the path to your ascension—defined by you only. It can be walked by you only.

The false teachers will do everything they can to make you believe that there is some aspect of the separate self that you do not have to shed because it either already is perfect in the eyes of God or it can become so by following the teacher. The ascended masters, the true teachers, will tell you: "*It all has to go.*" There is nothing you can take with you into the ascended realm, except what is already in your causal body.

This is the illusion that you truly need to overcome in order to shed the dream, the dysfunctional dream, the impossible dream, of the perfect guru. What is it that happens to you psychologically when you think you have found a guru on earth who lives up to your standard of perfection? Take my own example. I can see so clearly now that many of my students came to me, and they accepted: "Oh yes, Elizabeth Clare Prophet is a messenger of the ascended masters, she was anointed by the masters, she has had all these wonderful embodiments, she is karma-free, she can see everything, she can see my aura, she can see what I am thinking, she knows everything that has ever happened and will ever happen, she has all these superhuman qualities." They had never seen these qualities, but they were convinced that I had them.

What happened in the psyche of the student? When you think you have found the perfect teacher, what does that say about you? When the student is ready, the teacher appears. Here, this perfect teacher has appeared to me; that must mean that I am the perfect student. That must mean I have certain qualities, that I have a certain value, a certain attainment.

Why spiritual people are so judgmental

What is it that happens psychologically? You now begin to believe that because you are such an advanced student, there are certain elements of your outer self that you do not need to shed in order to ascend. Why don't you need to shed them? Because they live up to the standard of perfection defined by your perfect guru and the perfect teaching. You think you do not need to look at the beam in your own eye. Instead, many students begin to believe that they are now qualified to look at the splinter in the eyes of their brothers and sisters.

When I look back at the church that I was a head of for so many years, I can see today so clearly how incredibly judgmental our organizational culture was. I can then also look at the broader field of New Age, spiritual and religious organizations and see that the vast majority of them are also very judgmental.

It is all because there is this dream of having found the perfect church, the perfect organization, the perfect guru whereby you have suddenly become one of these students who, although you may not be perfect, there are at least some aspects of your human self that you do not need to look at—and thereby your ego feels safe.

Your ego has managed to use your spiritual teaching, to use your guru, to create a safe zone in your own being that you think you do not have to look at. Then, the ego *is* safe because when the ego has managed to make you believe that you do not need to look at the ego, then you have no chance of freeing yourself from that aspect of the ego—or rather from the ego in its totality. As long as there is some aspect of illusion and the fallen consciousness in your being, your ego is safe. Your ego is like the chameleon who can hide behind even the smallest splinter in your eye.

This is the illusion that I had vowed to take on myself and to help my students overcome. The teachings were given, both by me and the ascended masters in dictations, that could help students overcome that illusion. When it became increasingly clear that the majority of the students could not follow the teachings, then I did allow myself to be taken down from the pedestal upon which both I and my students had put me. I allowed myself to experience the ultimate humiliation, not only of a failed prophecy, but of truly having taken the church into such an unbalanced position that it threatened the very survival of the church.

Yes, I freely admit from the ascended state that the way we as an organization handled the shelter cycle was completely out of balance. I am not thereby denying that there was a reality. The ascended masters wanted us to build those shelters. They wanted to do this for a reason and that reason was fulfilled. Nevertheless, it is one thing to know *what* to do. It is another thing *how* you do it. This is a principle that you need to know in order to be an ascended master student and work towards the ascension.

The all-or-nothing approach to a guru

What is it that the fallen beings will do as their next level in their strategy to sabotage the guru-chela relationship? They will try to make you believe that when it comes to a guru, you only have two options. It's all or nothing. You either submit yourself as a slave of that guru or you have to remove yourself and reject the guru entirely.

In reality, the true gurus have total respect for your free will. As I have explained from the beginning of this series of discourses, you created a divine plan before you came into embodiment. You have yourself defined certain goals for what you want to see happen in this lifetime. Now, listen carefully. Your divine plan defines *what* will happen to you but your divine plan does not define *how* you deal with what happens to you. The ascended masters, when you are willing to work with them, have the right to help you become aware of *what* you want to do according to your divine plan. They *will not,* they *cannot* according to the law, tell you *how* to do it, *how* to carry it out.

All of the many people who were involved with the shelter cycle in one way or another had vowed to be in that situation as part of their divine plans. You had all chosen it. The masters had the right in their dictations to make us aware of *what* we had chosen to do. What they *did* not do – what they *could* not do, what the law will not allow them to do and what we did not want them to do – is to tell us *how* to build those shelters.

This was *our* decision because this is our opportunity to grow. What the fallen beings have attempted to do is to deny this. They want you to either blindly follow the teacher so that you feel like you are wearing a straightjacket and have lost your free will, or they want you to completely rebel against the teacher and refuse to follow the guru. As always, beyond the two opposite polarities defined by the fallen beings there is the Middle Way. This means that you do recognize *what* the guru is telling you to do. You recognize that this is accurate, but you also recognize that *you* must choose *how* you do it.

The *how* is the Omega aspect, the *what* is the Alpha. The Alpha is defined by *you* in your divine plan, and therefore it is the right thing for you to acknowledge the *what* and to carry it out. The Omega, the *how,* is not defined in your divine plan. The only way you grow is that you decide on the *how* while you are looking at the situation from *inside* the physical body and your soul vehicle.

Do you see why this is so? When you are out of embodiment, looking from the wider perspective that you use to define your divine plan, you see everything clearly. It would be easy for you to pass the initiations, but you cannot actually pass the initiations that way. Why not? Because passing an initiation means that you come to see a choice you made in the past, see why it was limited and you undo that choice. The choice was made from a limited perspective in the first place, and therefore you only learn by undoing the choice from the same limited perspective.

You need the wider perspective that the guru gives you as a contrast, as a co-measurement, so you can see the limitations of your perspective. You still need to be in the body, in the outer self, in order to undo the choice. That is how you pass your initiation. If the guru gave you everything on a silver platter, if the guru made the choices for you, how would you learn, how would you grow and how would you ascend?

The shelter cycle of the church

If you were one of the people who were involved with what we called the shelter cycle in the church, it would be wise of you to recognize that you had chosen to be part of that experience as part of your divine plan. You can look at the two potential reactions that are chosen by many of the people who were involved with this. You can see that some chose to say: "But it must have been all true, and we were under the leadership of a genuine messenger. Therefore, what we did must have some higher purpose and some higher meaning that we did not know about. So I don't need to think about it. I don't need to discern. I just need to keep believing in this perfect messenger and then I will ascend." There are people who have taken, and who to this day still take, this approach and refuse to reflect, refuse to discern.

Then there were those who immediately afterwards or later reasoned that: "A prophesy was given, it did not come to pass, it was a false prophesy. This means that Elizabeth must be a false prophet, she must be a false messenger. The whole thing must have been a hoax, an illusion and therefore I reject everything." These people likewise refuse to discern, they refuse to think.

What the wise students will do is to apply the approach I have given you in these discourses and to say: "I acknowledge the *what;* I was meant to be part of that experience. We were meant to build those blasted blast shelters but now I am wondering: What was I meant to learn from that experience?"

I order to know what you are meant to learn, in order to learn the lesson, you need to look at your reaction to the guru. I was the outer guru who got everyone to build those shelters. I fully admit this and take responsibility for it. I am now ascended and you are not, so the question for you is: "What does your reaction to that situation say about the still unresolved aspects of your psychology that you need to shed in order to ascend?"

The wise student realizes that the *how* of how you did what you did and the *how* of how you reacted to what happened is a product of your personal psychology. This is *your* personal psychology. *You* created it, *you* are responsible for it, *you* need to uncreate it in order to ascend. What the unwise student does is to focus on the psychology of the guru and analyze what was wrong about what the guru did. This is not necessarily entirely unproductive. You can look at my life, my psychology, the shelter cycle or other aspects of church life. If you can objectively see how my psychology caused me to do the things that I did, then you can use that as a stepping stone. You can realize that you were attracted to me as a teacher because you have certain elements in your psychology that you need to overcome.

You were attracted to me as a teacher because I was the one who was best suited for bringing out in you what you need to see in yourself. If seeing the splinter in *my* eye helps you see the beam in *your own* eye, then it is perfectly fine for you to look at the splinter in my eye—or you may call it a beam if you like. It is fine to look at it, analyze it and understand it, but if you take the approach taken by so many people in the world of only focusing on what *I* did wrong and what was wrong with my psychology without looking at *yourself,* then you will not grow from the experience.

Using a guru to define a safe zone for your ego

I do not blame or condemn you, I am simply stating the fact that you will not grow until you look at yourself. Looking at me, looking *out* from your perception filter, will not help you grow. You will not grow until you reverse the direction of your attention and say, as Truman said: "The buck stops here."

What is it that happens to those who accept a guru that appears to be perfect and think they have now become the perfect students? They create a safe haven for their egos by defining a zone in their own self, their own soul vehicle, that they think they do not need to look at.

What happens to those who come to the conclusion that the guru that claimed to be perfect, and that they thought was perfect, was not perfect after all; it was indeed a false guru who fooled them? They have also defined a safe zone in themselves, for there is some aspect of their ego that they think they don't need to look at. In fact, they have reinforced the safe zone that caused them to accept that guru in the first place.

Can you begin to see what is behind both of these reactions? If you accept a guru as perfect, what is the underlying reaction? You think you are able to tell what is perfect. You think you know what a perfect guru is like. You think that the perfect guru can be defined according to your present perception filter. What have I said is the key to your ascension? It is that you shed that perception filter. How can a true guru help you step out of your perception filter? By challenging your perception filter. There is no way that a true guru can help you ascend without challenging any and all aspects of your perception filter.

When you need a guru on earth and when you say: "This guru is perfect, has some superior authority or has reached a high state of consciousness based on my criteria," then you are actually saying subconsciously: "I know better than God or better than the ascended masters what the perfect guru on earth should be like." You have come to accept the standard for a perfect guru defined by the fallen beings. You have accepted their arrogance that this standard actually defines the reality of what a perfect guru is like. What happens when you see that this particular guru no longer lives up to your standard, what happens when you reject the guru and say this guru was not perfect? Well, you are reinforcing your standard. Now you are saying: "I know better than God what a perfect guru should be like, and therefore I know why that guru failed. That guru failed to live up to my criteria, my perfect standard."

Questioning your standard for a guru

Ah yes, my beloved, I, when I was in embodiment, did fail to live up to the standard for a perfect guru created by many of my own students, or at least accepted by many of my own students. I did! I failed to live up to it, but in failing to live up to your standard, I still gave you an opportunity to question your standard.

I demonstrated to you that one can actually be a guru and not live up to the standard of perfection held by the students. I demonstrated that in order to be a true guru, you need to be willing to disappoint your students, to challenge their standard. If they can see beyond the outer form of the guru, then they can still follow the guru as he or she goes higher. If they will not look beyond the outer form, if they will not stop judging the guru by the outer standard, then how can they free themselves from their own standard?

What is it that happens when you use your standard of perfection to judge me as having failed as a guru, as being a false prophet? You are also saying that God will judge *you* according to the same standard. My beloved, if you think that God will judge you according to the standard you have defined, if you think that standard was defined outside of yourself by some superhuman authority, how will you ever question the standard?

How will you ever realize that the standard that you have for what it means to be perfect is precisely what holds you back from ascending? How will you ever acknowledge that you need to look at your standard, question every aspect of it and get rid of it because it is all illusion?

If you cannot allow a *guru* to be imperfect, you cannot allow *yourself* to be imperfect. If you cannot allow yourself to be imperfect, you cannot enter the kingdom of God for in the kingdom of God there is no standard.

You will not enter the kingdom of God by thinking you are *perfect*. Nor will you enter the kingdom of God if you think you are *imperfect*. You will enter the kingdom only when the whole consciousness of judging everything based on a standard has fallen by the wayside. You have looked at this consciousness, the dualistic standard of two extremes that you either live up to or fail to live up to, and you have said: "Get thee behind me Satan, for thou art an offense to me. Thou savourest not the things that be of God but the things that be of men."

We judge ourselves based on our standards

One of the hardest things to shed for many of us, and certainly for myself, was precisely this belief that the ascended masters have a standard whereby they judge me and whether I am worthy to ascend or not ascend. It was tough for me to acknowledge and recognize that El Morya was not sitting up there in Darjeeling and judging me according to a standard.

I was the one who had created the standard according to which I was *judging myself*. Not only did I have to get rid of the standard, but I had to get rid of the entire tendency to judge myself. As long as you are judging yourself, you cannot accept God's invitation to his kingdom. You will be evaluating whether you are worthy to enter the kingdom. As long as you are evaluating whether you are worthy to enter, you are standing there on the doorstep, letting "I dare not" wait upon "I do."

You cannot take that final step and walk into the kingdom. There is no gatekeeper that is keeping you out. Well, there *is* the gatekeeper of your own ego, your Dweller on the Threshold, your own unresolved psychology—but that is not an external gatekeeper set there by God. The door to the ascended realm is always open. Surely, you do not enter the marriage feast except through invitation only, but you are all invited, as Jesus described in his parable.

What did Jesus actually try to say in his parable about the wedding feast? First, there were those that were bidden because they were worthy. Was he referring to those who had the highest spiritual attainment? Perhaps there is another interpretation of this wonderful parable? Perhaps the first ones that were invited were the ones who had set themselves up as the overlords on earth, those who judged themselves to be superior to others based on the standard they had accepted. Why were they not willing to go to the wedding? Because they were not willing to give up their standard. They would rather remain outside the kingdom where they could still feel superior than enter the kingdom where superiority and inferiority is left behind.

I wish I would have had these insights while I was still conscious in my physical body. Many things might have been different. The *how* of how I did things would have been very different. Again, there is no point in looking back and regretting. I am not saying this with regrets but in order to help you see that if you can accept these insights while you are still in the body, you still have time and opportunity to change the *how* of how you live your life, how you react to so many situations, how you treat other people, how you treat yourself.

My goodness, how I can look back at my life today and see so many situations where I reacted a certain way precisely because I had this standard of perfection against which I was judging myself, judging the other person and judging what should be the outcome of that situation. Again, I perfectly see from the ascended state that everything was a product of my psychology and the psychology of the other person, going all the way back to my father and my mother.

My father was abusive because of *his* psychology. My mother accepted the abuse and was codependent, and actually *wanted* the abuse, because of *her* psychology. My father exposed me to this trauma because of *his* psychology, my mother could not defend me from this trauma, could not remove me from the trauma, because of *her* psychology. Yet I responded to the trauma the way I did because of *my* unresolved psychology. I did not remove myself or speak out because of *my* psychology. If I had not had this standard of perfection, there are so many things I could have done differently. It may not have had any effect on my father or my mother, but it would have had a profound effect on how *I* experienced the situation. I could have gone through the same situation – my father would not have changed, my mother would not have changed – but *I* would have come out of there with far less trauma than I actually did.

I see so many situations later in life with my own children where I could not give them the love that they were pleading for, or even provoking me in order to get, because I had this standard of perfection that was always standing in the way. I could not give *my children* the love that my parents could not give *me*. I didn't know how; I had never received that kind of love. I didn't know how to give it, but it was again this underlying standard of perfection for how love should be given and received that prevented me from doing better with my children than my parents had done with me. I see so many times with my students where I was judging the situation based on this standard of the perfect guru and a strict, disciplinary El Morya that I had created in my own mind. I was applying it to my students.

Everything is in order

You can take the position that this was what my students were ready for, and, yes, that is true. This is the amazing conclusion you come to when you ascend: Everything that happens on earth is in order—in the sense that it is an outplaying of the unresolved psychology of the parties who are part of that situation. You also see from the ascended state that by just turning the dial of your consciousness a little bit, you can have such a profound impact on how you respond to outer situations. This means you can potentially have a very profound impact on how you affect other people, for better or worse. You can certainly have a very profound impact on how *you* experience those situations, whether you are traumatized or whether you grow.

You are still in embodiment, my beloved, or you would not be reading this. Whatever age you are when you read this, you still have some time left in the body. You can switch your consciousness, you can turn the dial of consciousness. You can look at your own standard, you can start throwing it away bit by bit. You will find that it will have the most profound impact on the rest of your time in embodiment.

The impact will be more profound than you can possibly imagine right now. I tell you that if you heed these words, you will, when you leave the body, look back and look at it as the most important instruction you have ever received. The choice to heed these instructions was the most important choice you ever made, for it had such a profound impact on the rest of this lifetime—that could be your final lifetime on this earth.

Why not make the best of this final lifetime? Why continue, in your final lifetime, to hold on to the standards of the fallen beings? *Get rid of it!*

Look at life on earth through the innocent mind of a child, through the childlike mind that is truly the pure awareness, the nonjudgmental awareness, of the ascended masters.

My beloved, I am an ascended master. I do not judge you. I became an ascended master by transcending the consciousness that judges you or judges myself. If you are to become an ascended master, you must transcend the consciousness that judges others, that judges me and that judges yourself.

11 | WANTING A GURU TO TELL YOU WHAT TO DO

I AM the Ascended Master Guru Ma, and whatever you think of me, I am *more*. Whatever you think of me based on how you experienced me while I was in embodiment on earth, I am today more. I am ascended, and the image that you formed of me has not ascended with me. How can I say this? Because you are still in embodiment, are you not? You will not know me fully as an ascended master until you, yourself, have ascended.

I thought I knew El Morya as an ascended master while I was yet unascended, but today I know that there is no way that you can know an ascended master from the unascended state. Only after I ascended, was I able to merge my being fully with the being who is today Master MORE—because he too wanted to signal that you become ascended only by becoming *more*, more than you could possibly imagine while on earth.

How can you make the best possible use of your experience with me if you *did* experience me while I was on earth? Only by realizing that your image is a product of your psychology. I was the way I was, I did what I did, I said what I said. That was a product of *my* psychology, but your experience of me was not created by me. Your experience of me is a product of *your* psychology. The only way you can come to know me as an ascended master is by transcending, not only the image of me that you formed while I was in embodiment, but the psychology that caused the formation of that image.

The spiritual path has distinct stages

Do you perhaps begin to see the underlying message, the underlying theme, that I am seeking to give people in this book? I am seeking to help you see that the spiritual path has stages. There is a certain stage where you need to do certain things in order to get through that stage. If you think that you have to continue doing what you did during that stage, you will not be able to get through the next stage up—and so it is over and over again until you ascend.

I was a genuine guru and a genuine messenger for the ascended masters. I was meant to give teachings and an example that could help people get through a certain stage on the spiritual path. I did fulfill that mission. I brought forth, through the dictations, the teachings about this. I gave my own lectures and teachings. I gave my own example. The teaching is there. What I also did was to give the hints of what was the next stage up.

What I did not fully do while in embodiment is give the teachings of showing you what were the limitations of what I could teach while I was in embodiment. It is therefore a unique opportunity to be able to speak through a messenger from the ascended state and give teachings on my last embodiment and my work as a spiritual teacher in embodiment. This is an unprecedented opportunity for which I am grateful.

I have given you the image that you are crossing the Sea of Samsara and that there is an area of the Sea of Samsara with very rough waves. In order to get through that stage, through that area, you need to have a boat that is so closed off that it does not take on water and sinks. I have also given you the image that when you get through the area of rough water and get closer to the farther shore, the boat will not take you onto the shore. Before you can move onto the shore, you need to dismantle the boat. You need to dismantle the decisions that make up the vehicle, the soul vehicle, that you used to navigate the previous stage on your path. You need to undo the choices where you closed off your mind to a higher and lower view.

A closed mind is also closed to the masters

I have said that you closed your mind off to the false teachings of the fallen beings. This is very true; you *did* close your mind off to the false teachings of the fallen beings and you needed to do this in order to avoid taking on water. What you do not realize is that in closing your mind off to the false teachings, you in most cases also closed your mind to the true teachings of the ascended masters.

A closed mind is a closed mind. It does not take in; neither the higher nor the lower. A *closed* mind is not the same as a *discerning* mind. There is a point on your path where you need to close your mind to the false teachings of the fallen beings. This is the challenge they present to the people on earth. There are so many false teachings; there are so many things and conditions on earth where the fallen beings are trying to force you into a negative reaction. You need to close your mind to this.

In doing so, you will, as I have now attempted to explain, close your mind off and say: "Ah, there are certain things I don't need to look at in myself. There are certain decisions I don't need to make because I have decided how to do things and I am just going to keep doing them." You *should* continue to do them until you have made it through the area of rough seas. When you get through, you must dare to open your mind enough that you can begin to acquire discernment rather than simply closing your mind.

It is good to close your mind to the false teachings. It is necessary, but that is not discernment. Discernment comes only from opening your mind again and looking at things from a different perspective—now that you are through the choppy waters. You have more calm seas so you can stand at the railing and look out over the sea and reflect. If you do not do this, but continue to power your way, then you will not make it onto the farther shore.

This is my message: Whatever you learned from me while I was in embodiment, it was in most cases valuable for you. It helped you navigate the rough seas. As I said in my last discourse, while you still have time in the body, you can advance your spiritual growth tremendously if you will only stand back and reflect a little bit on what you actually learned from me. What was the deeper lesson? What is the more long-term lesson?

There was in my teachings two levels. The one level was meant to get you through the rough seas, but the other level – that is much harder to see – was meant to get you beyond and onto the farther shore.

Guru Ma, tell me what to do with my life

Let me now talk about another way that people abuse gurus, even true gurus. What I saw many times while I was in embodiment was that people came to me and they had accepted me as a very high guru. They thought I was a genuine guru who had a high attainment, the highest authority and all of the things that they needed in order to feel that I was special, that I lived up to their personal superhuman standard. I was their superhero.

Now they come to me – whether they meet me personally, whether they are just sitting there at a conference and listening or whether they are reading a book – and what they are really saying subconsciously is: "Now, Guru Ma, tell me what to do with my life! Tell me what decisions to make! I accept you as a superhuman guru, and I am willing to do whatever you tell me to do in my life. Just tell me what to do, and I will do it."

There were especially two areas where people sought my advice. One was whether they should come on staff or not, whether they should come and move to where the church headquarters was and work on the staff of the church. This, for most people, meant completely breaking off their life, breaking off whatever career or job they might have had. It might in some cases mean they had to leave families and friends behind and really make a very radical change in their lives. Many people were willing to do this, were looking to do this, and they were asking me whether they *should* do this. If I said "Yes," many of them would come and work on staff. They would now reason that this was the highest possible service that they could give in that lifetime, and this is where they were meant to be for the rest of their lives.

The other area where people often asked my advice was in relationships. Many people came to the church and they had a spouse who was not supportive of their spiritual pursuits. When I say "not supportive" that is in many cases an understatement. It is rather incredible the stories I heard of how spouses will seek to deter their partners from pursuing the spiritual path. I can tell you honestly that in many cases it is the entire forces of death and hell that take over the mind of the spouse in order to discourage one person from walking the spiritual path. I can also tell you that in other cases it is actually the spouse that is more balanced than the person who is walking the path. The person who is walking the path is unbalanced, and the spouse sees this and is trying to balance that.

This is one situation where people come and say: "Should I divorce my spouse in order to be free to pursue my path?" In other cases, people came and said: "Should I marry this person or should I not?" Even many of the people on staff wanted my feedback on whom to marry or not to marry. I was willing to, in some cases, tell people what to do. In other cases I did not tell people what to do.

Why some were given advice and some not

This may from a superficial viewpoint seem quite arbitrary, but it was actually to a high degree – to as high a degree as I was able to free my mind from my own perception filter – directed by the masters. People got direction if that was the biggest opportunity for them to grow, and they got no direction if *that* was the biggest opportunity for them to grow. This depended on where they were at on the path.

I have told you that I was meant to guide people through a certain stage on the path and then give them teachings that could help them move on. What is the stage that I was meant to guide people through? It is the stage where you have not yet taken full responsibility for your own path. That is why you think you need an outer guru and that is why you come to a person who presents him or herself as an outer guru. You come to an organization that claims that it has a high teaching and offers you a path that you can follow. If you had gone beyond the stage of needing an outer guru, why would you have been attracted to that organization? When the student is ready for a certain type of guru, that guru appears. Until the student is ready for a higher kind of guru, the higher guru cannot appear because the student cannot see that guru.

You know that I gave teachings about the Age of Pisces, which was the last 2,000 years, and the Age of Aquarius, which is the next 2,000 years. Jesus was the main master, or hierarch, for the Age of Pisces. He came to demonstrate the path to personal, individual Christhood. This path was, as he describes himself in his book [*What Would Jesus Say about Christianity?*], taken away by the outer churches, or rather by the fallen beings. The fallen beings attempted to set themselves up as the intermediaries between God and people on earth. The fallen beings attempted to set themselves up as the true gurus, the *only* gurus, and they wanted people to follow them blindly.

The challenge in the Age of Pisces

The challenge in the Piscean age for humankind, and especially for the more mature spiritual seekers, was to get through the stage where you think you have to follow an outer guru blindly. You need to get to where you have developed enough discernment that you use an outer guru only as a tool for expanding your attunement with your ascended guru, with your Christ self, your I AM Presence and the ascended master that is your personal guru. You overcome the stage where you allow any institution or person on earth to stand between you and God, to stand between you and a direct relationship with the ascended masters.

"Thou shalt have no other Gods before me. Thou shalt not take unto thyself any graven image." When you allow something on earth to be more important to you than your direct inner relationship with the ascended masters, you are having a false God. When you have a certain image of the perfect guru on earth – or even of the ascended masters or yourself – then that image is standing between you and a direct experience and a direct encounter with the Spirit of the Ascended Masters. I was meant to help people get through that stage so that they could come to the point where they at least started to take full responsibility for their path.

They could not necessarily yet take the full responsibility, but they could at least begin to take responsibility. This was my task because this is what is needed at the end of the Piscean age. It is needed because the fallen beings were so successful in destroying the path given by Jesus and his example. Otherwise, it may not have been necessary, but as things stand it is absolutely necessary that there is a bridge to freedom from the fallen beings. That is why I gave many teachings about the fallen beings, the fallen consciousness, fallen angels, the power elite, what have you. That is why the masters are still giving such teachings today.

Even a false guru can be used for your growth

There is a stage on the spiritual path where you need an outer guru, and then there is a stage where you need to transcend the outer guru. I talked about this in my last discourse, and I promised I would give further teachings on it. We can now begin to consider this topic.

Let me go back to the maritime image that you are on the ocean and the seas are very rough. Your boat springs a leak, takes on water and sinks. You have to jump overboard in order to avoid being pulled down by your boat. What is the symbolism here? The symbolism is that you have created a very elaborate structure of a separate self in order to get through the rough seas. If that vessel fails, if that vessel gets taken down by the force generated by the fallen beings, then it actually becomes a dead weight that, when it goes down, will create a suction that will suck you under until you drown.

You will know that this has happened to many people after a shipwreck. They have been sucked down by the ship. In order to avoid being sucked down, the wise students will jump out early and swim away from the boat. But now you are in the water, the waves are rough, they are washing over you. You are drowning and you realize you are drowning. What do you do? Well, you seek to grasp for something to hold on to. You cry out for help. The Law of Free Will is such that the ascended masters, the true gurus *in* embodiment or *out of* embodiment, cannot offer you help until you ask for it.

When you do ask for it, the help will be extended in whatever form you are able to grasp given your state of consciousness. There are any number of gurus on this earth, ascended or unascended. Whichever one you have encountered, even false gurus you have encountered, was what you were able to grasp, given the state of consciousness you were in when you found that guru. This is important to keep in mind because it empowers you to learn from any guru, true or false.

It does not really matter that you have found and followed a false guru *if* you are willing to look at yourself and see what was the consciousness that caused you to attract that guru. Once you see the consciousness, undo the choices and overcome that consciousness, you have taken a major step forward even by following a false guru. If you do not reflect on why you attracted a certain guru, then you cannot actually make progress even by following a true guru. You turn the true guru into a false guru in your own mind, and the same way you can turn a false guru into a true guru by learning the lesson of what it is in your psychology that attracted the guru.

When to let go of your guru and move on

What happens when you are lying there in the ocean and you are drowning and you cry out? Suddenly, your hand feels something and you grab a hold of it. It may be a lifeline, but it is something that you can use to pull yourself above the waves so you are no longer drowning in the astral sea.

As time goes by, there is a pulling action from the rope. You are holding on and you are pulling. Gradually, you are pulled in towards a rescue boat, and in the rescue boat is a captain of the boat. This captain may be a somewhat rough character who just happens to be piloting that particular rescue boat. When you are aboard, the rescue boat will turn around and head for shore and the question now is: Once you get to the shore, what do you do?

Do you decide with your outer mind: "Oh, this boat and its captain rescued me from drowning; I would have died without them. I need to show my loyalty, appreciation and gratitude by living on this boat for the rest of my life and following this captain in whatever he tells me to do." Or do you say: "Great, now the rescue boat has fulfilled its mission, I'm gonna jump ashore and get on with my life. I am grateful for what they did for me, but the captain is a captain and he needs to go out and rescue others. I need to honor what he did for me by making the best possible use of the opportunity I have been given by having my life." This is how you make use of a guru in the best possible way.

I have earlier talked about why you decide to get on to the spiritual path. The entire plan and plot of the fallen beings is to prevent you from walking the spiritual path. First, they want to prevent you from finding a guru, from finding the path. Then they want to try and get you to follow a false guru. They also have another line of defense, and that is to try to make you so loyal to the first true guru you have found that you think you have to stay with that guru for the rest of this lifetime.

In some cases, it is perfectly alright to stay with that guru for the rest of the lifetime. That is an individual matter, but for many people it will not be alright. It is not part of their divine plans. If your outer mind decides: "Oh, I have to stay with this guru because he rescued me from the astral sea," then you are not open to the inner direction that could tell you to move on and when it is time to move on.

It is always difficult to make your own decisions

What is it that prevents you from hearing the inner voice and moving on? It is that you are not willing to take responsibility for your own path. So many of the people who came to me and wanted me to tell them how to live their lives were not willing to make their own decisions, to take responsibility for making those decisions. This is perfectly understandable, my beloved.

Again, I am an ascended being. I may have appeared judgmental while I was in embodiment, but I have transcended the consciousness I had while I was in embodiment—and that is why I have ascended. My only aim here is to help you see that if you are to ascend, you need to transcend, not the consciousness *I* had while I was in embodiment, but the consciousness *you* have in embodiment. You do that only when you are willing to look at yourself and make your own decisions. I know very, very well how difficult it is to make decisions. I experienced it myself, and I went through a very long phase in my life of being trapped in this perfect trap by the fallen beings.

The fallen beings have done everything possible to make life on earth so complicated, so difficult, that you feel like no matter what decision you make, things only get worse. They have attempted to create an environment with this standard of superhuman perfection where you feel that if you make a mistake, it has some epic importance. Either you will go to heaven because you made the right choice, or you will burn forever in hell because you made the wrong choice.

Can you not see how absolutely insane it is to believe that one choice you make can either send you to heaven or hell? What kind of a God would allow your future – your future *forever* – to depend on one choice you make here on earth when you have a very, very limited perspective? How could you possibly believe that the real God would create an environment as limited as the earth is, force you to make choices based on the limited perspective you have on earth and then send you to hell for all eternity if you make the wrong choice?

My beloved, I chuckle as I say this as an ascended master, but I realize very well that I wouldn't have been able to laugh at this while I was still in embodiment, at least not in my early years. I understand exactly how difficult it is to be in embodiment, to be faced with a situation that you feel you did not choose—and that in many cases you did not *entirely* choose yourself because it depended on the free-will choices made by other people. Even beyond the free-will choices made by you and the people in the situation, the entire situation on earth is so affected by the fallen beings and the fallen consciousness, and has been for so long, that there are so many things on earth that are out of balance. There are so many situations people are in where no matter what choice they make, it leads to unpleasant, negative consequences.

This is the very dilemma on earth. I have been in embodiment, not only once but many, many times. I have had many difficult embodiments where I faced very harsh consequences of my choices and faced very difficult situations. I am not saying this to stand out. I know that you have had many different, many difficult, embodiments. I am simply saying this to help you see that I have experienced the situation you are experiencing. I know what you are going through and I know how difficult it is to make decisions when you are in embodiment on earth.

I know full well how tempting it is to believe that you have now found some superhuman guru who can tell you what to do. If you do what the guru says, then there will not be negative consequences. Suddenly, you will be free from the negative consequences that have haunted you in your life because when you do what the perfect guru tells you to do, everything must turn out well.

A reprieve from your karmic return

I totally understand why so many people are at this stage where they feel damned if they do and damned if they don't. They are looking for a way out of this dilemma, and they think finding the right guru and doing what the guru tells them to do is the answer. I totally understand this. I also understand the deeper reality that this is just a phase on your path. It is a necessary phase, but it is necessary in only one way: It is the only way that you can actually get to the point where you start taking responsibility for making your own decisions. This happens when you realize that there is a way to avoid the negative consequences, a way that you have full power of inside yourself.

Again, there are phases, right? There is a phase where the seas are rough and your own karmic return, the choices of other people and the general situation on earth are just coming at you with such ferocity that you need to batten down the hatches and just get through it. There are many, many students who came to me while I was in embodiment and they asked me: "Mother, should I come on staff?"

In some cases I was allowed to see from the masters that these students were facing a very intense karmic return over the next coming years. If they were out in the world, they would experience the fullness of that karmic return, and it could either take them out of embodiment or cause them to get into situations and create consequences that they would be struggling to overcome for the rest of their lives.

I could also see that by them coming on staff, they could avoid creating quite as difficult consequences for themselves. There was a much better chance that they would be able to work on fulfilling their divine plans, rather than simply having the rest of this lifetime being spent dealing with negative karma and negative consequences. They were allowed to come on staff because it was a growth opportunity for them. However, the important thing to consider here is what happened when this cycle was over. The current of karmic return had come back, had not created the negative consequences, had been partly transmuted by the students' decree work, by their service and by them being in a spiritual environment where they were protected from the consequences.

It was like the student was drowning and it was pulled up on a rescue boat, and the rescue boat had now entered the harbor. The question was: What would make the student go on? This depended very much on the student's reaction.

When a student does not follow the guru's advice

The test was that the students had asked me to make a decision for them about whether they should come on staff or not. I had said: "Yes, come on staff" because that was what helped the student get through a very difficult phase. What is it that happens once you are through the rough waters and you have a little more smooth sailing? Now you have to start taking responsibility for yourself. When you are in rough seas there may only be one course you can take, and you have to just keep to that course to get through it. When you are in smoother waters there are more opportunities open. There is more than one course you can follow and that means what? It means you must *choose* your course. *I* cannot choose for you at that point; *you* must choose.

Do you see that I am allowed to tell you to do certain things, but I am not allowed to continue doing this when you no longer need it, when it is actually time for you to start making your own choices? In some cases, I could tell people: "Yes, come on staff" and it was right of me to tell them this. In some cases, I could *not* tell them to leave because that was something they had to decide on their own. There were other cases where I did tell people *not* to leave because I knew that their karmic return had not come full circle. There was still more turbulence coming, and it was still a better opportunity for them to stay on staff. Some people then decided to go out anyway and even this is okay.

If a student asks for the guru's advice and decides to *not* follow it, then that still shows that the student is now beginning to be willing to take responsibility for itself. You recognize, of course, that there is such a thing as rebelling against the guru through the ego. But there is also such a thing as being willing to make your own decisions. In some cases the guru might actually have to tell you to do one thing, not because this is what you are meant to do, but because this is actually what you are *not* meant to do. By telling you to do it, the guru forces you to make the choice to do what *you* feel you should do.

I realize, my beloved, that this can seem contradictory and can seem very complex. I realize full well that there are many people who have looked at how it was on staff, who have looked at what I told them, who have compared it to what I told others and who have come up with the conclusion that in one situation I said one thing to one person and in another situation I said the exact opposite to another person.

All of this is perfectly true from a linear perspective, but what you need to realize is that every person is in a unique situation. Every person has a unique psychology and a unique inner topography of the ego, the outer self, the dweller and the past momentums and habits. The guru cannot take the same approach to everybody. If you think that the guru should be consistent, you are actually demonstrating that you still have a superhuman standard.

Judging the guru as being inconsistent

You still think that making it into heaven is a matter of following an objectively defined, never-varying standard. You are applying that standard to the guru and using it to judge the guru. You say the guru must have been wrong because the guru didn't follow the standard here or there, the guru wasn't consistent, and the guru contradicted herself and so forth and so on.

I am not trying to tell you here that everything I did or said was always perfect. The fallen beings attempt to take every situation and say that there are two opposite polarities. The situation must be judged based on the existence of these two polarities so that it is either one or the other. It is either-or, black or white. Either the guru is a true guru and everything she did and said was perfect, in order and guided by the spirit. Or she is a false guru and everything she said was wrong, false and came from the astral plane or whatever. My beloved, it just doesn't work that way in reality.

12 | THE DANGERS OF BLAMING YOUR GURU

The situation on earth is murky. It has become that murky by the deliberate engineering of the fallen beings, but also by the unknowing participation of humankind. The collective consciousness on earth is extremely complex, extremely turbulent, and has so many undercurrents that it is very difficult to navigate the sea without being caught up in these undercurrents.

You might know that along the East Coast of the United States is something called the Gulf Stream. This stream flows North at a certain speed, and I have experienced myself that you can be out on a boat and you think you are navigating the waves, but in reality you and the waves are being carried North by the Gulf Stream. You need to take this into consideration if you are going to get to the harbor. You need to adjust your course based not only on the wind and the waves that you *can* see, but also based on the undercurrent that you *cannot* see.

Even a true guru is not entirely neutral

The reality is this. I was a guru, I was the sponsored messenger of the ascended masters. There are many, many cases where I was guided by the ascended masters to give people directions, but those directions still came through my mind, my psychology. They could in some cases – not in all, but in *some* cases – be affected by my psychology. The direction you got – and which *you* thought and *I* thought came from El Morya through me – was not necessarily the completely neutral direction coming from El Morya that he could have given you from the ascended realm.

It was the direction that came from El Morya but descended through the identity, the mental, the emotional realms of *my* mind. Then it was given to you, being interpreted through the four levels of *your* mind. This is the reality of how things work on earth, this is the reality of even how a true guru works on earth. As long as you are in embodiment, even if you are a true guru, everything must flow through the four levels of the material realm and it will be affected by whatever is in those realms. Again, you can take the view and say: "But this is completely wrong." Then you are trapped in the standard of wanting perfection or nothing.

The reality is that this is perfectly in order because "when the student is ready, the teacher appears." The teacher you are ready for is exactly the kind of teacher that appears to you. If you had attracted yourself to me as a guru, you were ready for that kind of a guru. The important thing is: What does that say about you that you can use to free yourself from what is holding you back?

The important lesson here is that whatever direction you got from me, or from another spiritual guru, did not have to be perfect according to some standard for there is no such standard in God. It had to be whatever it was. Whatever it was, was the best opportunity for you to see in yourself what you need to see in order to take the next step on your personal path. If you use it that way, it will help you grow. If you refuse, it will not help you grow.

Do you understand what I am saying here? Even if you had the perfect direction from a perfect guru and followed it blindly, that would not help you go beyond a certain stage on the spiritual path. When you are dealing with a very intense situation of karmic return and it is a matter of either sink or swim, then it is extremely important to have a good guru who can give you valid direction. I am not saying *perfect* direction but *valid* direction. It is extremely important to follow that direction blindly without looking right or left, without questioning it. You follow it because it is the only way to get through the choppy waters.

Once you get through the rough seas, it is equally important to now look back and reflect and consider: "What is the next step? What will it take for me to take responsibility for my own path so that I can not only get directions from within, but so that I can actually come to the point where I am willing to freely make decisions and freely learn from them?"

The ascended master purpose for relationships

There are many of my students who came to me as an outer physical guru and wanted me to tell them what to do. I told them what to do, and they followed it. Then, after some time, they realized that even though they had followed blindly what they believed was the perfect direction from a perfect guru, they were still experiencing unpleasant consequences.

This was especially true when I had told people whom to marry. Two people would come to me and say: "Mother, we are in love, we are thinking about getting married but we want your blessing. Should we marry or shouldn't we? We will do whatever you say." I say: "Yes, you can get married." They get married and now they expect that because the messenger of the ascended masters, the perfect guru, had told them to get married, their marriage will be happily ever after.

Why were they told to marry? Because marrying was the best possible opportunity for both of them to grow. Why was it the best opportunity to grow? Because their psychologies were matched so that they would inevitably bring out in each other what each of them needed to see in order to take the next step. A marriage arranged by the ascended masters, or recommended by the ascended masters, is not given to be happily ever after. It is arranged in order to create maximum opportunity for growth, and that often means people bring out in each other exactly what each person needs to see and overcome. The two people are in essence making more visible in each other what they have not been willing to see on their own. They are now forced to deal with something they otherwise could have covered over.

They are now standing there, realizing that their dream – again, the dream created by the fallen ones, by the perfect standard and the entire Hollywood movie industry of happily ever after – is not being fulfilled. What do these people then do? They say: "Mother told us to get married. She must have been wrong. She must have gotten the wrong direction. She must not be a true messenger after all." All of a sudden, the whole house of cards they have built comes crashing down.

The dilemma faced by the ascended masters

Do you understand the dilemma faced by the ascended masters and any true guru, especially a guru who is meant to do what I did? I was meant to take people beyond the stage of blindly following an outer guru so they could start to take responsibility for making their own decisions. I had to take on students who wanted me to tell them what to do. This was part of my assignment.

There were students who came to me and did not have that need. They did not ask for my direction, they did not want me to tell them what to do, they wanted me to give them teachings that would increase their inner attunement.

I had many students who came to me because they were not quite ready to take that step. Many of these students believed there is an outer standard: "If I make the right choices, I am guaranteed to make my ascension. If I do the right outer things, I will make my ascension. If I do the wrong things, I will go to hell, or at least I will have to re-embody. How do I then do the right outer things? Ah, I have the perfect guru here, the messenger of the ascended masters. If she tells me what to do and I do it, then it must be guaranteed to be right." Do you see what I have said all along here: You do not make your ascension that way. You can indeed make it through a time, a cycle, of very intense karmic return, but you will not make your ascension by following *outer* directions. You will make your ascension by making your own *inner* choices.

You need to get beyond that phase of wanting to follow an outer direction, of not wanting to make your own decisions. How do you do this? How do I, as a guru, teach you to do this? Well, in some cases I have no other option than by pushing people's buttons, by exaggerating a situation in order to make it obvious to people what is going on in their psychology so that they will hopefully be able to see what they have not seen so far. Again, we have the model: You give a teaching, but if the student does not heed the teaching, then you have to put the student in a situation that forces out what is unseen in the student's psychology so the student has another opportunity to finally see it.

People come to me because they are not willing to make their decisions. They want the perfect direction. I give them the direction, now they are facing the consequences. They don't like the consequences. How do they then respond? Do they respond by saying I must have given wrong directions, I am a false guru, I am this I am that I am the next thing? Or do they finally say: "Oh, maybe I need to look at myself here?" Do they look *out* or do they finally begin to look *in*?

That is the question. To be or not to be? To look *out* or to look *in*? To always project your attention out, looking for faults in others, or to finally begin to look in, not to look for fault but simply to look at what you need to let go of.

How you really balance karma

This mechanism of getting you to look out is set up by the fallen beings to sabotage your growth. Again, I have been there, I have seen it, I have experienced how difficult it is. One of the most difficult things on the spiritual path is to overcome this idea that your salvation, your entry into the kingdom of God, your ascension depends on the outer things you do or don't do.

This is created by the fallen beings. It is even to some degree reinforced by many spiritual teachings, including the Eastern teachings on karma. You have taken an action in a past life. It is now coming back as a karmic return. If you killed somebody in a past life, somebody will try to kill you in this life, an eye for an eye, a tooth for a tooth. You did *this,* what is coming back to you is *that.*

Again, I am not denying the Law of Karma here. It does to some degree work that way, but the purpose of it working that way is not that a certain action taken in the past will generate an action in the present and when the two actions meet they cancel out each other. This is not the way it works. Let me give you a higher teaching on karma that I was not able to give you while I was in embodiment.

There is a common belief – not only in our church but also in many spiritual and New Age movements and in the East – that if you have killed somebody in the past, for example, then if you are killed in this lifetime, it will have balanced your karma from the past. You did something to someone else, now the same thing is done to you—you have balanced the karma.

This is not the way it works. Why did you kill somebody in the past? Because you were in a certain state of consciousness. The karma does not come instantly back to you, it cycles through the four levels of the material realm and then it comes back in a future lifetime. What is the purpose of this delay? It is that you now have an opportunity for several lifetimes to get out of the state of consciousness you were in when you took that action. The purpose of life is *not* that you make karma, balance karma and then ascend. The purpose of life is that you expand your consciousness, your sense of self. You expand your consciousness by taking an action, looking at the consequences of the action, seeing what those consequences say about the state of consciousness that you are in and then using that to expand your state of consciousness, to raise your sense of self. That is how you grow and *that* is the purpose of life.

Say you killed somebody in the past and you are killed in this life. If that would balance your karma, what would you learn from that if you haven't changed your consciousness? The Law of Karma works differently. It does say that if you killed somebody in the past, there is a possibility that you will have that karmic return come all the way to the physical. If you have made a sincere effort to change your consciousness in the meantime, then it will not come through as a physical return. You don't have to be killed. You may experience a life-threatening situation or it may be completely consumed at the emotional, mental or identity level before it becomes physical.

Karma does not have to become physical, and karma is not balanced by becoming physical. It is balanced by you transcending the consciousness that caused you to make the karma. *That,* my beloved, is the only way to balance karma. Say you killed somebody in a past life and you have not changed your consciousness one bit. If you then are killed in this life, you will make more karma because of the way you react to being killed. You are likely to believe that this is unjust, this is something somebody did to you. You might even be angry at God for allowing you to be killed in this lifetime. You have not started to take responsibility for yourself, and therefore you are blaming it on somebody else. This causes you to create more karma, which will only generate a more intense return in the future. Many people are only intensifying their karmic return.

Your ascension depends on your state of consciousness

Just go and look at the Middle East. Go and look, right when I am speaking this, at what is happening in Syria. If you could see what I see from the ascended state, you would see that many of the people who are involved in this conflict have been fighting each other going back thousands of lifetimes in the Middle East. They kill somebody in one life. In a future life that person comes back in embodiment and kills them. Neither of the two have balanced their karma by doing this, they have only created a more intense karmic spiral. This is what they are still trapped in today, thousands of lifetimes later.

When will this end; this outplaying of these karmic spirals on earth? It will end only when the top ten percent of the most mature spiritual lifestreams on earth decide to free themselves from this consciousness by honestly looking at themselves and saying: "Oh, what do I have to learn? What do I have to let go of?"

Do you see what I said? It is not a matter of the actions you take. Everything concerning your ascension is a matter of your state of consciousness. You cannot be a mature spiritual student and think that you will make it to heaven by doing the *right* things and not doing the *wrong* things.

12 | The Dangers of Blaming Your Guru

Many people came to the church and they were at that state of consciousness where they wanted some higher authority to tell them: "Do this, don't do that and you will make it to heaven." This is essentially what the mainstream religions – especially in the Western world, certainly the three monotheistic religions – have been doing for thousands of years. They have set up this standard of the angry, judgmental God in the sky, and they have set up an outer set of rules on earth that says: "Do this, don't do that and you will make it up to the angry God in the sky."

Why anybody would want to go to the angry God in the sky is not discussed in these religions, right? The reason they give, the *only* reason they give, for why you want to go to the angry God in the sky is that the alternative is that you go to a very hot place and burn forever in hell. That is the only way they can motivate you to go to the angry God in the sky because no sane person wants to go to that God. Why would you want to spend eternity being locked in some heavenly world with an angry God that judges everything?

13 | TAKING YOURSELF AND LIFE TOO SERIOUSLY

The only way to make it to the ascended state is to transcend these graven images of the false God that have been put before the real God by the fallen beings. In order to do that, you must look at yourself. In the context of what we are talking about here, take a look at what is your attitude about making decisions. Do you actually believe that it is only a matter of making the *right* decision and avoid making the *wrong* decision, in terms of your outer actions and their outer consequences? If this is what you believe, then you have not yet started to take responsibility for yourself.

When you do start to take responsibility, you realize that the outer actions and their consequences are not actually important in terms of making your ascension. *Do you understand what I am saying?* I am not denying karma here. If you take a certain action – let us say you killed someone in a past life – you are creating a karmic impulse that will come back to you. All this karmic impulse will do is keep you trapped at the level of karma. You can – for a very, very long time, for thousands and thousands of embodiments – keep creating these karmic circles for yourself, and all you are doing is dealing with these karmic circles. You are not taking steps to get beyond this wheel of rebirth, as it is called in the East.

In order to get beyond the wheel, you have to shift your consciousness. You don't shift your consciousness by thinking that you have to avoid doing the wrong things and do the right outer things. You shift your consciousness by questioning why you feel the need to do the right thing and avoid the wrong thing. Why do you have the image of the angry and judgmental God and the standard of perfection that you must live up to in order to please that God? What is it that causes you to be attached to this? Why do you believe this is so important?

We have given the teaching that planet earth and the material world is just a sandbox. I know that when you are in embodiment it seems as if you can create terrible consequences, and you do have the ability to create terrible consequences. I am not making light of things on earth. I know very well the suffering that people are going through right now in Syria, Ukraine and other nations around the world, such as in Africa. I can tune in to this very easily as an ascended master.

Conditions on earth are ultimately unreal

I am not making light of the fact that people are creating terrible consequences and atrocities. I grew up learning about the Holocaust, and it was an absolutely astounding atrocity. It is still astounding that people could actually be sucked into such a downward spiral. Nevertheless, when you come to the ascended level, you see that all of these terrible things that are happening on earth are – from a higher perspective – simply the playing of children in the sandbox. Regardless of how this seems on earth, it has no eternal reality to it. *It is all unreal.*

If you go into a movie theatre, you are in a closed environment. It is dark, all external distractions are withdrawn from you—especially if you have turned off that cell phone of yours.

You are sucked into the environment created by the movie. If you watch a very intense movie about war, for example, you may experience how terrible it was for the soldiers to be in that war. You may be entirely engrossed in the movie while it is playing, but at some point it says: "The End" and you walk out of the movie theatre. Even though you are still very much affected by the experience you had and the intensity of it, you know that what happened in there was not absolutely real. It was a movie.

When you ascend from earth, you see that regardless of the terrible things that are happening on earth, it is really no more real from an eternal, ongoing perspective than a movie. I am not here trying to make excuses. I am not here trying to make light of things. There *are* terrible things happening on earth every day. It is creating terrible karmic consequences that people will have to face in the future, and you *will* reap what you sow.

Nevertheless, from the ascended perspective the actions that are taking place on earth are taking place in a realm of lower energies. *All* of these energies can be erased, requalified, transmuted.

This is the gift of Saint Germain with the violet flame, and it is the gift of all of the seven rays. Earth and everything that happens on earth in the physical octave is happening in a realm of lower energies that have no enduring existence or reality. It can all be erased. It could be erased in the blink of an eye if an ascended being with a high enough state of consciousness came to earth and released the full fire of its being to consume it.

This would also take away the opportunity for growth, and that is why this is not happening. This is why Jesus will not come back and roll up the world as a scroll and solve all of humankind's problems. The earth, regardless of the terrible things happening, is still a platform for growth. It is certainly one of the lower platforms in the material universe, but it is a viable platform for growth.

Learning to look beyond physical consequences

What you need to do – if you are to make your ascension in this life or the next – is to start looking beyond physical actions and physical consequences. Making your ascension is not a matter of choosing to do the right thing and choosing not to do the wrong thing. It is not the outer actions and their consequences that will determine your ascension. It is the shift in consciousness.

In order to shift your consciousness, you need to stop looking at everything that happens on earth as being so serious, so epically important. You need to start giving yourself a little bit of slack and realizing that the choices you make – what happens to you and what does *not* happen to you – do not have this epic importance of sending you to heaven or hell.

It is just a choice, and the importance is not what you did or what happened as a result of what you did. The importance is how you look at it, how you process the experience, what it did to your consciousness. The important thing is not the *physical* impact of your action, but the *psychological* impact of your action.

This means, my beloved, that any choice you make, any action you take, is not in and of itself a mistake. It is what you do in your mind that determines whether an action was a mistake or not. If you fail to question the consciousness that caused you to take the action, then the action was a mistake. If you do question the consciousness, see it for what it is and make a conscious decision to transcend it, then no matter what the action was and no matter what the consequences were, it was not a mistake because you have grown closer to your ascension.

You might still have created a karmic impulse that will be returned to you, but that karmic impulse can be transmuted by the violet flame—when you have changed the consciousness that caused you to make it. All of this is just mechanics. This is the importance of having the knowledge of the spoken word and the violet flame and using spiritual energy to transform the lower energy impulses in the four levels of the material realm. There is no consequence that cannot be consumed because whatever consequence you have created, is created in the lower energies and they can be transmuted by invoking higher energy. However, they cannot be transmuted from the same level of consciousness where you created the karmic impulse. You can give violet flame until you run out of breath, and it will not transmute your karma if you have not shifted your consciousness.

Being too focused on yourself

When I look at myself in my last embodiment – when I look at most of the students I attracted, when I look at all of the people on earth who are sincerely striving on the spiritual path and who are close to making their ascension – I see one overriding mechanism. It is the mechanism that causes people to take themselves and what happens to them, very, very seriously.

You take whatever happens to you, whatever other people do or say, you take it so personally. If you look at my life, you will see that I was the typical example of this. I had a very difficult childhood with an abusive father and a mother who did not protect me. The psychological effect of this – as you will see in many, many children who have been in a similar or worse situation of abuse – is that you become very focused on yourself.

Well, my beloved, now consider that you have had many lifetimes on this planet, and consider that the general environment on this planet is abusive. The fallen beings have created such ragnarok, such chaos, on this planet that the general environment is highly abusive. Most people do not think about this because the human mind has an ability to adjust to even the most extreme conditions and label them as normal. The effect of this is a necessary survival mechanism. In order to get through a certain phase, you have to label it as normal because once you accept it as normal, you can at least deal with it without completely falling apart.

You will see, even if you read about some of the survivors of the Holocaust, that those who were able to survive psychologically came to a point of accepting conditions the way they were and trying to make the best of it. This was what enabled them to survive. The fallen beings have attempted to create a situation on this planet where you are exposed to such abuse that you have to do this in order to simply survive, in order to make it through.

When you have done this for many lifetimes, what is the effect? The effect is that you become very, very focused on yourself. You think everything you do is somehow very, very important. Everything that happens to you is very important. What other people do or say to you is very important. Your own feelings and thoughts are very, very important. Now again, we come to a subtlety.

What you must do to qualify for your ascension

The collective consciousness on this planet *is* very low. You can go to some parts of the world where there is relative peace and relative prosperity and you can see that people are living lives that are really not that bad. They are still living in the collective consciousness of earth and this sets certain limitations. You are supposed to do what the people in your environment consider acceptable. You are supposed to live according to the prevailing standard in the environment where you grew up.

Just about everywhere on earth, that standard is not very conducive to you following the spiritual path and qualifying for your ascension, doing whatever is needed for you in this last embodiment to qualify for your ascension. In some cases, when you have only one embodiment left and you want to qualify for

13 | Taking Yourself and Life too Seriously

your ascension in this embodiment, you may have to do some things that are pretty radical compared to the norm in the environment where you grew up.

Look at the life of Jesus. What did he tell his disciples: "Leave your nets and follow me. If your father, mother, sister and brother is more important to you than following me, then you are not ready for the path that I offer." If you are in your last embodiment, you may have to do things that are considered absolutely radical and abhorrent by the people who are closest to you. They don't understand it and maybe they *cannot* understand it because they do not have the opportunity to qualify for their ascension in this lifetime, no matter what they do.

You do have that opportunity, but it may necessitate that you take some actions that seem radical to other people. You may have to join a spiritual organization, you may have to practice certain spiritual practices, you may have to take certain actions, you may have to marry certain people, you may have to divorce them, you may have to go on, you may have to do this, you may have to do that, you may have to change careers several times. All of these things might be necessary for you to make that last push of qualifying for your ascension.

How can you follow that path unless you are willing to go against the grain, to swim against the current of the mass consciousness? If you are blindly following the currents of the mass consciousness, you cannot qualify for your ascension; you cannot walk the spiritual path in any capacity. The very fact that you are a spiritual seeker, a spiritual student, means you are going against the mass consciousness. What does this mean? It means you must be focused on yourself. You must say: "I am different, I have a different goal than most people, and I am willing to be different even if I get flak from other people who want me to be normal."

Do you see that in order to actually get through the choppy waves of the collective consciousness and the resistance from your own environment, you have to batten down the hatches, close the openings in your mind and ignore what people are telling you. What is the effect of this? It makes you very focused on yourself. If you have, as we all had, many past lifetimes where you were exposed to abuse, either general or personal, you have also there built the tendency to be focused on yourself.

Healing your relationship with God

There is a level on your spiritual path where it is perfectly alright to be very focused on yourself, to ignore what the fallen ones are projecting into your mind, to ignore what other people are saying, to ignore the currents in the mass consciousness. You need to do this in order to make it through that area of turbulence, but if you are to make your ascension, you cannot continue to do this. For many of you, you will not qualify for your ascension in this lifetime if you continue to be so focused on yourself, your own growth, your own health, your own psychology, your own this and your own that. You cannot make it if you continue to take yourself and everything that happens to you so seriously.

In my very last years I started softening up—*just a bit*. The reason I had to spend so many years still holding on to the physical body, but not being conscious in the body, was to some degree that I needed to get over this tendency of being so focused on myself and interpreting everything that happened to me as having some great importance.

You see what I am saying here? When I was a child and experienced the abuse of both my father and my mother, I was so traumatized by this that it created a conflict in me about my relationship to God. I always knew there was a God. I always felt that God is just. In your mind you think: "Well, if God is just, he should not allow this abuse to happen to me unless I have done something to deserve it." Since I could not see with my mind what I had done to deserve this kind of abuse, it was impossible for me to explain this. Why was I being exposed to this abuse when I saw no reason for this?

As I began to grow older, what came to my mind is that this abuse could be justified if my exposure to it served some greater epic cause. If, for example, I had taken on karma that lessened the suffering of other people, giving them an opportunity to grow without suffering such severe abuse, then I could feel that my suffering had served some greater purpose. *That* could explain why God had allowed me to suffer. I might even have chosen to suffer myself. If my father was a fallen being and his abuse generated his final judgment that got him off this planet, then me being exposed to this abuse could have helped the forward progression of the planet and therefore have served a greater cause. Now, I am not saying that these two concerns are not valid.

Why you might choose to take on karma

What you understand here is that there is a very complex situation on earth. I just said that there are many people in the Middle East who are simply trapped in a karmic spiral where they are creating karma in this life by responding to a return karma from a past life—and they never get off this treadmill. Most people on earth are like this, but there is also a certain group of people on earth who are not trapped in these karmic spirals. This means that when something happens to one of these more mature lifestreams, it is not necessarily your own returning karma. In my case, for example, my father's abuse towards me was not a return of my karma. It was not that I had abused him in a past life and now I was exposed to his abuse and that settled the score. That was not the case.

There are many people – the more mature spiritual people, the ones who are closer to their ascension – who choose to take on karma that is not their own. Some choose to take it on for a particular other person in order to give that person an opportunity, and it can be a parent, a spouse or a sibling. There are other people who choose to take on general karma for humankind. There are also some of these lifestreams who choose to embody in a certain situation in order to give another lifestream an opportunity to either overcome their abusive tendencies or to outplay them to such a degree that it brings about their judgment and they are removed from the earth. These are valid scenarios that take place all the time.

Many of the spiritual people on earth are precisely in this situation, but what does this mean? It means that inside of you, you have a sense that the difficult consequences you are living – the outer situation, the outer abuse or whatever the situation may be: diseases, handicaps or other things – that these are not the just the return of your personal karma. If you do not have a spiritual awareness, you can feel that this must mean that God is unjust because he is allowing you to experience this even though you do not deserve it.

If you, like myself, have a firm belief that God is just, you need the explanation that your suffering serves some greater cause. Again, the explanation is true, but the psychological effect can very easily be that you become very focused on yourself and your own importance. You are now doing something very important for God or for the ascended masters. The suffering you have gone through has some epic importance, and what does this do to you psychologically? It actually reinforces your ego, your dweller, your outer self because it makes this outer self feel that it has epic importance and it is doing something for God.

The "epic" importance of ascending

I know this will seem contradictory and confusing to many. Did I not just say that it is true that you *are* doing something of great importance? Yes, you *are,* but the question is how you use it psychologically. If it is used to boost the importance of your ego, you will trap yourself more firmly in the outer self and it does not help your ascension.

What is it going to take to qualify for your ascension? In a sense, you can say that walking the path towards the ascension and qualifying for your ascension is the most epically important thing you can possibly do on planet earth. It raises the collective consciousness, it brings about the judgment of fallen beings, it raises the entire earth to a higher level. You can look at Jesus and you can see that it was of epic importance for the earth that he took embodiment and that he qualified for his ascension. I felt – when I was in embodiment, when I was a messenger and a teacher – that my work as a messenger, my work of qualifying for my ascension, was of epic importance. Many of my students felt exactly the same way.

Again, in order to make it through the rough seas, in order to pull ourselves beyond the downward pull of the mass consciousness, we need to have a motivation, we need to feel that what we are doing is important, that it has some greater importance. Why else would we do this that is so difficult? Why wouldn't we just follow along with the mass consciousness and enjoy life? We need this in order to get through a certain phase, but my beloved, you will not make your ascension by continuing to be so focused on yourself and by thinking that everything you do has some epic importance and therefore you should take it so seriously.

Qualifying for your ascension *is* of epic importance, but if you feel that what you are doing is of epic importance, you will not qualify for your ascension. Why not? What have I said earlier? In order to ascend, you must leave behind not only everything on earth but every illusion of your outer, separate self.

What is your motivation for wanting to ascend?

Yes, it *is* important to qualify for your ascension, but your outer self cannot qualify for the ascension. It can never ascend; it must be left behind. This means that there comes a point where you need to recognize that part of your motivation for walking the spiritual path – for following an ascended master teaching, for seeking to qualify for your ascension – is based on the ego's desire to reach some ultimate status where it can enter the wedding feast and be accepted by God. If you do not acknowledge this, you will not be able to shed those last elements of ego. It is precisely what has carried you to the point where you are standing just outside the gate that leads to the ascended state, and now you need to become aware that what has carried you this far cannot carry you into the ascended state.

You must see this tendency to focus on yourself and to think that everything you do is so important. You must see it for what it is, namely an element of the separate self. You must decide to leave it behind. You must realize, as I have said, that whatever takes place on earth is just a playing out of the sandbox of life. It has no ultimate reality. It has no ultimate importance in the great scheme of God.

Unless you see this, you cannot ascend. You will have to come back into embodiment. You will have to outplay this epic mindset in a more and more extreme form until you finally see it. You will not understand my last lifetime, my church and even the teachings given through me unless you recognize that I was very much in the epic mindset and that it affected many of the things I did, many of the things I said, and first of all the way I looked at everything.

Now again, this was in order. This was exactly the kind of teacher that people needed here at the end of the Piscean age. They needed to overcome the illusion created by the fallen beings and projected into the collective consciousness on earth.

The fallen beings think they are important

What is one of the deepest illusions of the fallen beings? It is that they are so important that they can force God to change his mind, that they can prove God wrong. Can you not see that the fallen beings are precisely trapped in this consciousness that they have become as gods, knowing good and evil, defining good and evil, being able to tell God how he should run the creation? It is the extreme form of self-focus that you see in the fallen beings. It should be easy to see that you will not ascend if you hold on to the consciousness of the fallen beings.

The ascended masters do not have this sense of self-importance. You will see, if you look carefully in the words of Jesus, that he did not have it. Did he not say: "I can of my own self do nothing?" When someone called him "good master," did he not say: "Why callest thou me good? There is none good but one, that is God?" Jesus ascended because he did not have this consciousness. He had overcome it. He demonstrated this after his stay in the wilderness where he was tempted by the devil. The devil attempted to make Jesus feel that what Jesus was doing was so important that he had to prove it to the devil, or that he needed to have all the kingdoms of the world in order to save people.

My beloved, it just isn't important in a cosmic sense what has happened to you on earth. Now, take care here. I have said that whatever you have done in the past creates a karmic impulse. You need to transmute that by invoking the violet flame and other spiritual energies. There *is* work to be done; it *is* important to do this. I have said that everything that has happened to you is an opportunity to see something in your consciousness and let go of it. It is important to do this. It is all important for following the path; it is very important to follow the path and to strive towards the ascension. All I am trying to say here is that striving is not what will get you that last step through the door to the ascended state

The real path is about letting go

In a sense, the real path, the *inner* path, is a path of letting go. You have come to identify yourself with a certain perception filter, a certain outer self. When you look at life through that perception filter, everything that happens seems very, very important. How do you get out of that perception filter? By coming to see that nothing is as important as it appears from inside the perception filter. Thereby, you can say: "Hey, but this is unreal; I am letting go of it."

When you walk the spiritual path, you have already made many of these decisions, even in this lifetime, of letting go. You have friends and family who are pursuing a career. They have a position in society, they are making lots of money, they have big houses and you have said: "That is not as important to me as following the spiritual path. I am letting it go." You have seen many things in your own psychology and you have come to see: "Oh, that isn't important to me anymore, I can let it go."

All I am trying to say here is that you come to a point when you are standing right there, and there is the gate. If you walk through that gate, you have ascended. Well, what is it going to take to take that last step? You are going to have to look back on earth and the question is: Is there anything on earth – including anything in your own consciousness or anything that is happening on earth – that is still important to you? Is there some problem on earth that you still feel you need to solve? Is there some change you need to make? Is there some epic cause that you feel you have to fight for; you cannot ascend until this or that or the next thing has happened in society?

My beloved, if there is *anything* on earth that is still important to you, you cannot leave the earth behind forever. It cannot be done. Free will reigns supreme. When you grasp this, you can make the rest of this lifetime so much easier for yourself by simply considering: "What is important to me? What is it I take seriously? What is it that offends me? What is it that I am attached to? What is it I think I need to solve? What is it I think I need to do?"

I am not saying you let everything go. There are still many things that are important to you. You have a divine plan, it is important for you to follow and fulfill that plan. It becomes so much easier for you to fulfill your divine plan if you don't take everything personally, if you don't take everything so seriously.

Again, there is a *what* and a *how*. If you look at my last lifetime, I did follow the *what* of what was in my divine plan. If I had been able to take myself less seriously, I could have done so much better concerning the *how* of why it was done. I would actually have been more successful, more effective in spreading the teachings of the ascended masters, if I had been less serious. I would have attracted more students. More than that, I would have made it so much easier for myself and the people around me if I had not been so serious about everything, if I had not taken so personally many of the things that happened in my life or that happened on the planet as a whole.

Feeling responsible for what happens in the world

Do you realize that many of us have come to take it personally when certain things happen in the world? What is the guideline here? The guideline is very simple: Everything on earth revolves around the Law of Free Will. You have free will. You are personally responsible for what you do with that free will. You are one hundred percent responsible for your own sphere of self, your own mind. You are one hundred percent responsible for what you do within that sphere. This is your sanctuary on earth.

You have an inner sanctuary where no one and no force on earth can enter unless you let them. You are not meant to let *anything* enter that inner sanctuary. You are not meant to let other people, even the ones closest to you, enter that sanctuary. You are especially not meant to let the fallen beings or the collective consciousness influence your inner sanctuary.

You have an inner sanctuary that is the core of your being, and you are one hundred percent responsible for what happens *inside* that sanctuary. In terms of what happens *outside* that sanctuary, this will to a very large degree depend on the free-will choices made by other people. According to the Law of Free Will, you have no right to control the choices of other people and you have no responsibility for their choices.

This means that you should not feel responsible for what happens outside your inner sanctuary. It is *not* your responsibility. God has not made you responsible for everything that happens on this earth. It is when you feel responsible for what is not your responsibility that you begin to take everything very seriously. You begin to take everything that happens to you very personally.

What does it mean to feel responsible for what happens outside your inner sanctuary? It means that you feel responsible for something over which you have no influence and no power. You cannot change what is going on outside your inner sanctuary by your inner choices, by your own choices. This means that you, by feeling responsible, automatically make yourself feel powerless. This means that you now have a standard of perfection for what *should* happen and what *should not* happen in the world.

The things that you think should *not* happen are nevertheless happening because other people are making choices. You feel powerless to change those choices, but you nevertheless feel that people should not be making them and these things should not be happening. The inevitable psychological consequence is that you become very serious. You think this is a great injustice that is happening, and you just cannot let it go. Your whole life becomes this spiral, this struggle, of struggling against conditions outside of yourself over which you have absolutely no influence. God has not given you this influence because it is not God's goal to change conditions on earth. God's goal for you is that you ascend.

Stop judging the light and the darkness

You will ascend only when you take complete command over your inner sanctuary and do not let any condition on earth influence what is happening in your inner sanctuary. You let nothing on earth influence how you feel, how you think, how you look at life and how you look at yourself. You are being the living spirit that you are, being the open door, letting the light from your I AM Presence stream, and you are not judging how the light should flow.

You can only be the open door for the light of your Presence if you are not judging how the light should flow. You can only avoid judging the light *if you do not judge the darkness*.

Again, the fallen beings have created the standard, and then they have projected that you are supposed to judge everything according to some standard of perfection. You will not be free of this until you stop judging *anything*.

What is happening on earth: *It just is what it is*. It is neither *this* nor *that*. As long as you think it is *this* or *that* and it should be *this* and it should not be *that*, you are attached to it. You will take it personally when it is not the way you think it should be. You will take it seriously because you think it has some epic importance that things are not the way they should be.

This will trap you and keep you from your ascension. I very nearly missed my ascension by not being willing to question this consciousness. You may think – based on what I said and what was said in dictations before I ascended – that my ascension was in the bag, it was a given. I tell you, until you have stepped through the gate, nothing is a given. How could it be when free will reigns supreme? At every stage towards your ascension, you are facing a choice. If you choose one option, you will stay where you are or go down. If you choose the other, you will go up. You must make a choice, and you do not have a choice if you can only go up. In the unascended realm there is always the possibility of going up or down. Until you have walked through the gate, it is a possibility that you can miss your ascension. You will miss your ascension by having something on earth to which you are attached, something that you feel is important, something on earth that you have taken into your inner sanctuary and have not let go of.

No man can ascend back *to* heaven save he that descended *from* heaven. The Conscious You descended in a state of formless purity and it will only ascend in a state of formless purity. I have ascended to that formless purity, and I ascended to the formless purity by transcending the very form that I had created.

I have transcended the form that I had in my last embodiment. I am giving this teaching because I hope that those who encountered the form that I had in my last embodiment will also be willing and able to transcend that form.

More importantly, I hope you will use my example to be willing and able to transcend your own form. You will not make or break your ascension by drinking *my* Kool-Aid or not drinking *my* Kool-Aid. You will only make your ascension when you stop drinking *your own* Kool-Aid.

14 | TURNING A TRUE GURU INTO A FALSE GURU

Guru Ma I AM, and I come to give you the next level in my teaching on the guru-chela relationship. I have said that there is a period on the path where you absolutely need a guru. I have talked about the fact that you go through a turbulent period where you are dealing with the return of your personal karma. You have to pull yourself beyond the mass consciousness, including your own family and your immediate environment. I have also said that you are being attacked by dark forces and therefore you have to have a safe vessel that can carry you through and shield you from these outside influences. A true guru can help you in many ways when you go through this phase.

Why you created internal spirits

There is another level where a true guru can be of incalculable assistance to you. There comes a period where you are still in choppy waters. You are still very much dealing with turbulence, but it is not so much an *external* turbulence but an *internal* turbulence. You have, in the subconscious levels of the mind, created an extremely elaborate structure that makes up your separate self, your mortal self.

In the church we talked about the Dweller on the Threshold, the carnal mind, the subconscious mind, and we also talked a little bit about the ego. What we have given today is the concept that you have internal spirits. When we talked about the dweller in the church, we were in a sense talking about such internal spirits. The importance of this teaching is that you have these internal "computer programs" that spring into action in certain situations and take over how you react to those situations. They take over how you look at the situation, what you think about it, what you think about how you might respond to it, what you feel about it and how you feel compelled to respond to the situation.

The reason you have created these spirits is that there came a point where you did not want to make certain decisions about how to react to conditions on earth. You created a spirit and said: "Well, in these situations I don't want to consciously deal with this. I don't want to consciously make decisions. Let the spirit take over. Let the subconscious computer take over." This was part of what you started creating when you turned your back upon your spiritual teacher and started walking away.

It is part of your not wanting to take full personal responsibility for your life and your path. You will see so many people in the world who are going through life and they are technically and physically conscious, but from a psychological and spiritual perspective they are barely conscious. They go to through life unawares. They go through life almost without being consciously aware of what is happening to them. They have, in a sense, withdrawn. They are living their lives on automatic pilot.

As you go through the initial phases of the spiritual path, where you are dealing with so many external challenges, this tendency can almost be reinforced. If you look honestly at many spiritual students, you will see that they do have a tendency to withdraw themselves from the world and to refuse to deal with certain topics, issues or problems.

I have said that there is a period where this is a valid approach. You are going through turbulence and you need to stay focused on your goal of getting through this turbulence, instead of being pulled down in all kinds of downward spirals that simply take you away from your goal. Your goal is ultimately the ascension, but in the short term it is to get through the turbulence so you can get your head above the water and start becoming more conscious again.

Knowing which internal voices are real and unreal

I said in my last discourse that when you are drowning, you cannot look right or left. There comes a point where you can get your head above the water and can start looking around, wondering: "Where do I go next?" There comes a point on the path where, as part of taking responsibility for your life and your path, you need to start consciously dealing with certain conditions and issues in your life.

You need to look at your outer life and you need to make choices; you need to say: "What is the consequence of me being in this particular situation? How does this affect my general well-being, my ability to focus within, my spiritual growth?" Then you need to make some choices where you choose *out*, you choose *away*, certain worldly activities that simply pull you away from the spiritual path or even pull you into negative patterns and spirals. You must do this consciously, by taking a conscious look, instead of running on automatic pilot.

There also comes a phase where it is not so much the outer things you are focused on, but you can begin to now look within. You can look at the beam in your own eye, look at your psychology, look at these patterns, these subconscious programs, these spirits. There are many spiritual students who are hesitant to do this, and I fully understand why. It is a very difficult process. In the beginning, you literally feel like there are so many voices speaking to you from inside your own mind. They are so confusing, so contradictory and so persistent that you feel like you are being pulled in many different directions just from inside your own mind, let alone the outside pulls on you.

In the beginning, it seems like it is impossible for you, with your conscious mind, to discern what is real and unreal, what is constructive and not in all of this internal turbulence, these internal voices. I am not here talking about people who physically hear voices in their heads, although that certainly does happen to some spiritual students. I am more talking about the inner thoughts and feelings that are pulling on your conscious mind.

The guru is pulling you out of negative spirals

A typical example is if you are going through a difficult situation, such as a conflict with another person, and you find yourself constantly thinking about the situation, going over it again and again.

You are feeling like: "Should I do this, should I do that? I wish this *would* have happened, I wish this *would not* have happened. I wish the other person would do *this* and not do *that*." You go over it and you add emotional energy and momentum to the entire situation. You are sucked into a spiral that you cannot pull your mind out of. We have all experienced this in our lives. I certainly experienced it in my life, both as a child and even as an adult.

This is just an example of how there is something inside of ourselves that almost takes over our ability to remain centered, focused, attuned to the I AM Presence and to the Christ self. The internal turbulence pulls us away from that balanced state where we can make balanced decisions, and we often end up making unbalanced decisions that we quickly regret because they lead to unpleasant consequences. There is that phase where there is so much inner turbulence – so many voices speaking to you, so many energetic pulls pulling on you – that you don't know what to do.

You need something that can help you move forward, and that is where a guru can be extremely helpful. There comes that point where you are not yet ready to fully tune in to your Christ self or your ascended teachers, meaning the inner guru, and therefore it can be of great value to have an outer guru.

It may not be one you have the opportunity to interact with personally, but it still may be a guru that has given teachings or written books that you can take and use as a foundation for navigating these choppy internal waters. The reason this is so important is that you are not yet ready to discern between what truly comes from the ego, what comes from the dweller or internal spirits, or what comes from your higher self, your Christ self. You are not yet ready, with the conscious mind, to actually be able to tell the subtle energetic difference between the internal spirits and your Christ self, the ascended teachers and I AM Presence.

You don't know who to believe, you don't know what to think, you don't know what to decide. It is therefore helpful to have a guru who can give you some guidelines, some rules that say: "Do *this,* don't do *that.*" Then you know that you are at least not getting yourself into deeper trouble than you are already in, and you might even make some progress by following the guru because now you have a guideline.

You will notice, I am sure, when you think about this that there are many times in your life where you have been so pulled from so many conflicting directions inside or outside yourself that you have felt almost paralyzed. You have felt under such stress, under such turbulence, that you could barely keep things together, as they say.

The value of making firm decisions

The real reason for this is that you are, as Jesus said: "a house divided against itself." You have at least two, or possibly many more, internal spirits that are talking to you, pulling on you at the same time. The reason they can pull on you is that you are divided in your conscious mind, you have no firm guideline, you have no firm decision. Ultimately, you need to come to the point where you have the ability within yourself to sense the energetic difference between all the internal spirits and your Christ self and I AM Presence. You know, you simply *feel*, what is real, what is unreal.

Until you can do this, these spirits will pull on you mercilessly unless you can do something else to neutralize their influence. That something else is to make a firm decision. For example, many, many people – when they first find the spiritual path – have been engaged in certain outer habits or activities. This could be smoking, drinking alcohol, taking drugs, sexual promiscuity, various forms of rock music, partying, all kinds of lifestyles that are common in today's world. Many find themselves going through a period where they do sense that these activities are not truly spiritual and they do sense that: "Yes, I probably should go beyond this, I probably should stop doing this." But they don't have a firm decision in their minds.

Because they don't have a firm decision, the spirits that want them to continue these activities have an easy time of pulling on their emotional and mental bodies. The more they pull, the more difficult it becomes for you to have the firm resolve, and therefore you find yourself lapsing into these old habits. You might make a decision that you are going to stop smoking, for example, but after some time you are pulled back into the habit. It is so excruciatingly difficult to stop, but the reason for this is that you are still vulnerable to these pulls of the spirits. You are vulnerable because your mind is divided. You do not have a firm resolve: "No, I am not doing this anymore." This is where an external teacher can help you come to this resolve. The teacher can help you make the decision, have the firm inner resolve: "No, this activity is no longer acceptable to me as a student of the ascended masters or of this guru. I will follow the guru; I will obey the guru regardless of what my internal spirits, my dweller, my carnal mind, my ego, is telling me." Once you get to that point – where you now have a firm resolve that you will follow the guru regardless of what your ego and your internal spirits are telling you – then you are no longer so vulnerable to them.

You are able to navigate through the choppy waters much more easily because they are not as choppy anymore; you are not pulled in different directions. Imagine being water skiing and you have two skies and there is a rope attached to each ski. There are some pranksters in a boat on either side of you that are pulling your water skies away from each other. When does there come that point where the skies are pulled so far apart that you simply crash and hit the water hard? The guru can help you "keep it together," avoid being divided but being firm so that you can keep a straight course towards your goal. This can be extremely helpful, and it is a necessary phase.

The outer guru can become a limitation

Let me put it this way. You have certain internal spirits. They have pulled you into engaging in certain outer habits that either drain your energies, cause you to misqualify energy or to even dull your awareness to the point where you cannot in any way tune in to your higher being. There is absolutely no way you can make the maximum spiritual progress as long as you are engaging in these outer habits, they are too costly energetically. You *must* stop the outer habit, but the problem is that as long as you are engaged in the outer habit there is such a drain on your energy, there is such a lowering of your awareness, that you cannot in any way see or resolve the spirits that are pulling you into the habit.

You absolutely need to stop the habit, to stop the energy drain, and to start freeing your conscious awareness to where you are not pulled into these outer activities or these emotional and mental reactionary patterns. If the outside guru can help you do it, this is a valuable service for you.

Here comes the next phase. Once you have created some inner peace and tranquility, you have to realize that this is not enough in itself. This is where many spiritual students get caught. They think: "But I am so much better off today than I was when I had all these bad habits. The reason I am so much better is that I have blindly followed the outer guru. So I just need to keep following the outer guru, and then I will make it to the goal." (Whatever the goal is defined as being—whether the ascension, Nirvana or enlightenment.)

This simply cannot be done because the only way to truly make it to the ascension is that you expose your internal spirits. You must look at them consciously and see the decision you made in the past that caused you to create that spirit. Then, you consciously undo it by making a higher decision. It is the *only* way you can ultimately make it.

This is where the outer guru can become a limitation. If you feel you have to be loyal to the outer guru, if you feel that you can just continue to do what the outer guru tells you to do, then that guru – even if it was a true guru sponsored by the ascended masters – becomes a false guru. The outer guru is now preventing you from seeing the spirits in yourself and dismissing those spirits so that you can come into attunement and later oneness with your inner guru. This is the true goal. An outer guru is only meant to take you to the point where you are ready to lock in to the inner guru and come into oneness with that guru. If the outer guru detracts you from this goal, he is no longer helping your spiritual progress but hindering it. This goes for *any guru whatsoever.*

It is difficult but possible to see your spirits

What you need to do is to come to a point where you are willing to start consciously looking at your internal spirits, looking at the beam in your own eye. I know very well how difficult this is, especially in the beginning. I can also assure you that if you use the tools, including the decrees and invocations and the teachings given by the ascended masters, it is not beyond you to go through this process. Anyone who is a sincere spiritual student, and who is committed, will make it, will make progress on this path. In the beginning, yes, it will seem very difficult.

I can look back at my own life and see how there were certain periods where I was being forced by outer circumstances to look at my internal spirits. This even happened while I was functioning as a guru, as a messenger for the ascended masters. Many of my students thought I was above this, but I realized internally that I was not because I felt how there were certain things that came up and that I had to look at. Now, I will say that while I was still conscious in the physical body, I did not realize the full extent of how much I actually had left, how many spirits I had left that I needed to look at. I did not realize fully how my actual involvement with spiritual activities, even my position as a guru and messenger, had created or reinforced certain spirits. Again, given that I was in a certain position where I had a certain goal, I could not have dealt with all of this at once and at the same time fulfilled my outer obligations. There is a balance that has to be made. Nevertheless, no matter what your outer situation is – no matter how busy you are, how important you think your work is, how much you think you have to do, how much you think other people depend on you – it is necessary to have some awareness of the need to look at your reactionary patterns, to look at your spirits and to dismiss them one at a time—or rather *two* at a time for they are always created in pairs.

If you do not do this, then your outer position actually becomes an excuse for not growing. That means your outer position keeps you from making progress towards your ascension. This is not something you can afford if you are determined to make your ascension in this lifetime. You cannot let *anything* – including your outer position, including your family, including your work, including your spiritual pursuits – stand in the way of you making progress towards the ascension.

Making progress towards the ascension means dismissing the spirits that you cannot take with you into the ascended realm. They must *all* be gone before you are ready to ascend. They all don't need to be gone at once because as you move upwards, through the 144 levels of consciousness, you dismiss one at a time, one for each level, and that is sufficient.

After I became less conscious, but still in a physical body, I went through a very intense period where I was doing some catch-up of looking at and dismissing these spirits [This happened at inner levels beyond conscious awareness]. What I wish to convey to you here is that this is a process that you come to at the higher stages of the path and it is a necessary process.

You can make your path so much easier for yourself by becoming consciously aware that you have the internal spirits and how you need to dismiss them. Again, tools have been given that are valid and valuable tools. The tools given in the church about the teachings on the Dweller on the Threshold, the Cosmic Clock and many of these other tools given can be valuable for people at a certain level or from a certain background.

Finding a tool that works for you

You need to find the tool that resonates with you and use it to the best of your ability, but first of all – beyond using outer tools – you need to recognize that this is not an automatic process. Yes, we have given you decrees, for example for the binding of the dweller, we have given you invocations for resolving spirits. But you cannot get yourself into the mindset of thinking that by giving these decrees and invocations or by studying certain teachings, you will automatically transcend the spirits. You will not *automatically* transcend these internal spirits. I said they were created by you making a decision, and you must consciously see and undo that decision before you are free of the spirit.

You must invoke the light, such as the violet flame, to transmute the energies that were misqualified through that spirit. When you have consumed the energies and dismantled the structure, the matrix of decisions, then the spirit is gone and you are free. This requires work, dedication, but it requires first of all conscious awareness.

What the guru cannot do for you is make you conscious. The guru cannot give you the willingness to be conscious. The guru can give you all kinds of teachings, but I can tell you from experience that I have seen thousands of students come to me and sit there and listen to a teaching or listen to a dictation but take in very little consciously. They simply were not *conscious*. They were hearing the words – if they were not asleep – but they were not conscious of what was being said.

Obviously, I am not saying that you have to be conscious

of every word said in a long dictation, for example. Ideally, you should be able to listen to or read a dictation and there should be at least one thought that would stand out. Then you will hold on to that thought and integrate it, turn it over in your mind and see how it applies to you. You will ask for inner directions as to what this means, how you can go higher in understanding and how you can apply it in your life.

What you must supply to the guru-chela relationship

This willingness to be conscious is something that *you* must supply. The guru cannot do it for you. That is why I am saying that you cannot think: "Oh, now I have found this wonderful guru, I don't need to be conscious anymore. I don't need to think for myself. I don't need to look in the mirror. I just need to focus my outer mind on what the guru tells me to do and then do it—and then I will make it."

This is not so. This is abuse of a guru. It is turning a true guru into a false guru. It is abusing the guru, and it is actually abusing your own office as a chela, as a student. You have a certain obligation in life and the obligation is to recognize that you have a divine plan. You made that divine plan while you were out of embodiment and therefore did not look at life through the perception filter you have right now.

Your obligation to yourself, what you owe to yourself, is to connect consciously to your divine plan so you at least know the next step you need to take. This is your obligation to yourself. God is not forcing this upon you, the ascended masters are not forcing this upon you, the guru is not forcing it upon you. It is what you want in your higher mind.

You need to come to the point where you make the conscious decision: "Yes, I am willing to override the turbulence, the inertia or the plain, outright laziness of the outer mind and force myself to become more conscious and force myself to take the steps that I need to take in order to make maximum progress."

You need to do this if this is to be your last embodiment. You cannot dillydally, you cannot compromise. I am not trying to say this is all or nothing. I am trying to say that it takes awareness to walk the path. In the church we often talked about the will of God and we talked about those students who had the will to progress, the will to be disciplined, the will to continue to do the decrees and this and that. This is all valuable for a certain period, but there comes a point where you need to refine your will. It is not so much directed at doing the outer things but directed at doing the inner work of looking at yourself and becoming more conscious of what is going on in your own mind. You can then expose these spirits and dismiss them whereby you can become more conscious of what is going on *beyond* your mind, namely in your I AM Presence.

15 | THE CONSCIOUS YOU AND THE I AM PRESENCE

Your I AM Presence has the solution to every problem you are facing on earth, but if you cannot tune in to your I AM Presence, then you cannot sense the solution. An essential key to actually starting to integrate with your Presence is to realize that there is a fundamental difference between your I AM Presence and your concept of a guru. You see, my beloved, the concept of a guru can be very, very valuable, but the concept of a guru implies – by its very definition – that you are "here" as a distinct individual and the guru is separated from you.

This is why the guru is valuable to you because the guru is not inside your perception filter, is not blinded by what blinds you. The guru can give you directions that are not coming from inside the perception filter, and these directions, when followed, can help you go beyond the perception filter. It is necessary – by definition – that you see the guru as being outside yourself, at least outside your separate self.

Your relationship with your I AM Presence

Your I AM Presence is *not* your guru; your I AM Presence is *not* your teacher. It is not the purpose of your Presence to teach you *anything*. Even an ascended master will be an external being to you. I have said that while you are unascended, you often have an idolatrous, graven image of ascended masters. You must shed this as you ascend, seeking to come more and more into oneness with the Presence of the master.

Even after I ascended, I see myself as a distinct individual being. I see Master MORE and Saint Germain as distinct individual beings. I can come into complete oneness with Saint Germain – which, by the way, is a most wonderful experience – but I still know that *I* am coming into oneness with a distinct being. You will always see an ascended master as distinct from yourself, even when you become an ascended master.

How do you then become an ascended master? Well, in the beginning – when you find the teachings of the ascended masters and begin to hear about the I AM Presence – it is inevitable that you look at the I AM Presence as being outside yourself. When the Conscious You is looking at everything from inside the perception filter of the separate self, then truly the I AM Presence *is* outside that separate self. The I AM Presence is in the spiritual realm.

An ascended master, such as Master MORE or Jesus, is always meant to be your teacher, but your I AM Presence is not meant to be your teacher. Your I AM Presence is not your guru that is *external* to your self. How do you ascend? By coming into oneness with the Presence, but here is the subtle difference that it is almost impossible to grasp until you reach the very highest levels of the 144 levels of consciousness.

As I said, I am an ascended master. I can come into oneness with Saint Germain, but I know I am coming into oneness with a distinct being. As you ascend, as you reach that 144th level and make the last quantum leap, you come into oneness with your I AM Presence. You do not come into oneness with your I AM Presence the same way you come into oneness with, say Saint Germain or another ascended master.

I am a distinct being from Saint Germain. I can come into oneness with Saint Germain and I can go out of oneness with Saint Germain, but we are still distinct beings. When you are at the 144th level and come into oneness with your I AM Presence, you are not coming into oneness with a *distinct being*. You are coming into oneness with *yourself*. Your I AM Presence is not your guru. Your I AM Presence is *you*. The subtle teaching here can only be grasped when you fully understand and experience, in glimpses, the pure awareness of the Conscious You.

The decision made by your I AM Presence

Before you first took embodiment in a denser sphere, your I AM Presence was in the spiritual realm. It looked down and made the decision that it wanted to serve as a co-creator by projecting a part of itself, an extension of itself, into a dense realm and taking on a body there. Thereby, it would be experiencing this realm from the inside and helping to co-create it, raising it up to become a permanent part of the spiritual realm. As I said, this might not have happened in this material universe. It could have been in a previous sphere but the mechanism is the same.

The I AM Presence sends an extension of itself, which becomes what we now call the Conscious You, but what we used to call the core of the soul. The importance of calling it the Conscious You and seeing it as pure awareness is that it truly has no form, no characteristics. It has awareness but no individual characteristics that sets it apart from the I AM Presence.

We might say that even the words that "the I AM Presence sends an extension of itself into the material world" is a primitive description. It would be better to say that the I AM

Presence focuses itself in the material world, not the totality, but it focuses an element, an extension, of its awareness there. This pure awareness of the Conscious You has awareness of itself as a distinct being. It has free will. It can determine where it will focus itself.

In the beginning, it chooses to go into a predefined role, whether it was in Maitreya's Mystery School or in another mystery school, and see what it is like to play that role. It is through this role, through the self, that it expresses itself in the physical realm or a mystery school. As the Conscious You decides to experiment with the duality consciousness, the fruit of the knowledge of good and evil, it takes on roles that were not defined by the spiritual teacher but were defined by the fallen beings, the false teachers.

The soul vehicle that appears spiritual

Through this process, the Conscious You begins to build the soul vehicle. As I have said, the soul vehicle can become a very elaborate, very sophisticated, structure that might appear very, very spiritual. The Conscious You comes to the point where it begins to realize there is something called the ascension, and it formulates the desire to ascend. This happens because in between embodiments you decide that you want to pursue your ascension. When you come down into embodiment, it is likely that your conscious awareness will grab on to the concept of the ascension, ascended masters and the spiritual path leading to it.

Many students still believe that walking the path towards the ascension is a matter of perfecting the outer self. I have attempted to explain that this is not the case. You need to *let go* of the outer self, and you do this by looking at the elements that make up the outer self – the spirits that make up the outer self – and dismissing the decisions, the illusions, that formed them.

What happens when you shed more and more of these spirits, more and more of these illusions, and you reach the 144th level of consciousness? Well, what happens is that you begin to shift your sense of identity. When you are at the lower levels of the path, you are fully identified with the outer self. You think: "I am so and so (your name), I come from this family, I live in this country, I live in this society, I have this occupation, I am this race, I am this ethnic group, I am this sex, I am this, I am that, I am the next thing." You let all of the outer things define you, and you are completely identified with it.

As you become aware of the spiritual path, you realize: "Oh, I am *more* than these outer things and I actually want to come more into oneness with that spiritual self." However you see it, you still see it as something outside yourself, and as you shed the elements of the outer self, you begin to shift your identity. Instead of saying: "I am this I am, down here in the material world," you start saying: "Oh, I am *that* I AM up there in the spiritual realm." You come to a point where you begin to have conscious experiences or receive inner sensations from your I AM Presence.

Your I AM Presence does not tell you what to do

There is a subtle difference that you need to be aware of at this stage. The awareness of this can make it so much easier for you to actually attune yourself to your Presence. Your guru will speak to you, and it will sometimes appear to you as an external voice speaking to you. If you have a physical guru, then obviously you are hearing that person speak to you with a physical voice. Even your ascended guru or your Christ self will often appear to you as an external voice, an external thought or an external Presence that is there giving you directions. In many cases, these might be worded directions.

You might not hear them as an inner voice in your head, but you might still sense: "Oh yes, I'm supposed to do this." This is clearly something you experience as coming from outside yourself. What did I say about your I AM Presence? Your I AM Presence is *not* your guru. I know well that there are many – even among my own students and even myself when I was in embodiment – who have felt: "Oh, I got this direction from my I AM Presence," "My I AM Presence told me to do this." This is actually *not* the case. If you experience something as a direction coming from *outside* yourself, it is not coming from your I AM Presence; it is coming from your guru. It may be the internal guru of your Christ self or an ascended master where you do not hear it as an outer voice but hear or receive it inside your mind, but it is still experienced as coming from somewhere *outside*. Many, many students have projected a graven image upon the I AM Presence and have thought that they are receiving directions from the I AM Presence, but it actually comes from the being who serves as your outer guru. It can still be genuine direction, and in many cases it *is* genuine direction. Only it is not coming from your Presence.

There is a period on your path where it is perfectly okay that you think it is coming from your Presence. As you reach the higher levels and go towards the 144th level, you actually need to shift your awareness. You need to realize that the goal of the guru is different from the goal of the I AM Presence. Your guru's goal is to give you directions that help you raise your consciousness and walk the spiritual path here on earth, doing the things you need to do here on earth, including fulfilling your divine plan, balancing your karma and so on.

This is the role of the guru, but this is *not* the role of your I AM Presence. The role of your I AM Presence is to simply be there for you as a Presence that is your ultimate frame of reference for what is real and what is unreal, not only in the physical world but especially in your own inner world. What did

I just say happens? You shift your sense of identity away from the outer self and towards the Presence. What is the goal of the Presence? It is to facilitate this shift in your sense of identity where you have an alternative to the outer self.

As you become more aware, you begin to sense your Presence, but you do not hear your Presence as an external voice. You begin to sense your Presence as an *inner* Presence. It gives you no directions, no teachings. It gives you a frame of reference for what is your true identity. When you sense this, you can compare it to what is coming to you from your outer self, from the spirits. You can instantly know: "That spirit, that voice, is not who I am. I am more than this; I am *that* I AM up there!"

You may still not experience your Presence clearly and fully, but you sense there is something there that is more than the outer self. That is what your I AM Presence does for you. That is the role of your Presence, and this is why you need to make the shift. If you are projecting onto your Presence that the Presence should be like the guru, should be like the external voice, then you cannot make it beyond a certain level. You cannot make it to the 144th level as long as you see the I AM Presence as an external voice or an external being.

You need to shed this image, this graven image, so that you do not hold it before the real God of your Presence. It is your I AM Presence that speaks to you out of the burning bush in the beginning, but then further along on the path there is no bush, there is no voice, there is nothing burning, there is just Presence. When you come to the 144th level, the last step you take is that you let go of the very core of the outer self, and here is again where there is a subtle distinction.

The last self you must shed before ascending

When the Conscious You first comes into embodiment, I have said that it takes on an outer self, a predefined role, and it gradually builds on to it. The very first thing that the Conscious You takes on is the sense of being a distinct individual being. It has a point-like sense of self that is different from the spherical sense of self of the I AM Presence.

The I AM Presence is not the Creator; it does not have God awareness. If you are in embodiment on earth, your I AM Presence is not a highly evolved being compared to Cosmic Beings and the Creator. It has the potential to grow towards full God awareness, but it has not reached it. In fact, it is sending you down as a way for it to grow towards higher states of consciousness. Your I AM Presence will continue to grow after you ascend, and you descending will help your I AM Presence grow.

When you have first descended, you suddenly become aware: "I AM, therefore I can think and I can be aware of what is happening in this material world." Then you take on this sense of being a distinct, individual, separate self. If you had full awareness of your Presence at that moment, you would see yourself as being separate from the Presence. You are *down here,* the Presence is *up there.*

As you rise towards the 144th level of consciousness, you gradually get rid of that sense of distance from the Presence. When you are at the 144th level, in order to ascend you have to shed that core of the separate self. This core is beyond what we in the church called the dweller. It is actually beyond what in most cases is called the ego. Or we can say it is the very core of the ego. It is not the dweller because the dweller is a spirit that you can shed, and there comes that point where you have actually shed all the spirits. You have gotten rid of all the spirits, but there is still that very core sense that you are a separate being from the Presence.

When you are at the 144th level – and when you are completely ready to ascend – then you shed that last sense of separation from the Presence and you become one with the Presence. This might take some contemplation. I fully realize that many people will find this teaching objectionable, questionable, even false. When I was in embodiment, I would not have been able to grasp this. I would have denied that you lose all sense of self because I still felt that there had to be a part of my soul vehicle that was becoming acceptable to God because of all the outer things I had done here on earth. Therefore, it *must* be possible to bring that perfected part into the kingdom.

What happens to the Conscious You

Even this messenger, who has had the concept of the Conscious You for several years, has struggled with this. What actually happens with the Conscious You when you ascend? Does it disappear?

This is where words become very inadequate for describing reality. What did I say earlier? The I AM Presence focuses itself as that Conscious You, it focuses itself as a localized self. This localized self is given free will so it makes a lot of choices down here as it goes through its journey. When it gives up the final aspect of the separate self, it gives up its free will, it gives up its localized awareness. It again becomes the Presence focused as its totality.

You might say that the Conscious You becomes one with the I AM Presence, merges back into the I AM Presence, gives up its sense of identity, individuality, existence. All of these words you can apply, but notice one thing. They are focused on how the Conscious You experiences it because what the Conscious You has done in its entire journey is experience the world as a distinct, localized self. The Conscious You has believed that: "I am a distinct being, and I am experiencing what I am experiencing."

In reality, you could say there has never been a distinct being. You could say there has never been a Conscious You because it has all along been the I AM Presence that has focused itself in a localized point. It is not that the Conscious You has ever done anything. That is why Jesus said: "I can of my own self do nothing." What he also could have said was: "I have no own self; it is an illusion."

This is an illusion that you simply cannot give up until you are at the 144th level. If you gave it up, you could not travel even from the 143rd to the 144th. You need a vehicle in order to climb the spiral staircase of the path to the ascension. You need to have a sense that there is a "you" that is qualifying, that is ascending, that is rising up through the levels of the material universe and the levels of consciousness possible here.

When you come to the top, you need to shed that final vehicle, that sense that there is a you who has been traveling. You again begin to become aware of yourself as the fullness of the Presence. The Presence is now *more* than it was when the Conscious You descended. The experiences the Conscious You has had, the decisions it has made, has risen to your Causal Body. Therefore, the I AM Presence is *more*. *You* are more.

You do not ascend until the Conscious You gives up the sense of being a Conscious You and becomes again the fullness of the Presence. At *that* point, your I AM Presence shifts its awareness. It is no longer focused as a Conscious You down here, it is now focused as an ascended being.

An absolutely incredible shift in consciousness

Again, words are very inadequate. Anything I say here, there will be – depending on your level of consciousness – an interpretation imposed upon my words by your outer self. It will be aimed at keeping you trapped in that outer self, making you decide that: "Oh, there *is* a part of my outer self that I *can't* give up, that I *don't need* to give up, that I *shouldn't* give up."

As you go higher on the path, you can make it so much easier for yourself if you will realize that the ascension means giving up the final aspect of the separate self, even the sense that you are a separate self. The higher levels of the path is where you begin to consciously see the need to give up some element of the outer self. You cannot give it up until you see it and see that it is not who you really are because you sense the Presence: "Ah, I am *that* I AM up there, not this little I am down here!"

You keep doing this, you keep becoming aware: "Ah, this is just a little I am down here that I have been experiencing and that I have been experiencing life through. But it's just a spirit, it's just another element of the outer self. Now that I see that this is an outer self, I am also aware that I am more than this because I am *that* I AM up there." You keep doing this as you go higher and higher, but then, when you are at the 144th level, you are seeing: "Oh, I am not even the self that I am *down here*. I am not separated from that I AM *up there* because that I AM up there is not "up there." It is *here* – or I am there – because there is no separation. I *AM* the Presence."

This is such an absolutely incredible shift in consciousness. I wish I could describe it to you with words, but I know very well that even trying to describe it will be misused by your outer minds.

It is such an incredible liberation. Suddenly, your I AM Presence becomes aware of itself as an ascended master, as an ascended being. It is an incredible transformation to go through. When you go through it, when you have gone through it, you can take a look back. Even before you go through it, you will take a look back. One of the important characteristics at this point is that as you go higher towards the 144th level, you begin to look at all these spirits and dismiss them. Then you look back at your life.

Seeing everything as an opportunity to grow

When you are dealing with a specific spirit, for example, you are looking at how you experience life through that spirit. You might see that there were certain decisions you made that were made through the filter of that spirit. You look at the consequences that it had, you see that they were probably very unpleasant for you to experience, that they may have caused all kinds of consequences, all kinds of suffering for other people. You clearly see that, from a certain perspective, you could say they were wrong, they were not right. You do realize that they are not an expression of who you really are. They are only an expression of that spirit, that separate sense of self.

You also see that regardless of what happened, regardless of the consequences, it was still an opportunity to grow. Yes, you might have done something through a certain spirit that created suffering for other people, but it was not what you did that created the suffering. It was the fact that these people *experienced* what you did through the filter of their particular spirit, their particular outer self.

What created suffering for you was that *you* experienced what you did through the perception filter of the same spirit that caused you to do what you did. You took an action based on the perception filter of the spirit, and then you experienced and judged your own action and yourself through the same perception filter. *That* is why it felt like such intense suffering as long as you were inside the filter.

When you begin to see the unreality of the filter – and disassociate yourself from identifying with it – you also see, as I said in my last discourse, that whatever has happened on earth is just the outplayings of children playing in the sandbox. It is ultimately unreal. The energies out of which it was created can all be transmuted.

You experience that you have transmuted the energies misqualified through a given spirit, and therefore you know this is gone. There comes that point where you look at what you did through that spirit and you have absolutely no regrets. All of your sense of guilt, shame, regrets, being stupid, having made a mistake, being a sinner, being worthless, all of these feelings you suddenly see are just a product of the very spirit through which this was done.

When you finally stop judging yourself

What is the point in judging your action through the very spirit that caused you to take the action? Instead, you are able to reach up and experience how your Presence looks at the situation. You experience that your Presence has none of the judgments of the spirit. It has no judgment whatsoever because to the Presence it was just an experience that can be used to define who you are in a positive sense.

You might say that as the Conscious You is going through the process of walking the path towards the ascension, your Conscious You looks at a given spirit, looks at what was done through that spirit, how it experienced life through that spirit, and then it comes to the conscious decision: "This is *not* who I am. I am *more* than this." The Conscious You is focused on what was done, what was not constructive, what was not the highest expression of who it is. It is focused on: "I am *not* this." It is the Conscious You that is experiencing it this way.

The I AM Presence has a very different experience of what the Conscious You is going through. It is not looking at the mistakes; it doesn't have any of the negative feelings. It doesn't even think: "This is not who I am." It actually experiences the entire situation with a completely positive approach. It does not say: "This was wrong" or "This is not who I am." It turns everything into a positive learning experience, and then it says: "Oh, *this* is who I am," in a positive way.

You may, for example, have an experience where the Conscious You has identified itself as a sinner. You may have been influenced by the Christian concept of sin, you may have done something that the Christian religion defines as a sin. You may have accepted for yourself: "Oh, I'm such a sinner. Why did I do that? I should never have done that. It was so wrong of me to do this."

This is a spirit. When that spirit was created there was one aspect of the spirit that caused you to do what is a sin, and then there was another aspect created simultaneously that condemns yourself for doing it. They are both part of that spirit. Or they are two separate spirits springing from the same decision, however you want to say it with words. Your I AM Presence looks at that experience and says: "I am a co-creator with free will and I can choose to be *more*. I am choosing to be *this;* I am choosing to express myself this way."

What was the point of all your struggles?

Do you see that in the beginning, before you start consciously walking the path, your Conscious You is building an outer, mortal self, a separate self? When you find the path and become consciously aware of it, you start gradually dismantling the self you have built. You build a separate self until you are so trapped in it that you can't stand yourself anymore. Then you cry out for deliverance. You make contact with a true spiritual teacher and you start walking the path that brings you back to the state of purity with which you originally descended because you have dismantled the outer self.

As you go to the higher levels of the path, the Conscious You begins to think: "What was the point of it all? Why did I have to go through all this mess of building this terrible outer self and having all these terrible experiences—and now I just have to dismantle it all again. Why would God pull such a trick on me?"

What you don't realize is that as you were building the separate self – even if you were going down the levels of consciousness from the 48th level to the lowest level possible on earth – your I AM Presence was having a completely positive experience. It was using every experience that the Conscious You had as a way to define itself in a positive way. "I am this. I am this way. I am doing this. This is how I express myself." When the Conscious You made the shift and started dismantling the separate self, your I AM Presence simply continued its positive experience.

Everything that has happened "down here" has, by your I AM Presence, been turned into a positive experience for how it defines itself, how it defines itself as an ascended being. Your I AM Presence has been building your identity as an ascended master while you, the Conscious You, was in the unascended state. Everything that you have experienced, everything you have done, has only helped to build your positive identity as an ascended master.

16 | HAVING NO REGRETS ABOUT LIFE ON EARTH

When you come to the higher levels, you look at your life and you say: "Why should I have any regrets for anything that has happened to me on earth?" I know well that there are many of you, many who will read this book, who are not yet at the level where you can lock in to what I am saying. There are certainly many who are at the point where you can become consciously aware of the need to go beyond having regrets about anything that has happened on earth. If you can make that shift consciously while you are still in the body, you can make the rest of this lifetime so much easier.

In fact, for many of the people who have it in their divine plans to ascend in this lifetime, it is crucial that you make the conscious shift to stop regretting, to stop judging, to stop condemning yourself. Just accept: "It was what it was. No regrets. It is just a matter of moving on. I am *not* that I am down here; I am *that* I AM up there." You move on; from this point you move on.

The ascension means depersonalizing everything

You become aware of the limitation of a certain spirit, you see what you have done, you see what the consequences were and you say: "From this point forward; I am moving on. I am not this I am down here. I am *that* I AM up there, I am more than this little self." When you can do this consciously, you can begin to make so much faster progress. Now you can do what I said in my last discourse: You can stop taking yourself and everything that happens to you so seriously. You can *depersonalize* your life, and I can tell you that making your ascension is the ultimate step of depersonalization. You depersonalize *everything*. Even the personal self is depersonalized as you ascend.

Why is this so important? Consider the figure eight. It has a lower part that is rounded and wide, then it has a nexus that is just one point and then it has an upper part that is rounded. When you first find the spiritual path, you are at the bottom of the figure eight. You have to move upwards, but the problem is there is so much confusion down here in the material world. There are so many pulls on you, there are so many spiritual gurus, spiritual teachings, false teachings, true teachings, more than one true gurus. What do you do; it's all turmoil, it's all confusion?

You have to do what I said earlier: You create a vessel that closes your mind to all of the influences that detract you from moving higher. As you are moving up towards the nexus, you are in a sense narrowing your choices. You are beginning to say: "As a spiritual person, I am not engaging in this that or the next activity." Jesus talked about the broad way that most people follow, and it does not lead to the ascension. This is the broad way of being divided, of having too many activities, of trying to do everything.

Narrowing your focus—but not too much

You select a way, and you say: "I am not doing *this*. I am not doing *that*." Then you narrow down your focus until you come to that nexus point, and the nexus point is when you begin to make contact with your Christ self and your ascended teachers. You get a sense for your I AM Presence, and now you come to the point where you are truly conscious of walking the path.

There is a point where you can say: "Yes, I am conscious of the spiritual path, I have even found the teachings of the ascended masters." As I said, I have seen thousands of students sit there and listen to dictations and they were not really conscious. From an outer viewpoint, their outer minds were aware of the spiritual path, the ascended masters and the potential to ascend, but they were not truly conscious within, they were not looking within themselves.

You stop looking at all these outer things, you come to that nexus and now you start looking at the internal spirits. In the beginning, this is turmoil, this is confusion, and you need a guideline, you need to hold on to something. You hold on to your guru, you hold on to your spiritual teaching, and you actually come to a point where many, many students are at. They have now found one teaching, one guru, that they believe to be genuine, possibly even the only true one, or the highest teaching, or whatever they need in order to motivate themselves.

You come to that point where you are now completely one-pointed in focusing on and applying that teaching. This is perfectly in order. It prevents you from being pulled in all these directions, but the thing is that when you do this, it is like I said: You create a boat that is all closed off, and a closed off boat prevents you from taking in water from the outside. It prevents you from taking in all these negative pulls. The problem is: The more closed your boat is, the less you can look out. Yes, you are protecting yourself from the negative influences, but you are also closing yourself in. You are actually closing yourself off to possibilities that are positive, creative possibilities. As I have said now many times, this is perfectly in order. There is a phase on your path where you need to do this. Instead of being pulled by the many choices made by ordinary people who are not spiritual, you come to the point where you feel like there is only one thing you can do. You have to follow this teaching, this set of rules, this diet. You have to do this, you have to do that, there is one road for you to take. And it is true: *there is*.

A graven image of what it means to be the Christ

When you begin to come to the higher stages of the path, you need to start recognizing that there is more than one way to follow the spiritual path. There is more than one viable path to follow, there is more than one way to express your Christhood. Again, there is a distinction here.

When you first hear about the concept that you can put on personal Christhood, your outer self will create a graven image of what it means to be the Christ on earth. I have seen this in my own consciousness because until I withdrew from the body, I still had elements of a graven image of what it meant to be the Christ. I still had a graven image of how Jesus was the Christ and how other people had been the Christ. I had a graven image of what it meant to express my Christhood.

I saw thousands of my own students also create a graven image, many of them based on the graven image that I had and that I had projected out in my lectures and talks. This graven image is actually helpful to you at a certain point because it helps you select away all of the activities that are not Christ-like. It is not that your graven image is necessarily wrong, but there comes that point where you have gone through the nexus and you now need to start tuning in to what is your individual way to be the Christ, what is your individual Christhood.

Jesus was a great example of a person who has put on his individual Christhood. Today, we have no outer record or awareness of how exactly Jesus was, unless we actually were in embodiment with Jesus and had a direct experience with him. Even those of us who were in embodiment with Jesus experienced Jesus through the perception filter we had at the time. We do not fully understand how Jesus experienced his Christhood.

What we tend to do is that if we accept that Jesus was the primary example of a being with Christhood, we think that *his* way of being the Christ is the *only* way to be the Christ. In order for *us* to be the Christ, we need to emulate what Jesus did. You even have the old book called *The Imitation of Christ*. It is based on the idea that you take Jesus' example and you emulate, you try to become like him.

Again, this is valuable in order to navigate the turbulent area of the Sea of Samsara. It helps you get beyond all the outer temptations and distractions, but it will not take you to the ascension. In order for you to qualify for your ascension, you must *not* express Christhood the way *Jesus* did it, but the way *you* are meant to do it.

The Christ is not the doer

What does it mean to be the Christ? What did Jesus say? He said: "I can of my own self do nothing." He realized, or at least the realization behind his words was, that as long as you are in embodiment, you will have an element of this localized, individual self. It is not this individual self that is doing, that is the doer. The ultimate doer is the I AM Presence.

The I AM Presence has an individuality that is completely beyond the individuality of your outer self. Jesus also said: "I am the open door which no man can shut." This shows that the

Conscious You, when it becomes aware of itself as pure awareness, can function as an open door whereby the I AM Presence can express its divine individuality even through the physical body and the outer self. It will to some degree be colored by the outer self, but it is still a worthy expression of the individuality of the I AM Presence. The individuality of your I AM Presence is unique, it was created unique, but it has become even more unique through your journey.

The ultimate culmination of your journey in the material realm is that your I AM Presence is allowed, is able, to express the fullness of the individuality it has created as the Conscious You was journeying in the lower realms. Do you see this? Do you see the importance of this? The Conscious You becomes aware of itself as being the I AM Presence, being an extension of the I AM Presence. It allows the individuality of the I AM Presence to shine through instead of expressing the individuality of the outer consciousness.

This is sort of the Conscious You's reward for all of the difficulties and suffering it has gone through. You now begin to experience yourself as an extension of the Presence, and you have the full joy of seeing your divine individuality expressed. How can you do this if your Conscious You believes that there is only one way to be the Christ, and it holds on to a graven image of what it means to be the Christ? The simple answer is that if you have a graven image – where you think there is only one way to be the Christ – then you will shut the door so that your I AM Presence cannot express its individuality.

Individual Christhood does not mean that you decide with the outer mind what it means to be the Christ, and then you force yourself to live up to it. There is a period where you can grow this way, but you cannot express your Christhood this way. Your individual Christhood means that the individuality of your I AM Presence is shining through the Conscious You.

The way *you* are meant to be the Christ is not the same way that Jesus did it—or Saint Germain did it, or El Morya did it.

The greatest regret people have after dying

You are a distinct individual. If I had been more aware of this – and I am not saying I had absolutely no awareness of it, but if I had been more aware of it, more accepting of this – it would have been easier for myself in my last years in the body while I was still conscious. If *you* can accept this and become aware of this, it will be much easier for yourself for the rest of this embodiment. You will also be able to express much more of your Christhood.

I can tell you that as you come to the higher levels of consciousness, one of the greatest challenges you face is that you begin to see the difference between your highest potential and what you were actually able to express so far. There are students who have diligently followed an ascended master teaching for decades. They have come to the point where they have balanced sufficient karma that they are not karmically forced to take embodiment again after they leave the body.

This is what we in the church said was the case for those who had balanced more than 51 percent of their karma and therefore did not have to re-embody physically. These students still faced a very difficult task of balancing the remaining 49 percent (or however much of their karma is left), of resolving their psychology and seeking to fulfill their divine plan.

The greatest regret that these students have is when they look back and say: "Oh, this was the highest potential for what I *could have* expressed in my last lifetime and this is what I actually *did* express. Oh, I wish there hadn't been that gap, I wish I could have done more. I wish I could have expressed my divine individuality much more than trying to follow this outer path or this outer image defined by my outer mind." This is one of the major regrets that people have, and that is why I am giving you this teaching. You can, if you are willing, make the conscious shift of allowing yourself to express your individual Christhood.

This is not something you can do at the lower levels. If you try to do it at a lower level of consciousness, it will be the ego that will define how you should express your individual Christhood—and *that* is not Christhood. At the higher levels you need to realize there is more than one way to be the Christ. It is not a matter of you being the Christ the way other people have done it or the way other people think it should be done. You need to be the Christ the way your I AM Presence wants it to be done—not your ego, not the spirits, not other people, not the fallen beings, not even a true guru or the ascended masters or the way they did it. It is the way your I AM Presence wants to do it, wants to express it. You are the open door, nothing *more,* nothing *less.*

What persecutes the Living Christ

I once said to the community in my church that if the Living Christ entered our community, he would be persecuted. I did have awareness of what I have just told you but not as much as I could have had. I, myself, would most likely have persecuted the Living Christ because he did not follow my rules. I might even have said that if the Living Christ was not willing to follow the rules of the community, he could not stay in the community.

Do not fall into this trap. I realize that what I give you here is a very, very delicate challenge. The ego is so quick to define what it means to be the Christ based on some outer standard, even a standard created by the fallen beings. Nevertheless, at a certain level of the path, you need to consciously look at what is your standard for what you think – with the outer mind – it means to be the Christ. Then you begin to dismantle it. You begin to question it, and you begin to tune in to your I AM Presence. You become aware of the need to become the open door, the truly *open* door that does not restrict or limit the I AM Presence by demanding that the expression of the Presence should live up to a standard defined by the outer self.

There are many, many people on this earth who have expressed their Christhood in ways that are highly unusual. While I was still in embodiment, I could look at some of these people and I would say: "That person could never be the Living Christ, there is no way such a person could be the Living Christ." In many cases, I would have looked at the life of such a person and seen certain things that they did that I knew were not spiritual. It was not that I wasn't right. They *were* not spiritual, but there are many people who have lived an entire lifetime doing many things that were not the Living Christ, they were not an expression of the Christ, but still doing one or a few things that *were* an expression of their Christhood and that did bring themselves or even society forward.

It is at a certain level of the path very wise and very necessary to give up judging according to any outer standard. You leave judgment to the ascended masters and the Karmic Board. You simply accept that things are the way they are. Whatever they are, there is always the possibility that your I AM Presence might be able to shine a ray of light through your being so that even in the seemingly most unspiritual conditions there can be an expression of the Light of Christ.

The trap of judgment

As I said, Jesus was born in a manger to signal that even under the most humble conditions there can be an expression of the Christ Light and Christ Truth. Judgment is truly a trap set by the fallen beings. I have earlier said that our own community in the church was extremely judgmental, as were many other spiritual and religious movements. Just look at the earth in general, look at political organizations, companies, look at so many endeavors where there is raised up a standard that is used to judge everyone.

You cannot attain your individual Christhood if you are judging other people. If you are judging others, you will be subconsciously judging yourself based on the same spirit. This is not Christhood. There will come a point where you need to recognize that the Living Christ follows no rules and no standard defined on earth.

Again, there is a point on your path where you need to have a standard, preferably one defined by a true spiritual guru and a true spiritual teaching. This is helpful to you for navigating through the rough waves. There comes that point where you have gone through the nexus on your path and now you need to throw away and dismantle the standard in order to be the open door for the expression of your individual Christhood.

As I have said many times, it is by looking at your own reaction that you can make progress. If you have a reaction to my words, be willing to look at that reaction: "Why am I so attached to having a standard? Why am I so attached to judging how the Living Christ should behave? What does that say about the spirits I have in my being and how they not only judge others but judge myself? What does this say about my I AM Presence and its ability to express itself freely through me?"

Why you can and cannot do anything you want

I know there are those who will say that when I say that the Christ follows no rules, I am saying that you can do anything you want. In a sense, you *could* say: "Yes, when you are the Christ, you can do anything you want."

The trick is that what you want is not what the separate self wants; it is what the I AM Presence wants. In a sense you – as the Living Christ – want nothing other than to be an open door for the Presence to raise up all life. You are not seeking to raise up the separate self, you are actually seeking to get rid of the separate self, to dis-identify yourself from the separate self and its desires so that you can be the open door for the Presence to raise up all life. This is the difference. When you begin to grasp it, you begin to be the *open* door.

Judge not that ye be not judged—by your own internal spirit. If you think that you can know with the outer mind how the Living Christ should or should not behave, I submit to you that this is because you have a spirit that is created from the very spiritual pride and arrogance of the fallen beings who think they know better than God.

Why does the Living Christ come into this world? To set you free from the perception filter of the fallen consciousness. How will the Living Christ be able to set you free if you demand that the Living Christ should conform to the perception filter of the fallen consciousness?

The Living Christ cannot set you free by conforming to your perception filter but must challenge it. This means that the Living Christ might do one thing in one situation and do the seemingly opposite in another situation. In each case, it was done to challenge the perceptions of a particular group of people.

As I have said, the most difficult challenge is to actually let go of what you have defined as "good." For most spiritual people it is easy enough for them to define certain actions as evil and say: "I need to transcend them." It is very difficult to see that if you have a definition of what is evil, you also have a definition of what is good—and even your definition of good springs from the duality consciousness.

In order to ascend, you need to transcend even what you judge as being good, right, true or spiritual. There are people who are so convinced that certain actions are good and spiritual that they are trapped by this perception filter. If the Living Christ is to help them in any way, he must challenge their perception filter, possibly by demonstrating that you can be a spiritual person without following these rules.

There are those who knew Mark who knew that sometimes he would define rules for the community. Then he would be the first one to go and break all of them in order to demonstrate that rules apply to a certain level of the path. When you are beyond that level, you cannot force yourself to conform to the rules because the rules no longer matter.

How the cookie crumbles

We have a wonderful saying in the United States: "That's just how the cookie crumbled." When you stop judging – when you stop analyzing and evaluating based on the outer mind, when you stop demanding that you should live up to a set of rules and regulations – *then* you can begin to see that in many cases a decision was not wrong or right according to an outer standard.

I have talked about the need to depersonalize your life, to stop taking everything so seriously. There are many spiritual students who believe that in order to become the Christ, they have to find the ultimate way to judge everything they do. They create this elaborate standard, and now they use the analytical mind to compare everything they do, everything they feel, everything they think to this standard. They become so focused on themselves that they have no awareness left over to tune in to the Presence and their ascended teacher.

They are all in the analytical mind, analyzing everything. When they do something, and it has a certain consequence that is not pleasant, they can only judge that they must have made a mistake. Then they start analyzing: "What if I had not done *this* but I had done *that?*" You see, my beloved, sometimes it is not necessary to analyze every decision that you made or every decision other people made or whatever happened in the world. Sometimes you need to look at a situation and say: "That's just the way the cookie crumbled."

The important thing is not the decision or its consequences, the important thing is the consciousness behind it, the spirit behind it. If I look at that spirit, I can see: "Oh, I am not *that* I am down here; I am *that* I AM up there." This is what you need to learn from every decision, every situation.

Don't be so focused on the outcome, judging and analyzing the outcome, that you forget to look beyond to the consciousness, to the spirit. I, myself, had this clear tendency. I thought that if you knew what is the Christ's standard, then you should be able to set up rules for how everything should be done. I even had the belief that in my own church we could create rules for how everything could be done. Everything could be organized to the most minute detail.

Where is the room for the ascended masters to take that organization in a new direction? Can we really claim to be the organization of El Morya if we have created so many rules that we say: "Well, you know what, Morya, we don't need you anymore. We don't need your divine direction, we don't need you to come in here and upset the applecart. We've got everything under control down here, Morya. Just let us follow our rules and we know we'll make our ascensions."

When to follow rules and when not to

Yes, my beloved, it's a nice thought isn't it? The ego feels very secure when it has these rules. *It just isn't going to cut it,* it's not going to bring you to your ascension.

There is a point where you need rules to take you to a higher level. When you get to that higher level, you need to throw away the rules. You need to transcend the rules, you need to tune in to your Presence. You need to have no limitations, no filter, that you impose upon what the Presence can do through you. You need to be willing to do things that your outer mind might think are wrong, ridiculous or unnecessary.

You will all have to go through a period where your I AM Presence will express things through you that your outer mind does not like because they do not live up to its standard. You face the test: "What will you do? Will you be loyal to the outer standard or will you be in oneness with the Presence and let the Presence be what the Presence will be."

Will you let the Presence crumble your own cookie, the cookie of the outer self, or will you eat that cookie and wash it down with your own Kool-Aid? The true goal at the higher levels of the path is simple: "Be the open door, nothing *less*, nothing *more*."

17| WHY DID THIS HAPPEN TO ME?

I AM the Ascended Master Guru Ma. I have spoken in previous dictations about the students who come to a spiritual guru, and they want the guru to tell them what to do. Then they become resentful when things do not turn out the way they expected. What I wish to talk about now is the students who come to the guru and they describe a situation that has happened in their life, and then they want the guru to answer the question: "Why did this happen to me?"

Underneath that conscious question there is often an unspoken question: "Why did God allow this to happen to me?" You will notice, I am sure, that when something unexpected or unpleasant happens to you, it is almost inevitable that a question comes up in your mind: "Why did this happen to me?" You will probably have noticed that this is the same for almost every human being on this planet. From this we can conclude a couple of things. First of all, it is almost a universal tendency that all people ask the question: "Why did this happen to me?" What is behind the asking of the question? What does the asking of the question say about the state of consciousness of the person asking it?

Well, does it not say that there is a universal, subconscious recognition of the fact that you live in a world of cause and effect? Therefore, you assume that when something happens to you there must be a reason why this happened. When you are a spiritual person, you tend to believe that there must be some spiritual reason. When you find a spiritual guru who has an elaborate and sophisticated teaching, you tend to assume that the guru should be able to answer all of your questions about life and therefore should be able to tell you exactly why something happened to you.

I freely admit that while I was an embodied guru, I projected out the image that there is a reason why everything happens to you. I even somewhat projected, and certainly reinforced, the image that I had many of the answers to why many things happened to people. I projected out the image that this could be explained mainly by your karma. What I wish to give you now is a more sophisticated understanding of this than I was able to give you while I was still in embodiment. Why I was not able to give this more sophisticated understanding then is unimportant in this context.

All people are connected in a web of energy

What I will focus on is giving you the broader view that you attain when you become an ascended master. What you can do from the ascended state is that you can participate in some of the council sessions held by other ascended masters who are more experienced than yourself. This may be the Karmic Board, the Darjeeling Council and other councils set up by the ascended masters to deal with the situation on earth.

What you realize from the ascended state is that what is happening on earth is incredibly complex. It would be almost impossible to fathom the complexity from the unascended state. In fact, when I say "almost impossible," I can say with certainty that it would be impossible to fathom the *entirety* of how complex the situation is. I still wish to give you at least some impression of what is happening on a planet like earth.

I did, while I was in embodiment, talk about the Antahkarana or the web of life. I taught that all people on earth are connected by this web, this Antahkarana. The web is made up of energy that has taken on certain forms, certain vibrations. What makes it take on form is the consciousness of human beings.

What you see from the ascended state is this intricate web of these threads of energy, literally like ropes formed by finer energies, that tie many human beings together. In a sense, there is an Antahkarana that ties *all* human beings together on earth. When you go to more specific levels, you see that there are many groups of people who are tied together by these ropes, lines or strings of energy.

Some of this energy vibrates in the emotional frequency spectrum, some of it in the mental and some of it at the identity or etheric level. You could compare this to a map of earth where all of the cities and all of the houses are connected by roads. Or you could look at one of the nighttime satellite photos that shows all the street lights and other lights that are lighting up the night and forming an intricate pattern.

You can begin to see how specific groups are connected by certain lines of energy, and certainly you can call this karma. What I wish to give you here is an understanding that goes beyond the traditional view of karma, given by Eastern religions and to some degree also by the teachings by the ascended masters. It is not that this view is wrong; it is simply that there is more to it. There is a higher level of understanding of how karma works.

A higher view of how karma works

There has been a tendency, especially in Eastern religions, to believe that karma is set in stone. If we are to talk about energy, as I have done here, we could say that in the past you made a choice. This sent a karmic impulse, an energy impulse, into the four levels of the material universe. If this karmic impulse is allowed to return to you without being changed, it can trigger a certain situation in your life. For example, this can be an accident, an illness, the loss of a business, the loss of a loved one, whatever tragedy people experience, even the death of your physical body.

You can say that, yes, this was your karma coming back to you, but what I desire to give to you here is the understanding that karma comes back only if you have not changed your consciousness. We could then say that karma is not the punishment of an angry God, as it is sometimes seen by people, neither is it an entirely impersonal law that simply returns to you what you send out.

Karma has the purpose of teaching you how to use your creative faculties. How do you co-create anything? You use the mind's ability to formulate a mental image. You project that image onto the Ma-ter light, which causes the formation of a matrix of energy. This matrix has a given form, it has a given level of vibration and it has a certain momentum or strength. You then project this matrix outside the sphere of your mind. Once it has left the sphere of your mind and has been projected outside your mind, it has generated an impulse that will cycle through and eventually return to you. However, this return is not simply mechanical, impersonal or guaranteed. This return *can* come to pass or it can *not* come to pass.

There are two main reasons why it may not come to pass. The one reason is that the Karmic Board, or the ascended master who oversees your personal evolution, sees that you have a karmic return coming back to you, looks at your growth in consciousness, sees that you are close to breaking through to a higher level of consciousness and then decides to hold back the karmic return for a time. This is done in order to give you an opportunity to break through to that higher level before the karmic return comes back.

What is the point in you having the karmic return if you have learned your lesson and shifted your consciousness? This does not mean that the karma is completely gone, but it does mean that you can now balance it from a higher level of consciousness. It will be much easier for you to consume the karmic impulse in the identity, mental or emotional level before it manifests as a physical event in your life. This is only possible when you have shifted your consciousness.

The other reason a karmic return may not come back as a physical consequence is that you have changed your state of consciousness, you have transcended the state of consciousness in which you generated that karmic impulse. Therefore, you are now free of that former state of consciousness, that former self. This means that when the karmic impulse comes back, it is – often without you being consciously aware of it – consumed in the three higher bodies before it becomes physical. This is especially the case if you make the calls and use the violet flame.

We can now go back to the question: "Why did this happen to me?" You can now see a more sophisticated answer. It did not happen to you because there is an angry God in the sky who wants to punish you for something you did in the past. You will notice that even many people who are aware of karma and reincarnation still think that there must be an angry God who wants to punish them, and that is why he has created a universe in which karma is returned to you. This is simply not the case.

Why did this happen to you? Because in the past you made certain choices that generated an energy impulse, a karmic impulse. You have not sufficiently changed your consciousness, and therefore the karmic impulse from the past came all the way full circle and descended into the material frequency spectrum where it manifested as a specific event in your life.

Many people will take this teaching and say: "Yes, but that still does not explain why this happened to me. What did I do in the past to deserve this or to generate this impulse?" Here is where we come to another layer of complexity.

The belief that you must have deserved it

On the one hand, you most likely *did* do something in the past. Your past actions are not the only reason things happen to you, as I will talk about shortly. In many cases, the reason is that you did something in the past, probably in a past life long forgotten, and it is now coming full circle as a karmic impulse. However, here is where you need to be more sophisticated and step up to a higher understanding.

The fallen beings have for a very long time projected a very complex consciousness that includes the image of the angry God, that you are a sinner or an imperfect being and therefore when something comes back to you, it is because you deserve it. If bad things happen to you, it must be because either you did something bad or you are a bad person and therefore you deserve what you are getting. This is a state of consciousness that is very, very persuasive while you are still in embodiment. Certainly, I, myself, was affected by it.

When you ascend, you see that it is absolutely and completely untrue. It has no reality whatsoever in the ascended realm. There is no ascended master, no member of the Karmic Board and no judgmental God up here in the ascended realm who is looking down upon you and evaluating what you deserve based on you being such a bad person. In the ascended realm there is no judgment, no condemnation, no sense of guilt. What you did in the past was to experiment with your co-creative abilities. This is exactly what God gave you the right to do and what God wants you to do.

What am I telling you, my beloved? I am telling you that you were created to go into the world and be as the little child that Jesus said would be the only one entering the kingdom of heaven. You are meant to have the innocence of the little child who innocently co-creates, uses its co-creative abilities to formulate an image based on its current state of consciousness, its current sense of self, and then projects out that image.

The purpose is that you generate an impulse that is returned by the cosmic mirror. By experiencing the return, you can evaluate simply: "*Do* I want more of this, or *don't* I want more of this?" If you don't want more, you know you have to refine your consciousness so that you do not continue to send out the same kind of impulses. If you want something that is better, something that is higher, then you know you have to raise your consciousness.

You do so, and then you generate another impulse and you send that out. When it comes back, you evaluate: "Do I want more *of* this, or do I want more *than* this?" If you want more than, then you raise your consciousness again. If you want more of the same, well then you stay in the same state of consciousness and generate impulses through that state of consciousness until you have had enough of that experience. Now you say: "Yes, I do want more than this, and I am ready for something more."

This is how you are meant to be as a co-creator. There are many, many planets in the physical universe where the inhabitants are innocently co-creating like this because these planets are untouched by the fallen consciousness. Earth is not such a planet, and that is why the collective consciousness has been deeply affected by the fallen consciousness.

This is why many spiritual people believe that you must have deserved what is happening to you, implying that there is some higher authority who judges what you deserve based on your past bad actions. As I have said, there is no such evaluation in the ascended realm. It is not that you deserve what is coming back to you; it is simply that what is coming back to you is a reflection of the state of consciousness with which you created the impulse.

If you could look at this with the innocent mind of the child, meaning the non-judgmental mind of the Christ consciousness, you would not see what is coming back to you as something bad, as something you deserve, as a form of punishment for something you did in the past. You would see it as simply a reflection of the state of consciousness you were in at the time.

I realize that this is a catch-22. If you feel that what comes back to you must be something you deserved, then you have not shifted your consciousness. You have not completely freed yourself from the fallen consciousness, and therefore you can only see it this way. The fact that you asked the question shows something about your state of consciousness.

Overcoming the desire to change others

If we do go back in time, there was a point where the inhabitants of planet earth had descended to such a low level of collective consciousness that the fallen beings were allowed to start embodying on this planet. This was when the collective consciousness started becoming polluted and eventually completely dominated by the fallen consciousness. Before this happened, there was actually a limit to what the inhabitants of this planet would do to each other.

I, for example, taught in my church that there was a point where war did not occur on this planet because the inhabitants of this planet had not come up with it. Then the collective consciousness of this planet was lowered so that certain lifestreams from other planets were allowed to embody here,

17 | Why Did This Happen to Me?

and they carried with them in their soul memories the concept of war. They taught it to the people on this planet, and from that moment on war has been one of the dominating forces on this planet.

It has also been one of the primary ways in which people generate the kind of karma that can cause you to be killed in this life because you killed in another life. You allowed yourself to be sucked into fighting the wars that are truly the wars of domination between different fallen beings, and thereby you generated the kind of karma that comes from killing another human being. You generated an impulse that might very well result in you dying, either by being killed or through an accident or disease in a future lifetime.

You could say, in a certain way, that by you being tempted by the serpentine consciousness, and going into the serpentine consciousness, you created a karmic impulse that is now coming back to you. You might say that by going into the fallen consciousness, you deserve what is happening to you. Again, no ascended being looks at it this way.

As an ascended being you have absolute respect for the Law of Free Will. You cannot ascend unless you develop this uncompromising respect for the free will of others and for your own free will. You ascend only when you have such absolute respect for the free will of other people that you have absolutely no desire left to change any person on earth. If you have a desire to change anyone, you cannot ascend.

You can ascend only when you have such uncompromising respect for your own free will that you will not let any other person on earth prevent you from leaving them behind and entering the ascended state. You are saying: "Regardless of what anybody else wants or regardless of what the entire humanity wants, I am choosing to ascend. This is my right, my individual choice. *I am choosing to ascend right now!*"

18 | THE DETERMINATION TO ASCEND

As an ascended master, you know that even going into the fallen consciousness will not be condemned by God or the masters. The Karmic Board realizes full well that the fallen consciousness is a potential outcome of free will. You cannot give beings a will that is completely free if they cannot rebel against having free will, against God's plan for growth. You cannot give them free will if they cannot create a separate self and begin to believe that the separate self is as a God who can define good and evil.

As an ascended master you have an uncompromising respect for the Law of Free Will, but this is based on an absolute understanding of why free will is the only way for lifestreams to grow. The concern of the Karmic Board and the ascended masters is not to punish you, is not to give you what you deserve. It is not even a desire that you should see a karmic return of what you sent out in the past.

The Karmic Board has absolutely no desire and finds no satisfaction in seeing you reap what you have sown. Their goal is to help you transcend the consciousness in which you created the karmic impulse so that it does not have to come back physically. Their only concern is how to help you transcend the fallen consciousness once you have stepped into it. What I am saying here is that the very state of consciousness that causes you to ask: "Why did this happen to me, what did I do to deserve this?" keeps you tied to the fallen consciousness, prevents you from transcending the fallen consciousness.

There are actually spiritual people, and in fact many ascended master students, who have gotten themselves into a state of consciousness where they are sort of passively waiting for whatever life brings them. Then, almost like the stoic philosophers of Ancient Greece and many Christian and spiritual groups around the world, they are simply saying: "Oh well, whatever happens is whatever happens. I just have to bear it and make the best of it." Again, we have a subtlety.

Once something has happened in the physical, yes, you cannot turn back the clock. You cannot make it un-happened, and therefore you *should* make the best of it. You should accept what happened and make the best of it and go on from there as best you can. There is no point in rebelling against something that has already happened.

What I am saying here is that it is not constructive for your ascension that you go into this state of passively waiting for whatever life throws at you. If you are to make your ascension at the end of this lifetime, you need to go into a very active state of mind where you are saying: "I am stopping all of my karmic impulses from the past before they become physical. I am doing this by honestly and sincerely striving to transcend my former state of consciousness."

"I am looking at any element of the fallen consciousness in my being. I am taking the teachings of the ascended masters and using them to evaluate whether I have elements of the fallen consciousness. I am calling to my ascended teachers and my Christ self to expose this to me, and then I am invoking the violet flame and the other six rays to consume the karma before it becomes physical. I am not allowing a karmic return from the past to cause an event in my life that will make it harder for me, or impossible for me, to qualify for my ascension in this lifetime. This is *not* going to happen to me!"

It takes determination to make your ascension

If you are to make your ascension there has to be that kind of determination: uncompromising. You are not dilly-dallying, you are not drifting like a piece of wood that is being tossed around by the waves and thrown up on the beach. You are taking charge of your life. You are saying: "I *have* to make my ascension in this life!" Then you do whatever you can see to make that ascension.

That includes making an effort to come to see what you cannot now see by using the tools and teachings of the ascended masters to shift your consciousness, to shift out of these fallen lies and illusions that have been inserted into your consciousness. What does this mean?

I talked about the Antahkarana and how all people are connected in this web of life. If you could see what we see from the ascended level about yourself, you could draw a map that is centered around where your physical body is right now. You could then draw a map at the physical level, at the emotional level, at the mental level and at the identity level. You would see how you have, at each level, certain lines of energy that connects you to other people, to places, to situations. You could first take a map that shows you the connections that exist right now, independently of time, but then you could make that map three-dimensional by seeing how these lines of energy reach back in time where you are connected to certain places and events that happened in the past.

For example, many people who are in embodiment today have in a past life, many even in a recent past life, been through a war where you might have been killed or wounded in a certain battle or you might have killed or wounded other people. There will be a karmic thread that reaches back to that situation because in the Akashic records there is a record of that particular event. There is energy that was generated when the event took place, and it has not been dissolved because not enough people know about the violet flame and are invoking the violet flame to dissolve these old records. This means that if you went through the situation, you will have a tie to that. This is one of the things you need to cut in order to be free.

Even if you are not physically aware of what happened to you in all these past lives, by you giving the decrees and working on shifting your consciousness, you are cutting these ties. You are cutting your boat free from all of these anchors that are dragging behind. If you could see this, you would see how many of these karmic ties, these energetic ties, you have to other people and situations.

I realize that most of you will not be able to see this, but you can still ask for an inner confirmation and get some feel for the fact that you are tied. Then you can learn the lesson that is meant to be learned from this teaching, which is that what creates a karmic tie, or any energetic tie, is that you focus your attention on something and you generate an energy impulse that is lower than the vibration of love.

I am here talking about love in its pure non-possessive form, not the human possessive love that is what most people normally associate with the word love. Anger, hatred, fear these are obvious feelings that generate lower energies. Even what many people call positive feelings, such as a possessive love or wanting to control or own other people, generate karmic ties. Even the sense that you are doing something for the greater good can generate a karmic impulse if you are seeking to force the free will of other people.

Drawing a personal energy map

The conscious lesson you can learn is that you can take a look at your life. You can do this very simply by sitting quietly and you can just observe: Where is your mind going? Where is your attention going? Imagine this for yourself, or you can even take a piece of paper and draw this.

You can take a piece of paper and in the center you make a little circle that represents you. Then you simply sit there and observe your mind. When you feel that your consciousness is going towards a certain person or a certain topic, you draw a line (from the center) and then you start drawing a circle at the end of the line. You draw the circle bigger and darker, depending on the intensity you feel in the energy. Then you write a simple name to identify the energy.

You go back to the center, and now you feel where you go next. You draw another line and another circle, write down what it is. If you will do this several times, you can draw a map and it is an energy map. What is it that pulls your attention into going into these feelings of fear, worry, concern, anger, whatever you have? What is it that draws you into these seemingly benign feelings of wanting to change something, wanting to solve some problem, feeling like you have to do this or even that you are doing this for a greater cause? You can learn to observe that this is not because you are voluntarily choosing to focus on something; there is a pull, there is an obsession, a compulsion, that pulls your attention into focusing on this.

This can be a very helpful exercise for showing you what it is that pulls your attention into reinforcing a certain matrix of thoughts and energy. Let us take a practical example. Let us say that you become aware that there is a person in your life who is seeking to control you. This might be a parent, for example. You feel a certain powerlessness when you are dealing with this person, and this has created a certain resentment and anger in you. If you would draw a map, you would see that your attention is often drawn to this person. There would be a very dark circle where you have really pressed on the pen to draw the circle represented by the energies you feel when you think about this person.

What are you now doing? Well, in your present life you are feeding your energy into a matrix that is centered around this person. If this is a person that is close to you, it is a virtual certainty that this is not the first lifetime where you have encountered this person. You have been embodied with this person before, and the pattern you are now having with this person most likely started several lifetimes ago. The reason it is so intense is that it has been reinforced over several lifetimes.

Having embodied with fallen beings in your family

I am in no way blaming you for this. It is one of the consequences of the development of this planet that many, many people, especially the more spiritually mature people, have for various reasons incarnated with people in the fallen consciousness.

I, myself, had two parents who were very much trapped in the fallen consciousness. It affected me deeply. I have been embodied with these parents several times in various roles, and I originally started doing this, not because I had to, but because I volunteered to try and help them transcend their consciousness. Many spiritual people have done the same.

Again, there is no blame. It is very understandable that you have been deeply affected by certain lifestreams that are very much trapped in the fallen consciousness. The concern here is this: If you are to make your ascension at the end of this lifetime, you absolutely *must* break the tie to such lifestreams. The question is: "How do you do this? How do you break the tie?"

18 | The Determination to Ascend

Here is the absolute requirement: You must stop feeding your energy and attention into these old spirals. There is absolutely no other way, and here is another absolute law. *You will not break the karmic tie to someone else by seeking to change that person.*

You will break the karmic tie only by looking at yourself and seeking to change yourself. You must raise your consciousness to the point where the other person and the other person's state of consciousness no longer has anything in you whereby it can force your attention into reinforcing or creating any kind of spiral.

You are free from the pull of the other person's consciousness. In many cases, people who are in the fallen consciousness will directly and aggressively seek to pull you into a pattern with them. It is extremely common that a person who is trapped in the fallen consciousness will first seek to control you in various ways. When you seek to break free of that control, the person will turn on you and seek to destroy you psychologically in a way that has often been called soul murder.

When fallen beings try to murder your soul

This is a pattern you will see repeated over and over again. I have seen so many people in my own church that fit into this pattern. I have seen many people who were close to qualifying for their ascension, but the major thing that was holding them back was that they still had a tie, an energetic, karmic tie, to a person who was trapped in the fallen consciousness.

I have also had quite a number of people who were trapped in the fallen consciousness come to my church and start doing what they always do: seeking to control other people. I have had people who came seeking to control *me,* and when they could not control me, turned on me an attempted to destroy me. I have seen so many spiritual people who have been deeply hurt when a loved one turned on them and attempted to destroy them, attempted to murder their soul.

There are lifestreams – and I encountered quite a number of them when I was in embodiment – who have an incredible momentum on committing soul murder and who have no compunctions about doing so if it is within their power. My own father once blamed me for having caused my mother to leave him, and he stood there and literally cursed me. He knew that he could not kill me physically, but he attempted to use all of the momentum of his consciousness to put a curse on me that would result in my physical death. Or at least it would result in my psychological death so that I would give up on life and could not fulfill my mission.

He did not realize that this was not actually him personally being so angry with me. It was actually certain dark forces working through him at that moment, seeking to destroy me and prevent me from becoming a messenger for the ascended masters.

Now let us go back to what I said before: "Why did this happen to you?" Was it because you deserved it? No, but it was because you created an impulse in a past life that is coming back to you. It is coming back physically because you have not transcended the consciousness. Take the situation of my own father. Very far back in a very distant embodiment, I first chose to embody with this lifestream that was my father in my last embodiment. I chose this because I had a desire to help this lifestream transcend its state of consciousness. I was at that time in a fairly innocent state of consciousness. I saw how trapped this lifestream was in the fallen consciousness, and I desired to help it.

Once I embodied and was now in a physical body with this lifestream, it was such a difficult relationship that I started creating a karmic impulse where I very strongly desired to force that lifestream to change. This was not a destructive impulse where I wanted to destroy that lifestream or kill him or do other things, but it was still a violation of the Law of Free Will.

I chose to embody with that lifestream. When I first chose to do this, I had no karmic reason that forced me to do so. It was a choice I made. Once I was in embodiment, I had forgotten the choice, could not tune in to it. Because of the unpleasantness of being so close to this lifestream, I wanted to force him to change so that he would not continue to hurt me. Many, many people have experienced a similar situation.

I created karma with that lifestream, which meant that the next time I embodied with that lifestream it was not because I made a free choice. I did make the choice, but I made the choice because I saw that I had created karma and I wanted to balance that karma. I wanted to rise above the karma.

How to finally break a karmic spiral

Once I was in embodiment again, I was feeling the weight of this person's energy. Truly, nothing I had done while embodying with that lifestream had changed the lifestream one bit. He had, if anything, become more trapped in his state of consciousness by what he had done to me and the way I had responded to it. This continued for several lifetimes, in fact I had quite a few embodiments with the lifestream that was my father in my last embodiment.

Why did I choose to embody with this lifestream – that was so trapped in the fallen consciousness – in what had the potential to be my last lifetime? It was because I wanted to learn the lesson, and what is the lesson? It is that when you truly understand the Law of Free Will, you see that you cannot change any other lifestream. If you seek to force them, you only create karma for yourself, and you most likely cause them to respond in a way that only reinforces their state of consciousness. If you do *not* seek to force them, you will not change them. Many of these lifestreams in the fallen consciousness will never change on their own. That is why the karmic law is set up to return your impulses to you in what we have called the School of Hard Knocks. Once a person is trapped in the fallen consciousness, it most likely will not change until it experiences such hard knocks that it decides that it *has to* change because it can't stand it anymore.

You don't want to make yourself an instrument for giving such a person hard knocks because you make karma for yourself by doing it. You actually reinforce your own state of consciousness that is making you think you have to force others to change. What is the core of the fallen consciousness? It is a disrespect for free will and a willingness to force the free will of others. Even if you think that you are doing this for the person's own good, you are still acting from the fallen consciousness and you cannot ascend as long as you are doing this. What was the lesson I needed to learn? It was that *you cannot change any other lifestream.*

You can give them an opportunity, but the only way to really give them an opportunity is to be true to yourself, to be who you are, to let the light of your I AM Presence shine and to let them do with it whatever they want. You can only try to be an example by being yourself and then let them do or not do whatever they choose. You must be non-attached to other people's choices. Anything else, any kind of attachment, creates an energetic tie between you and that person, and it will prevent you from ascending. It is *that* simple.

Based on this, you can begin – if you are willing – to look at your life and see where your attention and where your energy is being fed into a spiral with another person, or a cause, or a situation, whatever it may be. Then you will know that when you focus your attention on something, it will feed energy into the matrix. It will reinforce the tie that you have to that something here on earth. This will prevent you from ascending. You can only ascend when you have no ties whatsoever to anything on earth.

What must you do if you know this is your last embodiment? If you have a desire to ascend, you must cut these ties. You do not cut the tie by simply physically breaking off from that person, although it may be necessary to do so. You truly cut the tie by transcending the state of consciousness where you have any desire to change the other person. You need to change your consciousness to the point where you simply don't have a reaction to that person. You set them free to be who they are, to do what they do, to have the experience they need to have.

Setting other people free is setting yourself free

You realize that whatever choices they are making, they need to have that experience. They may need to have it because they will generate such hard knocks for themselves that they eventually come to that hit-rock-bottom point where they can't do it anymore. They may need to have it for other reasons, but that is not important to you.

You do not need to analyze and judge with your outer mind why people are doing what they are doing and whether they should be doing it or not doing it. This you must free yourself from because it is another aspect of the fallen consciousness. How do you get to the point where you are not judging others? You must stop judging yourself, you must stop analyzing yourself: "Should I be doing *this,* should I be doing *that?*" You must become as a little child where you are willing to experiment with life.

What is underlying the consciousness where you ask: "Why did this happen to me?" It implies that you think that if you knew why this happened, you could change so that it would not happen again, it would not happen in the future or it would not be so bad.

What we see from the ascended state is the incredible complexity of these energetic ties that weave people together in this intricate web of life. We also see that with the capacity you have when you are in embodiment, it is impossible for you to know all of the intricacies that are involved in a particular situation. Say you look at your own life and a particular situation that happened in that life, and you ask me: "Guru Ma, show me why this happened." The reality is that the situation that you went through was the product of a very complex, intricate web of interactions between you and other people. This is so complex that your conscious mind would be unable to fathom it.

That is why many spiritual gurus have given a simplified explanation out of a desire to give their students something. This is not necessarily invalid if it helps you transcend the consciousness. If it simply puts you in a passive state of mind or satisfies some human curiosity, then it is not helpful—it can, in fact, be harmful.

You cannot ascend by living your life based on simplistic explanations. You must come to a greater understanding. The greater understanding you need to come to is *not* that you know every detail. The greater understanding is that you know that regardless of the intricacies of the situation, the central aspect is that you look at your *reaction* and ask yourself what that says about the state of consciousness that *you* need to transcend.

19 | WHY NOTHING CAN BE PREDICTED WITH CERTAINTY

You may have heard about scientists who are investigating these very complex events that are going on, for example, at the subatomic level. You can depict the interaction of subatomic particles, but if you looked at a situation ahead of time and asked a scientist to calculate the outcome of that interaction, then the scientist would say that this is impossible.

There are two aspects of why it is impossible to predict with certainty what is going to happen. One is the sheer complexity. Even the seemingly simplest events at these deeper levels of matter involve so many complexities that the best supercomputers on the planet could not calculate them all in a reasonable time frame. The other reason why it is impossible to predict ahead of time what will happen is the uncertainty principle. There is a certain uncertainty built into the physical universe, which makes it impossible to predict exactly what is going to happen until it actually happens.

Why nothing is predictable

This is something that you can benefit from realizing as a spiritual student because it helps you overcome what is one of the biggest traps on the spiritual path. I have so far talked about the desire to know: "Why did this happen to me?" One of the underlying mechanisms here is that people desire to know why this happened in the past so they can predict what might happen in the future and prevent bad things from happening to them.

I, myself, made extensive use of astrology while I was in physical embodiment. It is not that astrology is invalid, but what happens in your life is not written in the stars or anywhere else in the sense that it can be predicted with certainty. You can get something out of it if you know how to read this intuitively, but you cannot predict anything with absolute certainty and it is important for you to ponder why.

Let us now, instead of looking at a situation that *has* happened to you, look into the future. Let us say that you know you are going to make a big change in your life, such as start a new relationship, a new career, move to another country or another part of your country. You are naturally concerned about what might happen if you do this: "Is anything bad going to happen if I do this because then I won't do it." You come to a spiritual guru and you say: "Guru Ma, tell me what's going to happen." Would it actually be possible to predict what is going to happen in such a situation?

The answer is "No." You can, as scientists say, predict certain probabilities, but you cannot predict with certainty. You might think that if everything you do creates an energetic impulse that is sent into the four levels of the material universe, then it should be possible to look at the supercomputer that the Karmic Board has and have it calculate every possible karmic return you have generated in the past, calculate the track that this karmic return will follow through the four levels of the material universe and therefore be able to calculate exactly when a certain impulse is coming back to the physical realm. This is not actually the case.

The Karmic Board can look at your karmic impulses and see when a major karmic impulse is due to go into the physical, and therefore they can decide to hold it back in order to give you an opportunity. What I am saying here is that even the Karmic Board cannot predict with certainty what is going to happen when a karmic impulse starts descending.

The Karmic Board has a capability that your physical scientists do not have: They are not limited by time and space. They *can* calculate the interaction of all of the many energy impulses that will be involved in that situation, but they still cannot predict exactly what is going to happen and here is why.

The complexity of human interactions

Say you are moving to another part of the country and starting a new job. You will be working with other people, you will be interacting with other people. All of these people have their own personal karmic map and their own present state of consciousness. When you start interacting with them, your personal karmic map starts interacting with theirs, your consciousness starts interacting with theirs. What your consciousness and your karmic map forms is a very, very complex pattern of energy waves.

A scientist can tell you that when two energy waves interact, they create an interference pattern. When you are interacting with another person, your consciousness and your karmic map starts interacting in this very complex set of wave interference patterns. Take note that this is not an entirely mechanical process. There *is* a mechanical element in the sense that there is a karmic impulse from the past descending through the identity, mental and emotional levels and into the physical. As it descends, what happens? Well, it starts interacting with your consciousness and the other person's consciousness, first at the identity level and then at the lower levels.

When a karmic impulse comes back to two people's consciousness at the identity level, they most likely react without being consciously aware of it. The way they react will now determine how the karmic impulse descends to the mental level. There is a choice made, even if it is subconscious, and it changes, potentially, the karmic return and the exact form that it takes. The same happens at the mental and the emotional level so before the karmic impulse reaches the physical there has been a very complex set of interactions that involves choices you make, or at least how your consciousness interacts with a karmic impulse. You may not be making an actual choice because you are responding the way you have done in the past, given that you have not changed your consciousness.

The entire process of a karmic impulse descending through the four levels is so complex that there is no way you could, with your conscious mind, predict and foresee exactly what is going to happen when you go into a new situation. There is, for that matter, no way the Karmic Board can foresee and predict exactly what is going to happen because of the element of free will.

The Karmic Board could create certain probabilities that you would react a certain way based on the way you have reacted in the past. The uncertainty principle discovered by science applies to your personal life. There is no way to predict with certainty what is going to happen until it actually happens because it is not predetermined.

Karma can undermine your free will

This is another element of the fallen consciousness. What have the fallen beings been trying to do from day one: undermine and destroy your free will. Can you see that even the concept that you have created karma in a past life and that this karma predetermines what is going to happen to you in this life is an undermining of your free will?

Look at how many people in India have given up on life because they think: "Oh, anything that happens is a result of my karma so what's the point in even trying? I can't change my present because I can't change my past." Well, my beloved, you may not be able to change a karmic impulse from the past but you *can* change your state of consciousness and *that* will change how the karmic impulse descends into the physical level, or whether it even reaches the physical level.

There is absolutely nothing you can do with your free will that will take away your ability to make choices. Yes, you can choose to put yourself in a certain state of consciousness that makes you think that there is nothing you can do. If you think that there is nothing you can do, there *is* nothing you can do—as long as you think this.

You can, at any moment, use your free will to reactivate your free will and say: "No, there *is* something I can do. I can change my consciousness. I can choose to look at my reaction, see what that says about my attachments and my state of consciousness. I can choose to cut those ties, cut those attachments, and I can start right now. Yes, it's a complex process. Yes, it will take the rest of this embodiment. Yes, it will be a lot of work. Yes, there will be times when it seems like I am getting nowhere, but I *can* do something."

If you are not willing to do something, you will not ascend at the end of this lifetime, regardless of whether you have the potential or not. In fact, if you are willing to do enough, the vast majority of the people of this planet could ascend in this lifetime if they were willing to shift their consciousness enough. I realize that for the vast majority of the people on this planet there is a high probability that they would not be willing to do this, but the potential is there. There is only a small percentage of people who are so trapped in the fallen consciousness, have made so much karma, that it simply would not be possible for them to qualify for their ascension in a normal physical lifespan. For the majority of the people on this planet, it would be theoretically possible; not likely, but theoretically possible.

You will be amazed at how much room there is in the Law of Free Will for actually using your free will to shift your consciousness. What I have essentially been trying to tell you here is: God has put no limitations in the way of your free will. *You* have created the limitations you face, and that means what? Anything you have created, you can *un*create. This is the reality of the Law of Free Will.

Did I fully get this when I was in embodiment? No! Should that stop you from getting it? Well, that choice is up to you. I have presented you with the absolute truth that I have observed and experienced after I ascended. It is immaterial what I believed before I ascended because I only ascended by letting go of all of *my* illusions. You will only ascend when you let go of all of *your* illusions.

No external force limits your free will

I tell you that any illusion that makes it seem like there are external forces that are limiting your free will has to go before you can ascend. You will ascend only when you fully accept that you can walk through that gate to the ascended realm and you can do it *right now*. I am not saying that you could make this decision right now in your waking consciousness because you have not resolved enough of your past levels of consciousness, your past illusions. You have not balanced the karmic impulses and so on.

What I *am* saying is that when you do the work, there comes that point where you realize: "Now I am capable of making that choice." You still have to make the choice, and if you think there is anything – *anything* – in heaven or on earth that can prevent you from making that choice, then you will not be able to make the choice, will you?

You have to accept that God has given you a will that is entirely free. God has never restricted your free will. The fallen ones have attempted to restrict your free will, but they are not able to do it against your own choices. You may choose to accept an illusion that limits your free will, but you have chosen to accept it and that means you can choose to *un*accept it.

There is no choice you could ever make that cannot be undone by making a better choice. When you realize this, you can say: "I don't need to know everything that is going to happen to me before it happens. I am willing to experiment with life. I am willing to continue to experiment with life and see what comes back and then look at my reaction to what comes back and what that says about my state of consciousness, my attachments, my concerns, where my attention and energies are going. Then I choose to let go of that attachment, let go of that separate self, let go of that spirit, let go of those illusions."

Saint Germain has said that you are a slave of your attention because where your attention goes, there goes your energy. Your soul must follow, and thus your soul is trapped. Your soul vehicle is the anchor that keeps your boat from crossing to the farther shore. You must cut those ties.

Do not let past choices restrict present choices

I look today, as an ascended master, back to the people that I knew in my last embodiment. I can look at so many of them and how they have reacted to me. Their reaction to me has created an energy matrix that only reinforces the very state of consciousness that is the main thing that prevents them from making progress on their spiritual path.

They have used me and my behavior – and the flaws that they saw in me – as an excuse for not looking at the very things in themselves that are preventing them from growing. They are focusing their attention on how bad I was – as a mother, as a guru, as a spouse, as this and that – and they are feeding their energies into this matrix—and all it does is keep them tied to the matrix.

It is perfectly fine to write a book about your mother and what she did or did not do, but the question is: "Does writing this book help you resolve something in your own consciousness or does it simply reinforce an energy matrix that is holding you back?" It is perfectly fine to create a website denouncing your mother and father as false prophets and false teachers, denouncing the ascended masters as real. "Does this help you grow or does it just keep you tied to a limiting matrix and does it reinforce that matrix?"

It is perfectly fine to go around talking amongst your own select little group of people about how: Mother did this and Mother did not do that. Mother said this, or Mother did not say that. There was a time when Mother lost her mantle, and she made a false prophecy, and she made this mistake and she made that mistake. I have no condemnation of any of the students who do or say what they do or say about me.

I understand that it was my role to be there, to be "in your face" and to force a reaction in you. I am happy that I have forced a reaction in you, no matter what that reaction is, because this gives you an opportunity to look at your reaction and evaluate: Does it help me grow or does it feed my energy into a matrix that keeps me tied to earth?

When all is said and done, none of us are required to be perfect according to a standard on earth. You have an absolute right to be who you are and to be in the state of consciousness you are in right now. You have an absolute right to decide whether you will transcend that state of consciousness or whether you will reinforce it. You are the one deciding how you will spend the rest of this lifetime.

You have a right to be who you are

You have a right to be here. You have a right to be in the state of consciousness you are in, and you have a right to express it. How other people react to you is a product of the state of consciousness they have chosen to be in and whether they choose to reinforce it or choose to transcend it.

You see, the same goes for *me*. I had a right to be in the state of consciousness I was in. I had a right to be a spiritual guru even though I was not the perfect human being. I had a right to stand up in front of the world and expose my flaws for all to see and analyze. I had a right to, so to speak, force people to react to me.

Do you understand? The Law of Free Will does not give you the right to force the free will of other people to make certain choices. The Law of Free Will gives you the right to be who you are and to be in embodiment on earth. This means that your mere presence on earth will force the people you encounter to react to you. They may react very negatively. They may blame you for being who you are. They may blame you for being here. They may say, as many people said to Jesus, even the demons speaking out of the mouth of one person obsessed: "Leave us alone, thou son of God."

The ascended masters have a right to challenge you

You do not have a right to be left alone in your own self-created perception filter. God has a right to challenge you by allowing other people to embody who have a different state of consciousness than you do and therefore force a reaction in you. This is not forcing you to make certain choices because you have the option to choose how you react to other people. If you were not challenged by other people, then you would create a state of consciousness that was self-reinforcing and you would never get out of it.

There are so many people on earth who cannot hear an ascended master, who cannot hear their Christ self. God has a simple choice, the Karmic Board has a simple choice: How can these people be awakened? If the ascended masters did nothing, these people would create a self-reinforcing spiral that would lead to their own destruction and even the destruction of the planet. What could the Karmic Board do? They could allow other lifestreams to embody on this planet who were so different from the original inhabitants that they would inevitably clash. Because they are all in physical embodiment, they cannot avoid each other so they cannot avoid forcing a reaction in each other. This forces them to consider that there are other people who look at life differently than they do. Although this has created a lot of conflict and war, it has also prevented the original inhabitants of earth from going into a downward spiral that would lead to the destruction of themselves and their planet.

This is the School of Hard Knocks for sure, but you are the one who determines how hard the knocks are going to be for you. Will you continue to react the way you are reacting now? Or will you look at your reaction and consider what that says about your state of consciousness and then decide to transcend that state of consciousness?

How you react to a spiritual authority figure

I had a right to be in embodiment. I had a right to accept the position as messenger for the ascended masters and spiritual guru. I had a right to exercise that position according to my state of consciousness. I had a right to cause a reaction in the tens of thousands of people that encountered me in some form or another, even the millions of people who encountered me in the press. This was *my* right. *You* have a right to react to me in any way *you* want.

I am now ascended. Why am I ascended? Because I started looking at my own reaction to being in the position I was in and my own reaction to other people. I started wondering what that said about my state of consciousness, the state of consciousness that was keeping me tied to earth. Then I started systematically cutting those ties until I had cut them all and I was free to ascend.

You can do the same. Whatever reaction you had to me, whatever experience you had, whatever our encounter was, you can look at your reaction to me but look beyond and see that this is your reaction to the spiritual guru and to God. Regardless of how imperfect I might have been, I still have given you the opportunity to consider how you react to a spiritual authority figure and what that says about the decision that caused you to walk away from your original spiritual guru.

This will show you what prevents you from coming back—if coming back is what you want. If it is not what you want, then you are free to pursue whatever experience you *do* want in the material universe. If you want to come back, you must follow the only path there is. You must *un*do what you have done, you must *un*choose what you have chosen, you must *un*learn what you have learned.

You have created the incredibly complex being that you are right now. You will not ascend by making it perfect according to some standard created on earth. You will ascend only by uncreating it and letting the experiences stored in your causal body be the only thing you take with you from earth.

How can you move on from here?

My beloved, the question you face in any situation is not: "Why did this happen to me?" or: "How can I prevent something from happening in the future?" The question you face in every situation is: "Now, how do I move on from here? How do I take the next step up the spiral staircase towards my ascension?"

In order to take that step, you need to understand something, you need to see something, about your state of consciousness and your reaction. You do *not* need to know everything that happened. You need to have a certain largess, a certain willingness to look at the big picture and to just realize what I said in my last discourse. You need to realize that any situation you encounter involves an extremely complex interaction of karmic impulses, karmic ties, your consciousness and the consciousness of other people. Even the simplest situations are so complex that there is no point in fully understanding why things happened.

Sometimes you need to simply look at a situation, and instead of asking: "Why did this happen?" or "Why did I do this?" you simply look at it and you say: "Okay, but this is how the cookie crumbled in this situation. Now, how do I move on?"

"The cookie has crumbled. Let it crumble. Let the crumbles fall where they may, but I am moving on. How do I move on?" *This is the question that will make or break your ascension.*

There are all of these other concerns: "Why did I do this? Why did he or she do this? Why did this happen? Why did this *not* happen? Why did God not protect me?" All of these questions will at some point on your path become irrelevant. You are simply looking at: "How do I take the next step?"

You are not worrying about ten steps in the future. You are not worrying about the past. How do I take the *next* step? When you always focus on taking the next step, you will keep making progress towards the point where you realize that the next step to take is the step, the quantum leap, that brings you into the ascended realm.

When you come to *that* realization, you will have to cast one final glance on planet earth and see if there is any tie to anything on earth that pulls on your attention. If you can look at everything that *is* happening, everything that *has* happened and everything that *might* happen and there is nothing that pulls your attention, then you will know: "I am free to choose to ascend." Then the question is: *Will* you choose to ascend? Even *that* cannot be predicted with certainty. I *did* choose to ascend, and I AM the Ascended Master Guru Ma.

20 | THE DILEMMA FACING SPIRITUAL MOVEMENTS

I AM the Ascended Master Guru Ma. What is the main message I would like to get across in this book? The main message can be summed up in a statement made by El Morya: "The trek upward is worth the inconvenience."

When you look at earth realistically, you see that the collective consciousness forms such a strong magnetic, downward pull that it is extremely difficult for people to pull themselves above it and walk the spiritual path towards a higher state of consciousness. It is extremely difficult to ascend from earth, it is not an easy task, my beloved.

You also see that the fallen beings, the false teachers, have done everything they could think of to lay traps that pull you into blind alleys. They either take you away from the spiritual path altogether, or the delay your progress for a very long time. Quite frankly, they can think of a lot. They are very creative in their destructive way. If they could have turned that creative drive into producing something positive, something that raised up the All, well, then the earth would long ago have ascended to a higher level.

What I am saying is that it is very difficult on earth to walk the spiritual path and to qualify for your ascension. It is not by any means an easy task. This means that walking the path is inconvenient. It requires effort, it requires determination, it requires vision, it requires drive, an extraordinary drive.

The spiritual path can also be enjoyable

There certainly is a phase on the path where you need to be so focused on yourself – on the path, on the spiritual teachings and the spiritual disciplines that you know are valid – and you just do not have the opportunity to look right or left. It is very tempting to say that you have to be focused and disciplined for your entire lifetime, yet this is not necessarily the case. Yes, you have to be focused and disciplined, but you also have to be aware that the path has stages. There does come a stage on your path where you actually do have time, do have opportunity, do have attention to focus on enjoying life. The path is not all about sacrifice.

I know very well that when you look at the life of Jesus, you will see that he had a very intense life, especially the last three years. He was very focused, very driven, but yet if you could see him in reality – beyond what is recorded in the scriptures – you would see that he had moments of joy. He had moments where he just enjoyed life. I, myself, remember one time where I happened to come upon him sitting in the hills, looking out over the Sea of Galilee. Our eyes met, and I saw in him something I had not seen before.

I saw that he had no thought, no concern, for the future; no regrets about the past. He was just in the moment, he was living in the moment. He was one with God, one with everything, and he was radiating a vibration of joy that filled my being so that I started physically shaking all over. This only lasted for a split second, but that was all I could bear, given the state of consciousness I was in at the time. The experience has never left me. It has left an imprint on my being so that I know it is possible, even when you are in embodiment on earth, to tune in to the ascended realm, to the ascended state of consciousness, in which you see everything on earth for what it is: Outplayings in the cosmic sandbox, mirages projected by the minds of men and those disembodied beings attached to earth.

You are not here to produce a physical result

You see, as it says in the scriptures: "Vanity of vanities, all is vanity." You see that it is all unreal and that it has no real bearing on who you are as a spiritual being. When you see this, you see that your real task here on earth is *not* to do something in the outer, not to produce a certain visible result. Your real task here on earth is to be the open door for the light of your I AM Presence. When you are that open door – nothing *less,* nothing *more* – then you will feel the ultimate joy.

The ultimate joy you can experience on earth is to be attuned to the particular God quality of your I AM Presence and to be the open door for radiating that God quality in the material world. When you feel the light of your Presence flowing through you; *that* is the ultimate joy you can experience while you are in embodiment on earth.

There comes those upper levels of the path where you need to consciously set aside some time to just focus on your Presence and not let your attention be drawn into all these things that you think you have to do or accomplish on earth. I can assure you that when I look back on my last embodiment, one of the things that I would have done differently today was to spend more time just focusing on the Presence.

When I say this, I realize that it is an impossibility. I was not able to do this because of the state of consciousness I was in. Yet I do wish that I had had the prompting from somewhere to make a shift in consciousness so that I could focus more on just being one with the Presence, rather than being so pulled into doing all these outer things of what I thought was my ultimate task on earth.

The difficulty of being a spiritual guru

Again, life on earth is no easy task. It is difficult to walk the spiritual path, but how difficult do you think it is to be a spiritual leader, a spiritual guru and a messenger for the ascended masters? It is quite difficult.

There is enormous opposition. There are so many traps set by the fallen beings to prevent you from being successful in this task. You are dodging so many bullets coming at you all the time from the outside world, from the astral plane, from the mental plane, from the lower identity realm. You are dodging bullets coming from human beings, even those who are your own followers, those on your staff and in your own family. You feel like you are a living target and that they are taking potshots at you 24 hours a day and you have to be constantly alert.

When you become the open door for the Presence, you become transparent. There is a part of the path where you need to have the shield of Archangel Michael to deflect what is coming at you from the world. When you become one with the Presence, you do not need this shield for you now have become the open door, meaning that the bullets pass through your lower form and into the all-consuming fire of the I AM Presence. It is like building a cannon that can send a bullet to the sun, the bullet will be consumed before it ever reaches the surface of the sun—if one could define the surface of the sun, which you cannot.

There comes that point where it is possible to shift your consciousness so that you focus not so much on the outer tasks that you think you have to accomplish. It is understandable that this is difficult. I, myself, felt that I had made so many sacrifices in my life, that I had walked such a difficult path of overcoming so many obstacles, and why had I done this? Because I felt there was a goal, there was something I had to do for the ascended masters. My love, my drive, to serve the masters was so strong that I was willing to sacrifice virtually everything in my personal life in order to fulfill my mission. I was willing to set aside personal desires. I was willing to face many situations that I would rather have avoided and nevertheless still overcome, still keep moving, still keep going forward.

I felt that the legacy that I had to leave for the planet was the teachings and an organization that could promote the teachings. What have I said earlier? When you are too focused on something, you begin to drink your own Kool-Aid. You begin to think this is the *only* way you can be, this is the only thing you can do. Of course, this shuts down certain opportunities for your Presence to express itself freely through you. You are not completely the *open* door.

I was a sponsored messenger anointed by the ascended masters. I had very high spiritual mantles, higher than anyone is capable of holding right now. Nevertheless, I was not the completely open door. I was open to taking the dictations, but there were certain ideas I had about what it meant to be a messenger – what it meant to be a guru, what my mission and my work was – that actually closed certain aspects of my personal doorway to the full expression of my I AM Presence.

Each and every one of us has his or her personal service in life. It is not for all of you to be a messenger, to be a spiritual guru, to be a public personality, to have a public role. There are millions of people on earth who are meant to walk the path towards the ascension without taking a public role. For such people the ultimate service you can give is to be the open door for the light of your I AM Presence. For those of you who do have a more public mission, the best way to fulfill that mission is to be the open door for your I AM Presence so that you have the minimal amount of resistance in your outer mind that unwittingly, unbeknownst to you, controls the flow of the Presence.

Spiritual movements in the Aquarian age

If I could, I would gladly have shifted my consciousness much more than I was able to shift it while I was still in embodiment. I can see now that had I been able and willing to shift my consciousness more, I would not have had to go through the Alzheimer's disease, at least not at an early stage. It could have been postponed partially or even completely if I had been willing to shift my consciousness enough by questioning whether being so involved with the outer organization was my highest level of service.

You can say that I did make an attempt to withdraw from the organizational responsibilities, but that was only when I saw the handwriting on the wall and realized that the physical disease would limit my ability. Running a large spiritual organization is no easy task, but truly I had made it more difficult for myself by setting myself up in the position I was in so that I was the one who had to make all the major decisions.

Now again, why did I do this? Because I had had so many experiences of people who came to me, blinded by the fallen consciousness, wanting to make decisions for the organization, decisions that were clearly out of alignment with the goals and the principles of the ascended masters.

I was in a dilemma because I had volunteered to take on, as my students and even my staff, many people that were very entrenched in the fallen consciousness. These are the kind of people that you cannot let run a spiritual organization. If you do, they will take it into a blind alley, as you see with so many spiritual and religious organizations, even political and business organizations, throughout history.

This is one of the dilemmas that are facing spiritual organizations in the coming age. You can see a very interesting dividing line. You can see that there are many spiritual organizations on earth today, many New Age organizations and more traditional organizations, that do not have teachings about the ego, about the dark aspects of human psychology and about dark forces. You can look at these organizations and you can see a very clear tendency.

Some of these organizations are relatively small, and this means that they are no threat to the false hierarchy on this planet. The false hierarchy does not really bother to send their representatives into these organizations. This means that you can find some small organizations who have a much more harmonious community than we ever had in my church. This is not, as some would think, because these organizations have a higher state of consciousness or are more harmonious than others. It is simply because, by refusing to acknowledge the presence of dark forces on earth, they are not growing beyond a certain level and therefore they are no threat to the dark forces. The dark forces leave them alone and the people sit there feeling how wonderful it is to be where they are at, often thinking that they are really high spiritual beings, but not realizing that they are not fulfilling their highest potential.

Then there are organizations that are growing bigger, that are reaching more people and have more of an influence. As soon as an organization reaches a certain size and begins to have an influence in society, the false hierarchy will send their representatives into that organization. They are sent with one purpose only, and that is to destroy that organization from within. Many of these people are not consciously aware of who they are and why they are joining this organization. They just do what they do without realizing what they are doing and why they are doing it. If you confronted them with this, they would blankly deny it and feel that they were advanced students who were only wanting to do the best for the organization. As has been said for good reason: "The road to hell is paved with good intentions."

The serpents in spiritual movements

When you have an organization that has a messenger that is sponsored by the ascended masters, and the organization is bringing forth teachings directly from the ascended masters in the form of dictations, does it not stand to reason that this organization becomes a primary target for the false hierarchy? What do they do? They send their representatives into that organization, and they often come being very willing to serve and do something. They are willing to make great sacrifices and do a lot of work, and the question you face as a leader is: "Can you even build and run an organization without having people who are willing to sacrifice, willing to do the work, willing to put forth the effort?"

I am not saying there is only one answer to that question, but it is a question you face. In my case, I had vowed to allow these students to come into the organization, and this was done for a variety of reasons. One was to give them an opportunity to either grow or to receive their judgment, but the other was to give those who were not trapped in the fallen consciousness an opportunity to discern.

It was said that our community in Montana was Maitreya's Mystery School come again. Well, what happened in Maitreya's Mystery School, as hinted at in the Book of Genesis? There was a serpent in the garden, was there not? It was the serpent who tempted and deceived Eve into eating the forbidden fruit. What does the serpent represent: Those who appear to be normal and benign people but who are trapped in the fallen consciousness and therefore are more attuned to the false hierarchy than to the ascended masters.

How do you pass the initiations in Maitreya's Mystery School? Well, why did you leave Maitreya's Mystery School in the first place? Because you listened to the serpent! You could not discern the unreality of the serpent's temptation, for you did not have sufficient sense of the reality of Maitreya's instructions. How do you then re-enter the mystery school and come into oneness with Maitreya? You must overcome the temptation of the serpent, and how do you overcome this? By encountering people who are the modern-day representatives of the serpent, the serpentine consciousness. You must meet these people in the flesh. They must seem to be completely benign, they must seem to be just spiritual students like you, or even to be more advanced spiritual students than you.

What is not depicted accurately in the Book of Genesis is that the serpent did not appear as a serpent. This is all symbolism. In reality, those who were in the serpentine consciousness appeared as any other being in the mystery school, but they often appeared to be the more advanced, the more sophisticated, the more mature. From a certain perspective, they *were* more advanced, more sophisticated, more mature. They had fallen a long time ago, and they had become very, very sophisticated in using the duality consciousness to deceive and manipulate others.

Do you see that in order to function as Maitreya's Mystery School come again, we had to allow these students to come into the organization and even attain leadership positions in the organization. This was the only way that those of you who were not trapped in the fallen consciousness – but were certainly affected by the fallen consciousness – could be given the test of discerning without having any outer indication of what you were meant to discern.

Why the guru cannot tell you what the test is

Do you think I could have told you this while I was still in embodiment? Where would be the test if you were told what the test is, which people are in the fallen consciousness and which are not? The test of discernment must be faced by you in the state of consciousness you are in. The guru can put you in a situation where you face this test, but the guru cannot tell you how to pass the test. You failed the test by turning your back on the guru, and you must retake the test on your own by overcoming the consciousness that caused you to turn away from the guru. This I could not tell you when I was yet unascended, but I *can,* by the law and the grace, tell you this from the ascended state so that you have a more full understanding of what you faced if you were a member of my church.

As I said, you cannot allow these people trapped in the fallen consciousness to make major decisions. You have to allow them to be in leadership positions, but you cannot allow them to make the big decisions for it would destroy the organization. I sat there and faced the dilemma that I had to make the biggest decisions. I simply could not trust that some of those in leadership positions could make the right decisions. That is why I became a bottleneck and many decisions were not made or were not made in a timely manner.

Certainly, this was a hindrance to the growth of the organization, a limitation on the functioning of the organization, but it was a necessary phase. The question for any spiritual organization of any size is how it deals with the fact that it will attract people in the fallen consciousness and that these people will seek to attain leadership positions in the organization.

Here, in the beginning stages of the Age of Aquarius, this is the central question for spiritual organizations. It is a question that is not faced by most of them, and this will cause them to either not grow or to go through a phase of severe power struggles that will ruin many of them. With the teachings of the ascended masters, one would say that students have the *knowledge* of how to deal with this issue but do they have the *will* to deal with it—*that* is another question? You will see in my own church what happened after my retirement. I had set in motion a plan for liberating the church from its former organizational culture and structure. I had set in motion a plan for opening it up more, decentralizing control.

An Aquarian form of leadership

What you see here is another organizational dilemma. You will see that if you go back in time, the primary form of leadership of nations was that there was one king or emperor who had almighty power. Even today, you see this in many nations. This system can function if the leader has some attunement to the ascended masters and therefore can be guided by the masters. If the leader is not trapped in the fallen consciousness, then a totalitarian system with one undisputed leader can actually function very efficiently. When that leader is trapped in the fallen consciousness, then the totalitarian system can produce absolute disaster, as you have also seen in history and even today.

The question for the ascended masters is: "What is the next step up from these centralized forms of leadership? What is the more Aquarian form of leadership?" Well, it is democracy where you spread the responsibility so that one person cannot make all of the decisions. Some decisions are made by the broader body, such as the parliament or the congress, but other decisions must be made by all of the people voting on the issue. This was what I desired to see for the church because it was an Aquarian model.

Has it come to pass? You decide for yourself! You decide whether the movement I started was undermined by a small group of people who could not let go of their old state of consciousness and who therefore started to turn things back towards more centralized control. You decide whether there were power struggles, you decide where the church is at today compared to the track that I set it on and compared to the vision of the ascended masters.

The challenge of recognizing a new messenger

How will you truly know whether the church is in alignment with the vision of the ascended masters if you do not have a functioning messenger? Surely, you can have some of the leaders who have attunement with the ascended masters, but you can be fairly sure that some of the leaders also have attunement with the false hierarchy, even though they will claim they are getting their instructions from the ascended masters.

How do you resolve this if you do not have a sponsored messenger? Why do you not have a sponsored messenger? Is it because some have set themselves up as the judges, saying there can be no future messenger, or *this* person cannot be a messenger and *that* person cannot be a messenger? No one can live up to the criteria that we have defined, for we have decided that we are the ones who will define the criteria.

It was my intention to leave my church with a sponsored messenger, but this was subject to the free will of the people who had the potential to become a sponsored messenger. Given their free-will choices, it did not happen. This was not necessarily a loss in the sense that it simply provided the organization and its members with a new initiation.

Would they be able to open themselves to having a new messenger, even though it was not a messenger authorized by the previous one? It still remains to be seen whether the organization will pass this initiation or fail it. The I AM Movement failed it, the Bridge to Freedom failed it, the Roerich Society failed it, other organizations that have had some degree of sponsorship failed it. In all fairness, it is not an easy initiation to pass.

Why am I giving these dictations through a messenger who is not acknowledged by my own church? Well, partly because no messenger is acknowledged by my own church so through whom could I speak? Partly because it has to be easy for the members of my own church to deny the validity of these dictations. This is part of their test. Let me state that this messenger has no ambition of becoming a messenger for my church; neither do we of the ascended masters have that ambition. This is not to say that there are not other people who could become sponsored messengers for my church so that it could continue to have the delivery of the Living Word.

Of course, this is a difficult initiation. You would not want a person in a position as messenger who is still so trapped in the fallen consciousness that he or she receives messages from the false hierarchy impostors rather than from the real ascended masters. Surely, I understand the dilemma. I also understand that, given the state of consciousness of the students, this is the test you are facing. You have – by your own state of consciousness – created the test, as we all have created our tests with our own state of consciousness. It is *your* test to face—or *not* to face if you so choose.

I know full well how easy it will be for those who have been or are part of my own church to deny, denounce and explain away these dictations. I have deliberately made it easier for you by making certain statements that are so far away from what I said while I was in embodiment that it becomes easy to reject them as something that Mother or Guru Ma would never have said.

This is part of your test. I can only leave you with the test that you have created for yourself by clinging to your current state of consciousness. I have no other option, for I am not allowed to give any signs and wonders. Plausible deniability must be maintained, such is the law based on the current state of the collective consciousness.

21 | THE LAST STEPS TOWARDS THE ASCENSION

Now I would shift gears and return to my opening remarks about being the open door. How do you become the open door? By becoming *open,* meaning you have no preconceived opinions and expectations about how the light of your I AM Presence should flow through you, where it should go, what effect it should have, what form it should take.

How will you pass your tests? I know that even I created the image that when you are facing a test there was a certain outer result that had to be produced. I thought there was only one right way to pass the test, but it is not so.

There are situations where there are two options and you must choose one or the other. One can indeed be not constructive, and only one leads to constructive, ongoing growth. Nevertheless, attachment to outcome, expectations about an outcome, will cause you to fail the test.

What is the greater test? Is it that you produce a specific result that you can grasp, that you have defined with the outer mind? Or is it that you transcend the outer mind, expectations and standards and become simply the open door for the Presence? You are not knowing what the Presence will do, not having any expectations, demands or desires about what the Presence should or should not do through you. You have no expectations about what is the only right outcome, you are open to any outcome, you are open to the Presence doing something that your outer mind cannot even fathom. *This* is being the open door.

There is a part of you that will rebel against this statement. Your ego and your outer mind will desperately want to cling to the idea that there must be an outer standard, an outcome that is the right one, that is the one mandated by God or the ascended masters.

Many paths lead to the ascension

If you look at an organization, there must be some way that this organization should be and should evolve according to the plan of the ascended masters. Yes, there is, but there is not just one way that an organization could evolve.

What did I say in my last discourse? If you look at the situation on earth, you see an incredible complexity of all of these energy connections. What you need to realize, on the higher stages of the path to the ascension, is that there is not just one path that you can personally follow towards your ascension. There are several paths to your ascension. In fact, one could say that there are infinite variations on the path that you can follow towards your ascension.

Certainly, there are many paths that lead you away from the ascension as well. That is why I have said that there is a phase where you must avoid having your attention drawn into all these blind allies that take you away from the ascension. You must be very focused and have a vessel that can carry you through the turbulent waves.

When you get through, you need to open yourself up to the potential that there is more than one way to walk towards your ascension. If you do not, you will remain trapped by an outer path defined by the outer mind. If you are not open to there being different ways, different paths to follow, how can you be open to your I AM Presence?

How will you make the last steps to your ascension? How will you pass the last initiations? You cannot pass them through the outer mind. You cannot pass them by sitting there with the outer mind and determining: "Yes, this is the test, these are my options and this is the only right option. This is how the ascended masters want me to walk my path." *That is not how it works.*

At the higher stages, you pass the tests by looking at your reaction to the situation, by looking at what that says about the elements of the fallen consciousness, the consciousness of separation, that you have left in your being. Then you see those elements, you consciously transcend them. When you have transcended this element, you do not immediately shift into another way to define your path.

You are floating. You are just open and you allow the Presence to flow through you. Then you simply flow with the Presence. You are not deciding with the outer mind where the Presence should or should not take you, you are flowing with the Presence.

Flowing with the River of Life

You could compare your path to a river. I have talked about the Sea of Samsara and the big waves, but let us shift to another visual image. You are in a little boat that has a rudder and you are floating down the river. If you turn the rudder, you change the course of your boat.

You may look back at your life and you may see that in a past lifetime, or even in this lifetime, you made a decision that turned your rudder and put you on a distinctly different course than the one you were on before. You may see that this led to a very unpleasant situation where you crashed into a rock in the river.

You may have regrets and you may say: "I wish I had never done that." As I have tried to explain to you, it was a choice you made and whatever happened was simply an event. *It was what it was.* The important thing is how you can learn from your reaction to the event. The event itself is unimportant; it is your *reaction* that reveals your consciousness and gives you an opportunity to transcend that consciousness.

What happens when you float down the river and you bump into a rock with your little boat? Well, it is unpleasant at the time, but pretty soon your boat drifts past the rock and now it is flowing down the river again. This is what is important on the path: Not what happened, not where you went, not what you bumped into but that you are still flowing down the river.

As long as you are flowing down the river, what can you easily do? You can turn the rudder on your boat! You may see that back there you turned the rudder and took a different direction than what you now realize is the ideal path. Then just turn your rudder and get back towards the ideal path, or at least a better path, according to your current vision.

There is no turn of the rudder that cannot be undone by turning the rudder again. As long as you are flowing down the river, as long as you have momentum, a turn of the rudder will change the course of your boat. Really, does it matter so much whether the stern of your boat is going in this or that direction? Does it matter which direction you are going in, which direction the bow of your boat is pointed in, when you are still flowing down the river?

Overcoming the attachment to outcome

The attachment to outcome is the biggest hindrance for students on the higher levels of the path. At lower levels the attachment to outcome is what carries you through the Sea of Samsara and the rough waves. You have to be focused on making it through, and that is why you are fixated on an outer teaching and an outer set of practices. You keep practicing them until you have made it through.

You cannot keep practicing them forever for they will not carry you to the ascended state. You have to be in attunement and know when it is time to take a different approach to the path. I have attempted, in these previous discourses, to do everything I can think of, at my current level of ascended consciousness, to help you make this shift to the higher levels of the path.

I am doing this for those of my own students who have followed the path that I gave while I was in embodiment and have gone as far as they can go on it. I am also doing it for the many other people who might find this book and who have followed another guru and gone as far as they can go with that guru.

I am offering you an on-ramp to the higher stages of the spiritual path where you no longer follow an outer guru. You follow the inner guru of your Christ self and your ascended teachers. When you come to the point where you have gone as far as you can go with these outer-inner gurus, you realize that beyond any guru is the I AM Presence who, as I said, is not your guru. The Presence is *you!*

The higher stages of the path are those of oneness with the Presence, and the more oneness you can attain while you are still in embodiment, the more of an open door you will become and the more of a positive impact you will have on this planet. You will not become fully one with your Presence as long as you are in embodiment because just maintaining a physical body requires that some of your attention goes into and through the body. You *can* attain a high degree of oneness with the Presence. The ultimate state of oneness with the Presence will not come until you ascend, and then you are no longer in embodiment. You do not have a focus in the material realm that can be an open door for the Presence.

The ascension is the ultimate form of service

This does not mean that you are not giving service by ascending. Once you ascend, you actually see what an incredible service to planet earth you have given by ascending. You see the Antahkarana, the web of energy connections, you have with so many people on earth. You may think: "Oh, I am just an ordinary person who only knows my family and friends and a few co-workers." You have been in many different lifetimes and many different places on the earth. You have energy connections to a large number of people, and all of these people will feel an upward pull when you ascend. They may not notice this consciously, but it will be there and it will help to pull up the whole.

In my case, I was more of a public person. Millions of people had heard about me. Anybody who had heard about me, even if it was in a negative context, was pulled upward when I ascended. Yes, the ascension *is* the ultimate service you can give on earth, but before you ascend you have the option, you have the potential, to focus on oneness with the I AM Presence as the all-consuming goal. The greater the sense of oneness with the Presence you can attain, the more you become an open door for the Presence.

What I am saying here is that there are two ways to give service. One is to be an open door for light flowing from the spiritual realm into the material. The other way is to become a magnetic pull that pulls up on the Antahkarana of life. You are doing both as you are walking the spiritual path, but there is a limit to how much of an upward pull you can create while you are still in embodiment. There is, however, not so much of a limit to how much light you can let flow through you if you attain a high degree of oneness with the Presence.

When you do ascend, even though you no longer have a focus for light to flow through into the physical, you still create such an upward magnetic pull that it pulls everyone up so much higher than any other service you could give. Both are valid, both are needed, both are necessary. The ideal is that as you are walking the last steps towards the ascension, you become an open door for the Presence that can allow maximum light to flow through. Then, when you ascend, the light that has flown through you will form an even stronger magnetic, upward pull than if the light had not flown through you or had flown through you in lesser measure. You see the push and pull, the inbreath and the outbreath of God. A magnificent tapestry, *an absolutely incredible tapestry.*

What you see after you ascend

When you ascend, you see the intricacy, the complexity and yet the underlying simplicity of God's creation. I tell you that when you leave the body behind – when you leave the unascended consciousness, the separate self, behind for the last time – and you walk through that doorway to the ascended state, it is as if worlds within worlds begin to open up. Surely, the experience is a little bit different for everyone, but I tell you that after I left the earth behind fully and finally, I went through a period where I was simply so overwhelmed and overawed by the beauty and complexity and yet simplicity of God's creation that I spent some time just praising God, expressing my incredible admiration for the beauty of creation.

As I did this, every time I would express appreciation for what I saw, I would see more. Then I would be overawed and express my admiration for that, and I would see greater vistas. This went on; it was like wave upon wave upon wave. It was such an expansion of myself, my sense of self, that after some time I knew exactly what Lanello meant when he said through me: "*I AM everywhere in the consciousness of God!*" Back then, I could not quite fathom what he meant, for how can you fathom it until you experience it, and you cannot experience it until you are ascended.

I went through this period of just the expansion of self until I literally felt: "I AM everywhere in the consciousness of God." Then I was able to again begin to contract and realize that even though I had experienced being everywhere in the consciousness of God, I was still far from being one with my Creator, being at the level of the Creator consciousness. I was, after all, only a newly ascended master from earth, and I had a long way to go until I attained that full Creator consciousness.

I then came back in the sense of self of being a newly ascended master, and I have since then continued to grow from there, to consolidate my sense of consciousness, to look at the options I have and to decide where I want to go, what I want to do, how I want to serve in this unfolding of the most wondrous creation one could ever imagine.

What an incredible Creator we have. What an incredible Being that envisioned, that imagined, that "I-magicked" this incredible creation of which we are a part.

Wonders within wonders!

What an incredible opportunity to be a self-aware being who is part of this most wondrous creation. Such beauty in the ascended realm, but you can sense that beauty from the unascended state by becoming an open door for the beauty of your I AM Presence to flow through you.

I have truly no other wish for you.

I have no other wish for the many people who heard about me in my last embodiment than that they would become an open door for their own I AM Presence. Your I AM Presence is the ultimate beauty that you can fathom from the unascended state. You can experience your Presence, but you cannot experience your Presence from a distance. You can experience your Presence only by becoming the open door for the Presence to flow through you while you are yet unascended.

You experience the Presence only by experiencing the light of the Presence flowing through you in whatever way you see yourself. It is only when you ascend that you experience yourself as *being* the Presence and you are no longer experiencing separation. There is no light flowing through you. You *are* the light and you are the Presence from which it radiates.

I have given you everything that my heart desires to give you at this point, in what you call time and space, but which I see as the ongoing River of Life. Who knows what the future will hold? Before more can be given, that which has been given must be internalized by a critical mass of people to a critical degree.

More than giving you further teachings, I desire to greet you when you step through to the ascended realm. If you have read this book up until this point, I can assure you that I will be there along with the other ascended masters who are your personal teachers.

I am not seeking to hurry you on, for many of you have much to contribute to life on earth before you ascend. I *am* seeking to give you the vision that the path to the ascension is worth the inconvenience, *any* inconvenience.

You will know this fully only after you ascend and experience for yourself what an incredible joy it is to know: "Yes, I AM an ascended master!"

I AM the Ascended Master Guru Ma, and it is an infinite joy to be *that* I AM.

22 | WHAT IT FEELS LIKE TO ASCEND

NOTE: *The following three dictations were given before the previous dictations in this book. They were the first dictations given by the Ascended Master Guru Ma through this messenger. Although the following dictations touch on some of the same topics, they are included here in order to give a complete picture of what Guru Ma wants to convey at this time.*

Being a messenger for the ascended masters is no simple task. I know this well, for I used to be a messenger in embodiment, serving for many years in an organization with which some of you are familiar.

I ascended on July 4th, 2012. My ascended name is the Ascended Master Guru Ma, the name given to me while still in embodiment by Padmasambhava. I come simply to let you know that I have ascended, to give you some insight into what it feels like to be a newly ascended master and the contrast you have between being a person in embodiment and being ascended.

I wish I could share with you the immense joy that you feel when you stand there before that doorway, that pearly gate. You see that in the doorway is standing Serapis Bey, smiling as no one on earth could possibly smile. Behind him stands the ascended being closest to you – in my case, you know of whom I speak – and then other ascended masters who are ready to welcome you.

A dispensation and an opportunity

Before you can go through that doorway, my beloved, you must pause, you must turn around and take a long look at this planet we call earth. You must look long and hard to see: "Is there anything on this planet to which I am in any way attached?" Everyone who has ever ascended must go through this last initiation. You stand there and you must look into your own mind and being. You must look like you have never looked before and you must see everything that there could be to see.

If you have *any* attachment, you cannot make the voluntary choice to walk through the doorway to the ascended state. How can you when at this point you recognize the fullness of the Law of Free Will? If you discover an attachment, you must pause, you must look at it and you must evaluate: "Can I fully let it go, or do I actually, honestly, sincerely want to re-embody in order to live out whatever attachment I have?"

Do you know what is the hardest part of this initiation? It is precisely that the very service that you gave in your last embodiment – the very service that actually enabled you to balance your karma, fulfill your divine plan and fulfill these so-called outer requirements for the ascension – this very service is the one to which you might have unrecognized attachments.

Ah, how easy it is when you have served long and hard – when you have labored through much opposition, when you have given your all, sacrificed your all in service as best you could see it – how easy it is, my beloved, to develop an attachment to seeing a result of your labor and your service. This is potentially the most subtle and difficult initiation you will face on your path to the ascension. I certainly had to face it. Lanello had to face it, but he could not even warn me that I would face this initiation, for he saw that I already had attachments to seeing results of my service. Thus, I had to face this initiation without any outer guidance.

Do you understand that this is one of the reasons why I manifested an outer disease that caused me to withdraw from the organization to which I had given so much while still remaining in embodiment? You can look at the date I officially retired [in 1999] and you can count up to July 4, 2012, and you will see how long it took me to let go of all attachments, especially the attachments to my service.

Why am I telling you this when even Lanello was not allowed to warn me about this initiation? I am telling you this because I asked for a dispensation to be allowed to give this teaching so that others might work on these attachments before they leave embodiment. It is so much easier to overcome your attachments while you are still in embodiment, still have the clarity of mind, and still have the ability to work with other people. You can ask for their forgiveness where you have wronged and harmed them, ask that they understand you and what you were going through. Thus, I give you this opportunity from my heart.

The role of a spiritual leader in Pisces

This messenger was perfectly honest when he said that while he sat at my feet, so to speak, listening to dictation after dictation, he never had a desire to be in my position. Neither does he still have that desire, for the position I held was indeed an out-playing of the consciousness of Pisces and the tendency for people to have idolatry of spiritual leaders. I did speak of this. I did speak of this, but few heard me, and thus I would bow to their free will and allow them to project upon me.

I would bow to such an extent that I actually allowed myself to conform to that role. The hints were there for those who were willing to see them so that they could have transcended their idolatry no matter how formidable I might have appeared in my outer form. I say this with a glimpse of the humor that Lanello and I share. Although I did not share his humor fully while I was in physical embodiment, I certainly do share it now. I might say that I was indeed a very formidable guru, yet this was not without a purpose. It was partly because I had things to overcome from past lifetimes but also because many of the people who came to me had things to overcome.

There comes a point on the spiritual path where you realize that all form is but a mirage, that it is all camouflage, and you need to see beyond form to see the deeper reality. I would humbly ask that anyone who knew me in the past would be willing to look beyond the outer form that I took on and instead connect to the reality of who I am, to what is my spiritual flame as an ascended master.

Using a guru as an example

Did I show that flame while in embodiment? Indeed, I did. Many tuned in to it, many can tune in to it again today. Some have never lost their attunement to that spiritual flame, and those I truly honor for you are dear to my heart. This messenger many times would sit and absorb the flame that I truly am, and that once in a while would shine through the disguise of the "formidable guru." He saw behind the outer appearances, at least he saw that I AM beyond the outer appearances. His initiation was whether he could transcend his own involvement with my organization and not seek to emulate, but seek to transcend. This is the initiation you all face.

It is necessary, it is good, to have an example of a person who has been willing to become the open door for the ascended masters. It can be extremely valuable for you to have such an example because it helps you connect to the reality of the masters, but there are two problems.

One is that you elevate this person to an idol and think that this person can do something you cannot do. Have not the masters for many years said: "What one has done, all can do?" Certainly, not all of you have in your divine plans that you should stand in front of a group of people and let an ascended master speak through you. That is why you need to consider the second initiation that there are many ways to serve as open doors for the ascended masters. You do not all need to do what I did or what this messenger is doing, nor do you need to do it the same way. You have your own individual expression and this is the Aquarian potential. In the Piscean age, one of the main initiations was indeed conforming to some form of authority or structure on earth. In the Aquarian age it will be to transcend form and authority and be the open door for that which is beyond form and has no earthly authority other than the authority of the Light.

You all have a potential to serve for the remainder of this lifetime. Your service might indeed, if you apply yourselves, bring you to the point where you can ascend if you pass this last initiation. Your service can potentially become the millstone around your neck that prevents you from letting go of earth for there is still some result you want to see manifest.

Using a guru creatively

Dare to look at my life. I sacrificed everything in the service of the ascended masters, as I saw it at the time. Could I have seen more? Could I have seen it differently? Certainly, I can see it differently today. Many things I would have done differently; many, many things my beloved. First of all, my children I would have given more attention.

All any of us can do is do the best we can, based on the vision we have. If you want to do better than this, consider the necessity of always seeking to expand and transcend your current vision. Do the best you can according to your current vision, but do not continue to do the same things based on the same vision. Seek to transcend the vision so that you may see what you do not see today. This is the deeper meaning of the saying: "The reward for service is more service;" not more in volume but more in creativity, a higher vision of how to serve.

This is where many of my former students have become stuck, for they have accepted a pattern and they think they need to continue the pattern. They think that in order to remain loyal to me or to the ascended masters, they need to continue the pattern. If you truly want to be loyal to me, recognize that I have ascended only by transcending the consciousness I had when I was instrumental in you making the choice to accept the current pattern.

Notice my use of words. I did *not* – whatever you might project at me – force you to accept a certain pattern. I simply confirmed what you projected with your own consciousness, and that is what was one of my primary roles. Ponder this carefully, if you want to truly understand what various masters meant when they said that in the ascended realm I am considered a "guru among gurus."

I did not teach in the obvious way. Many of my actions and teachings were enigmas, riddles, that must be solved by looking beyond form. Many of the things I said and did were things you should *not* do. Many of the rules I gave were rules you should *not* follow—but not all. The challenge is to discern which ones to follow, which ones to go beyond. However, *that,* my beloved is *your* challenge, not *mine,* for I played my role to the best of my ability.

Letting go of your role

Could the teachings have been made more plain? Indeed, they could be made more plain, but they could not have been made more plain *at the time*. This is another attachment. You stand there, at the end of a long life of service. You see the organization that you created, you see how many people have come with sincere hearts and have applied the teachings and the tools you gave to the best of their ability. You also see that they have not transcended their consciousness.

You wish you could make the teaching more plain, more easy for them to grasp and understand. You wish you could go back and explain all the things that you could not explain at the time because *they* were not ready for it, *you* were not ready for it, *the planet* was not ready for it. This can also become a subtle attachment. You wish that you could give an ultimate teaching, but no ultimate teaching will ever be given on earth.

A teaching is just a tool for transcendence. For those who are not willing to look beyond the teaching and transcend, it becomes a trap just like the mainstream religions. You wish you could help your students see this, truly see it in their hearts. The reality is that you cannot make anyone see what they are not willing to see. You cannot *force* anyone to ascend, it must be the result of free-will choices. As Saint Germain has said, he had to make a million of them. These were not choices that were right or wrong, they were choices to transcend the old state of consciousness, the old vision, the old beliefs—even what you have come to believe was some ultimate or superior truth.

I gave the teaching that could be given through me, as I was, as the student body was and as the planet was at the time. Some of the teachings given through me were so high that it might be decades or centuries before a greater number of people will be able to decode the subtle messages. This is something you have to accept.

You have to give birth to the teaching, give birth to the organization. You nurture it, you nourish it, you see it grow. Then there comes a point where you must set it free. You must be like a child who has lovingly created a small model boat, as my father helped me do when I was a little girl. There comes that point where you put it in the water, and for a time you want to hold on to it. Then, you give it that last push and it floats out on the surface of the ocean, never to return to you—*never* to return to you, my beloved.

Never is a big word. You will never realize how big of a word it is until you stand before the gate that leads to the ascended state and you know that when you leave the earth, you will *never* come back. There is nothing you can do further on earth. You may do things from the ascended state but that is an entirely different thing than being in embodiment.

An incredible opportunity to be in embodiment

Most of you do not fully appreciate what an incredible opportunity it is to be in embodiment on earth and to have a physical body where you can get into someone's face and tell them things that they cannot ignore. Do you know how many times ascended masters stand before people in embodiment with the best of intentions of helping them? From the ascended state – as I have done this now for a year – we are standing there saying: "Will you listen to me?"

People cannot hear us physically, but when you are in a physical body, my beloved, you can go up and look someone straight in the eye and say: "Will you listen!" They can at least hear you. They still may not be willing to listen, but at least they have heard you and that is a good opportunity to have if you use it wisely. It is another thing, by the way, that you have to let go of in order to ascend. You do know that the moment you walk through that door, you do not have a physical body so that people can hear you.

My beloved, appreciate what you have while you are in embodiment, *appreciate what you have.* Do not appreciate it so much that it becomes another attachment, but appreciate it while you have it. Indeed, there comes that point where you have to choose: "Can I let it go?" There are many of you who may think: "I have been in embodiment many times on this earth, I have seen everything there is to see, I am fed up with the struggle, I am tired of these people that will not listen to me." Yet the moment you stand there and realize that now you have to leave this behind *forever,* that is when it dawns on you how wonderful of an opportunity it is to be in a physical body. I wish you would not have to wait until you are out of the body to appreciate having a body, and this is my humble wish for you.

Holding on to an image of Guru Ma

This messenger has for some time, quite frankly, resisted taking this dictation. He has no desire to set himself up and make any claim that a previous organization should acknowledge him or listen to him. I fully understand this. I had the opportunity, while in physical embodiment, to visit Mrs. Ballard, who was at that time a messenger for Saint Germain and the I AM Movement. During my visit, I was in training by Mark to become a messenger. I had the opportunity to tell Mrs. Ballard this, but I had no desire to do so. I saw that she was not ready to acknowledge this, and I had no desire to interfere with her free will, nor to even put down or make her doubt her own service, which was a magnificent example.

It is good not to be attached to recognition from those who are not ready. It is good to know what it truly means that as a guru you can appear only to the students who are ready. This messenger recognizes this; I recognize this as I am giving this dictation through him. Many will not be ready, many will not be ready.

I love you. I love all of you, even if you are not ready to acknowledge that I have moved on, that I am not the Guru Ma that you knew while I was in embodiment. I have transcended that a thousand times a thousand times. Have you transcended your image of me or are you holding on to an image that no longer exists?

Again, I love you even if you have not transcended. I love all who have ever come in contact with the Summit Lighthouse, with Church Universal and Triumphant, with the ascended masters. I have also come to the point of resolution where I see that my role was not to produce a specific result but only to give the opportunity for people to choose, an opportunity that they did not have before they encountered the light of the masters through me.

I have taken this opportunity, I have taken it here because, as you will see, we have a group of people here who honor both the old and the new. Thus, you have earned this dispensation, this dictation.

What it feels like to ascend

Let me end by returning to what I said in the beginning: "I wish I could give you a glimpse of what it feels like to ascend." It is the most incredible feeling when you have looked long and hard at yourself and your attachments, and when you let go of that final ghost, that final attachment. It feels as if the weight of the world is lifted from your shoulders. Truly, the weight of the world *is* lifted from your shoulders because through your attachment you were carrying a certain weight of the world.

If you give the devil one inroad, you get the whole ball of wax, the whole shebang, and through that one attachment you are tied to the entire consciousness of earth. When you let it go, it is such a relief that you feel so light, you feel so free, you feel so transparent. You have looked at yourself and there is nothing you seek to hide from yourself, which is the meaning of transparency, but it is also the meaning of freedom. How can you be free as long as there is something in your self that you are not willing to look at? It is not possible.

You feel so free, so joyful, that you feel like you could rise into the air. You have no weight, and suddenly you realize you *have* risen into the air. You are floating up, up, up, up, up into the ascended realm and there is brighter and brighter light. You are in this tunnel of white light, and suddenly you see, not a light at the end of the tunnel, you actually see a dark point at the end of the tunnel. Not dark as you consider it on earth, but you see something that is not the white light of the ascension for it embodies all of the colors of the rays, even the secret rays.

Then you plunge through that portal, and now you see that the light that you could see, that was not white, was the colors of the Causal Bodies of the ascended beings who are waiting to greet you. You look at them, and even though you don't have a physical body, you still feel like you have the biggest smile you could ever imagine! You are grinning from ear to ear, and there is your beloved Lanello with a grin even bigger than your own—and Master MORE and Saint Germain.

They all greet you, and you realize that for the first time you can fully accept yourself as one of them. You *are* an ascended being! You *are one of us!* That is a greater joy than anything you will ever experience on earth—anything, my beloved.

I am not giving you this to make you now feel like you need to ascend right now for this sounds so wonderful. Remember what I said about the opportunity to be in embodiment. Cherish it while you are here. Cherish it, for you have eternity in the ascended realm, and there is something to be said for time and space, which is why most of us descended in the first place.

What a joy it is to see those whose hearts are opened to the reality of the ascended masters and their own higher beings. What a joy it is, my beloved, what a joy! I greet you in the love of my heart, for *I AM the Ascended Master Guru Ma.*

23 | LETTING GO IN ORDER TO ASCEND

I AM the Ascended Master Guru Ma. You have no idea how good it feels to say that in the physical octave. It is indeed an acknowledgment of the fact that another human being has walked the path of the ascension and has proven the validity of this path, even the person who was much maligned and misunderstood while in embodiment.

"Beautiful Dreamer" is a beautiful song. While you are in embodiment it is often necessary for us to be a dreamer, to dream about something that clearly is not yet manifest and to pursue this goal with all due diligence of one's heart, mind and physical body. Yet you do not win your ascension by being a dreamer, you do not win your ascension by holding on to the dreams you had on earth. As I said in my previous release, you have to let go of *everything* on earth, even your dreams.

In a sense, my beloved, what is a dream but a mental image that confirms the illusion that there is a separation between you and what you see in the dream? The dream is just a dream and not reality. You do not ascend as long as you see a separation between yourself and the ascended state. You do not ascend by dreaming about ascending but only by coming to the point where you can look at yourself and recognize that you have looked at everything in your own being. You have let it go, you have dismissed it, you have dissolved it, you have resolved it and there is now nothing that the prince of this world can use to get you to react.

That is when you can come to that final point of acceptance: "I AM worthy to ascend." *That,* I tell you, is a difficult initiation for we all carry with us that sense of unworthiness. It has been put upon us by the fallen beings through so many lifetimes that it is almost impossible not to begin to believe it, at least at some level of your being.

Transcending unworthiness

If you will look at my life when I was a messenger for the ascended masters, you may see that I was working very hard, that I was very determined, that I left no stone unturned. I did everything I could possibly think of to do the work for the ascended masters as I could see it. When you are in the ascension spiral, you have to look at everything. I came to the realization that much of my striving, much of my hard work, much of my determination actually came from the fact that at a deep level of my being I did not consider myself fully worthy, fully worthy to be one with God, fully worthy to be a messenger for the ascended masters.

This is what I wish to discourse with you on because you all have to face this initiation. The earlier you begin to ponder it, the better is the possibility that you will pass the initiation before you leave embodiment. If you can pass this initiation before you leave embodiment, then you can give a much greater service than you can give while you still carry this heavy burden of unworthiness. When I look back at my life, I see how I carried the seed with me from past lifetimes, but my physical father in that last lifetime was very much instrumental in reinforcing the momentum.

Why did I carry this seed? Because I had in certain past lifetimes been in important positions of leadership and made serious mistakes. My father, God bless him, reinforced this momentum, not out of a conscious, deliberate, evil intent but simply because he was trapped in his own psychology. This is a situation that many of you will recognize from your own lives and your own parents. How many of you can say that you did not have parents that in some way reinforced the tendencies in your own psychology? I hope you can all say this for thereby you acknowledge an important fact: Your parents could only reinforce what was already in your psychology. They did not have the power to put something there that was not there. When you acknowledge this and you acknowledge free will, you can begin to free yourself from it.

Much more to say about the path

The path is a most wondrous process! If you go back to the teachings released through Mark and myself, you can find so many things said about the spiritual path. Then you can go even further back through previous ascended master teachings – through Geraldine, the Ballards, the Roerichs and even Blavatsky – and you can find other things said about the path, and you might ask yourself: "How much more could be said?" Then look at the teachings given through this messenger in a relatively short span of years about the ego, about the duality consciousness, about perception filters and see that so much more has been said than whatever was said before. Yet do not think that this is the final teaching that can or will be given. There are other layers: higher, deeper, more intricate levels of teachings about the path that can be given. It is an incredible process, an infinitely complex process, and I say this with the admiration that you have in the ascended realm.

I realize that when you are in embodiment, it is difficult to look at the complexities of your own path and look at this with admiration for you are going from one thing to another. I do not agree with many things that Winston Churchill said or did, but he did say: "War is just one damn thing after another." There are some times when we all feel that the path is just one damn thing after another. Is it not so?

It is difficult to see this while you are in embodiment, and that is why I desire to give you the perspective that when you ascend – or when you depersonalize your path before you leave the body – then you can see how wondrous it all is. This actually becomes a foundation for doing what is extremely important in order to transcend the past, namely forgiving.

Forgiveness is imperative

How did I deal with my father in my last lifetime while I was going through my ascension process? I had to forgive him unconditionally. I had to look at my past lifetimes and I had to forgive all people who had ever harmed me. I even had to look at this last lifetime and see how many people came to me in my capacity as a messenger and – deliberately, maliciously, subtly and with the serpentine mindset – attempted to hurt me, damage me or derail my service, derail my path.

My beloved, many of you have in past lifetimes, and even in this lifetime, volunteered to embody in very difficult situations where you dealt with people who had very severe momentums of various kinds of abuse. You did this in order to give them an opportunity to abuse you so that you might help enlighten them by reacting in a more loving manner than they expected. If that was not possible, you might bring about their judgment. I volunteered to play this role for a very large number of lifestreams.

I continued this vow almost through the end of my messengership. I can look back and I can see that I met tens of thousands of people who came to me with an impure intent. Some were projecting their own momentums as they would have done against any authority figure, it just happened to be me who was the target. Others came deliberately or were sent deliberately by dark forces to attempt to destroy me by inserting some thought, some feeling in my mind and being that would cause me to react negatively, possibly even just give up on being a messenger.

Do you know that one of the hardest things to experience on earth is when you have a dream of how much better life could be, yet people constantly reject it, ridicule it, put it down. Is it not difficult, my beloved? You need to realize that it was no different for me. I was exposed to it in a greater measure than most people because I had a public service and I met many, many people. I am telling you this in order to let you know that there comes a point where you see that this is simply part of the path—not only for you, but for all lifestreams embodying on earth.

You may look at many situations, and you may start with the analytical mind saying: "How could this happen, why are people doing this or why does God allow it to happen?" You can analyze, and analyze and analyze until you are fed up with analyzing. You can also step away from the analytical mind and realize that the analytical mind can never resolve this enigma. In your heart you can come to see that it is simply part of the cosmic dance for planet earth.

In reality, the outer event is not significant at all. When you begin to grasp this and when you begin to internalize this, you can truly come to see that even though someone comes to you with a deliberate intent of hurting you, what they are doing is not actually personal against you. They are either outplaying their own momentums and you don't really matter to them, or they are reacting against the light that you carry, for which you are the open door. When you recognize this, you can avoid some of these negative personal feelings where you feel a sense of injustice, a sense that this should not be happening to me when I have done nothing to these people.

Forgiving yourself

There were people I met in my last lifetime with whom I had karma from past lifetimes, perhaps because I was a queen who made decisions that affected many thousands of people. In such cases, I had to recognize that even though I made that decision in a lifetime long ago, I am no longer the same person. I have transcended the consciousness I had in that lifetime, and therefore I still do not need to take this personally. I do need to allow that person to either express it or even to be part of my staff, my family or in other ways be close to them and allow them to come up with various patterns that are strictly speaking abusive, but it is something *they* need to work out. They need to be given that opportunity so that they can come to the point where they can be free from me by doing the only thing that can set them free, namely forgiving me.

It is also my task not to look at them and react negatively and build on to a spiral so that I forgive them for what they are doing to me in this lifetime, and I forgive myself for what I did to them in a past lifetime. This applies to all of you, all of us, while we are in embodiment. Even those with whom you do not have karma, and who simply come to attack you, even those you need to forgive if you want to be free of them. If you can do this while you are still in embodiment, perhaps even while you are still being exposed to the abuse of these people, then not only will the rest of your lifetime be easier but you will also render an important service.

If you forgive someone who is abusing you, what do you do? You bring down the judgment of God upon the person who continues to abuse you even though you meet them only with forgiveness. If I had been able to fully master this, I would have made my life much easier. I would have made it easy for me to come to the point where I could forgive myself so that I could let go of my sense of unworthiness before God.

One of the most insidious effects of the serpentine mindset is indeed that we have the image of the remote God who is angry, who is condemning us or who looks upon us as not being worthy because we do not live up to the standard defined by the fallen beings. We think that it is God who thinks that we are not worthy, but in reality the only reason why we are not worthy is that we have not fully forgiven ourselves. We dare not look at God because we think that as long as we are not worthy, if we looked at God, we would somehow be burned.

The ascended masters do not shame you

My beloved, be honest with yourself and see how many of you, when you first came in contact with the ascended masters' teachings, had exactly this feeling. Some master, it might be Serapis Bey or it might be El Morya – who in his incarnation, so to speak, as El Morya certainly was more strict and was portrayed as being more strict than he is today – reinforced this image. You might have looked at the old picture of El Morya, and you might have thought: "If I really met him, I would burn up with shame or fear. He would see right through me, he would point out all my shortcomings. I would end up feeling so unworthy that I would have to crawl into a hole and stay there for three more lifetimes."

I, myself, felt that way when I met Mark and was introduced to the ascended masters. I sometimes felt that way when I dealt with Mark, who could be quite strict himself despite his genial humor in other situations. Mark had his own psychology, and there were times when he took himself awfully seriously. I tell you, you had better not crack a joke at those times for you would not get a smile back.

We all go through this period where we acknowledge the light of the masters and we sense with co-measurement that we still have impurities in our beings. We think we are not worthy to face the masters, and we project that they are the ones who are so strict, they are the ones who will reject us, criticize us, judge us. I tell you, when you ascend you realize the simple reality: The ascended masters are ascended and they are masters because they have overcome all of this dualistic nonsense of the fallen mindset. They have only love, a love that is beyond conditions.

Accepting yourself for who you are

I could not have brought forth the teachings on unconditional love that have been given through this messenger because I had not forgiven myself to the extent where I could fully accept that God's love is beyond conditions. My deepest wish for all of you is that you, while still in embodiment, would come to the point where you could fully forgive yourselves, where you could fully accept that God and the ascended masters love you with an unconditional, infinite, unbound love. They have only total acceptance, *we* have only total acceptance, of you.

I have only total acceptance for you. I accept you for who you are. I accept all those people I met through my last embodiment. I accept all who worked with me on my staff, all those who met me in the organization whether they accepted or rejected me. I accept all of you with unconditional love.

I accept you even if you reject this messenger and his dictations. You will one day come to the point where, in order to pass through your own ascension spiral, you have to acknowledge the truth of what I am saying. No one ever can ascend while rejecting unconditional love; it is not possible, my beloved.

23 | Letting Go in Order to Ascend

It is one of the hardest lessons for those who have been deceived by the fallen mindset of the remote, angry, judgmental God. The image of the angry God was the image that dominated the Piscean age. I was the last sponsored messenger for the dispensation of Pisces. I had to play a certain role, I had to portray myself – even the ascended masters, even God – a certain way. That was perfectly necessary in order to give a certain amount of people the initiations they needed at the end of Pisces. They might either accept a higher teaching or receive the judgment that would remove them from the earth so that at least future generations would be free of a certain downward pull.

I acknowledge fully that in the process of playing this role there were many gentle, loving lifestreams that came into contact with the organization, with some of the people in the organization or even with myself when I was playing this role, and they were deeply hurt or disturbed by this. I desire to, in the physical realm, set the record straight about unconditional love.

Every organization has its matrix

I was a guru that taught in subtle ways. I played a role. Sometimes, in order to play that role, I had to do things and say things that I would have preferred not to do or say. Other times I was, quite frankly, so caught up in the role that I thought it was perfectly necessary or justified to give that person such a discipline. In a sense it *was* necessary, for when you enter embodiment you are subject to the Law of Free Will.

When you enter a spiritual organization, you are subject to the pattern, the matrix, set for that organization. I happened to be the figurehead that in some ways was the open door for defining the matrix and in other ways defined it out of my personal psychology, even my higher individuality. I knew certain things had to be done a certain way to give my students the best possible opportunity. I knew certain things had to be done this way because this is who I am. As the leader, I had a perfect right to set a pattern for the organization to which I dedicated my entire life and being.

I am not here to apologize. When you pass through the ascension coil, the spiral, you also overcome the need to apologize for anything. You see that just as what other people did to you was part of the cosmic dance, what you did was also part of the cosmic dance. You did the best you could, given where you were at in consciousness at the time. None of us can do any better. We can strive to transcend our consciousness and therefore do better, but at any given time you are in a certain state of consciousness.

I hope I can inspire you to accept where you are today so you can begin to accept yourself as a chela on the path. You are a person who is on the path, but who is not at the end goal and you are not ready to ascend. You still have a ways to go, but you accept yourself where you are at right now. Then it becomes so much easier for you to look at the unresolved aspects of your psychology without condemning yourselves, without adding to this momentum of unworthiness or thinking God will not forgive you.

Instead, you can realize that God has already forgiven you; it is only up to you to forgive yourself. You cannot forgive yourself until you are free from the decision you made and you cannot be free until you look at it openly and honestly. It is such a simple process, but it is so infinitely difficult to do it when you are looking at the process from inside your current psychology.

What is the ego so good at doing? What are those in the serpentine mind so good at doing? They are so good at complicating everything! They keep you trapped in these infinitely complex patterns so that you do not see how simple the path really is.

I know you can go into the linear mind and say that I am now contradicting what I said earlier when I said there are many levels of teachings that can be given about the intricate layers of the path. There *are* intricate layers of the path, but the process of going from one layer to the next one up is still very simple.

You need to see the decision you made, recognize that *you* made it and therefore you have the perfect right to unmake it by making a different decision. This is the ultimate consequence of free will. You can make any decision you want, but you can also *un*make any decision you have ever made. Do *not* let anyone, including all of the false gurus on earth, tell you any different, for they are lying—all of them. Free will is *free,* limited only by your own previous choices.

My beloved, as you might be beginning to realize by now, it is wonderful for a newly ascended being to have a physical vehicle to speak through and to have an audience who will listen. I could go on for a very long time, but I recognize that there is a time and place for everything. I shall bid you a most fond adieu, and I shall speak again when the opportunity arises.

I give you my gratitude, I give you my gratitude. How wonderful to feel the love from so many people who did not even encounter me in the physical but have such love for the teaching that the ascended masters gave through me and the example, for better or worse, that I set.

With my fondest love!

24 | DARE TO LIVE YOUR OWN LIFE

I AM the Ascended Master Guru Ma, with Lanello. Thank you, our beloved hearts, for the outpouring of love. We then would outpour *our* joy, our joy of seeing that our teachings have been taken by people and used in ways that we could not always imagine while we were still in embodiment. We were so focused on bringing forth the teaching, doing the best we could see, and then not always being as open as we might have been to just letting the teaching go and let people do with it whatever they saw fit in their hearts.

I speak specifically for myself who faced an especially difficult task of suddenly being left alone with four children and a growing spiritual organization to run. After Mark left, there was such a hole in my life that I felt like I was adrift on a raging sea. In order to again get some kind of continuity in my life, I had to have some sense of being in control of life. This caused me to revert to some old momentums from past lives where I had been in leadership positions and thus had the power to institute certain elements of control.

Passing the test of Pisces

I created an organization that was perhaps more structured, more controlled, than it could have been. As I have said before, even *that* was still an expression, not only of my consciousness but the consciousness of the people who were meant to be given certain tests through that organization. There were many people who came and had expectations of how a spiritual organization, an ascended master organization, should function and should be run. It was the last organization to be sponsored in the Age of Pisces, and in Pisces what did people see? They saw these organizations – like the Eastern Orthodox and the Catholic Church and other religious organizations, such as Islam – that were very centralized and controlled, had many rules, doctrines and dogmas. What was the effect of it? It was that you did not really need to think, that you did not really need to go into your heart and feel from your Christ self what was the right thing to do in your personal life. You just blindly followed all of the rules.

We also had as the goal, both the ascended masters and Mark and I, to provide a record of the Path of Christhood and teachings about the Path of Christhood. The Path of Christhood is a path where you do not follow worldly rules, you do not even follow outer rules; you follow what you directly receive from within.

In the beginning stages of Christhood, you will sometimes make wrong decisions. You will even sometimes get incomplete or incorrect directions from within or you will interpret them through that filter of the lower mind. You can even, if you take an honest look at my life, see that I sometimes colored or interpreted the directions of El Morya in a certain way.

What else can one do? One will not attain Christhood, one will not qualify for the ascension, by following outer rules. We all have to be willing to go through a stage where we strive for a higher direction, a higher vision, but we are still willing to make decisions based on the limited vision we have now. Even if we make a so-called wrong decision, it can still become a step – when we honestly look at ourselves – for internalizing a greater degree of Christhood.

Being willing to look at your decisions

There comes a point where you must be willing to look at your decisions, look at your so-called mistakes. You must honestly acknowledge the decisions and their consequences, but when it comes to acknowledging them as mistakes, you actually need to step up to a higher level. You need to recognize that they were only mistakes when seen through a certain consciousness, and that consciousness is not the consciousness of Christ. It is an element of the human consciousness that you have elevated to the status of superiority, of being absolute, of being true in some higher way.

You have taken a lower consciousness, an expression of the consciousness of anti-christ, and you have put it in the place where the consciousness of Christ should be. It is, as the Bible says: "The abomination of desolation standing in the holy place where it ought not." You are judging yourself and others through that element of the consciousness of anti-christ. The very consciousness that causes you to make a certain choice is also the consciousness through which you will judge the outcome of that choice.

Do you see that if you look at an action and label it as a mistake through the same element of anti-christ that caused you to take that action, then you will not be free from the action? You will only pour more energy into it through your feelings of guilt or self-condemnation. You reinforce the spiral rather than transcending it, and that it why it is so important to consider that element of Jesus' teachings, mission, example and ministry which is that Christ can forgive all, that Christ can redeem all sins.

Christ as the redeemer

The misunderstanding from the churches of the world is that Christ is external to you and that he will take upon himself your sins and pay for them. The deeper reality is that you never need to "pay" for the sins. You need to invoke the light of God to consume the energy, but then you need to accept that the Christ in you can help you transcend the consciousness that caused you to sin—and then you are free. You are redeemed, not from without but from within. When you begin to lock in to this process, *that* is when you can begin the period that I have talked about in my previous releases that I went through after I withdrew from the physical body.

Imagine how difficult it could be for you to have withdrawn from your physical body, and your body is going into these later stages of what they called Alzheimer's disease where you basically cannot take care of yourself, you cannot remember your children and loved ones, you cannot speak coherently. You are basically like a drooling baby and yet you have in your mind the vision of how, in my case, I used to be the head of this large spiritual organization, a messenger of the ascended masters with all of the pomp and circumstance that I had created and that people in the organization had created around that position.

Can you imagine, my beloved, how difficult it could be for you, for me, to have been in such a powerful position where you really felt that you were doing God's work, you were doing the work of the ascended masters, you were doing the work for the ages. Now you were reduced to this drooling body and yet you had full awareness of your entire life.

How did I manage to even survive this test? I assure you, it *was* a test! None of us are beyond being tested until the point when we ascend. I did, as I just explained, pass the test through knowing the redeeming qualities of Christ. I did what I was not able to do while I was still in the position I held, namely looking openly and honestly at my life. I saw how I was judging myself through a certain element of the consciousness of anti-christ, and then I saw beyond it, seeing the consciousness of Christ. *Then,* I could set myself free from that consciousness of anti-christ.

I could look at my decisions and my actions, I could look at my feelings, my thoughts about myself, even my sense of identity. I could see the unreality, but I could also see the reality beyond it. I could set free the energies, the thoughtforms, the matrices of thought that I had created throughout many lifetimes, all those matrices that were part of my soul vehicle that I had carried for lifetimes. I truly had to look at and I had to let go of everything. You, my beloved, if you are willing, can start this process. I assure you that the earlier you start it, while you still have time left in the physical body, the more progress you will make on the path.

Stop living someone else's life

What I wish to bring to your attention in this release is how most people in the world have been brought up to live someone else's life. This goes back many lifetimes, but even in this lifetime I think you can see that as you grow up, you observe around you your parents, your family, your society. You absorb so many things.

Do you not realize and remember that Montessori talked about the absorbent mind? In the first six years of your life – and beyond, but especially in the first six years – you are like a sponge taking in impressions from the world. It causes you to build up this image of how you are supposed to live in the environment where you now find yourself. This is where society, any society, programs you, and the effect of this is that you are actually creating a mental image. The mental image is outside your self. Where exactly it is depends on your particular circumstances in childhood.

I had a very dominant father figure, and I created a certain mental image related to this external father figure. As I grew older, I began to become more independent yet I still had this mental image "out there." It was constantly a part of my attention, which was directed at evaluating myself and all of my decisions through that image. I was living my life "out there" through the image rather than in my own heart. When I met Mark, he became the substitute father, being older than myself. That is why I felt so distraught when he left. Who would be that father figure for me that I needed—or thought I needed?

Well, for me it became El Morya who took on that role. Even though I did have direct contact with El Morya, there was still a part of me that associated El Morya with that image of the father figure. I saw him through the coloring of that image. I was not, while in embodiment, able to grasp El Morya in his purest form nor was I able to convey this to my students. There was a period when I started to see this. I felt a deep sense of remorse and regret over having colored El Morya.

I can assure you, my beloved, that if someone had come to me while I was still fully functioning in my role as messenger and had told me this, I would have rejected it strongly and sternly. I would have rebuked that student as rebellious and not knowing the real El Morya whom I was convinced was the figure I saw through my own father image. When I came to see this and acknowledged the unreality of it, I also saw that my entire life I was in a way – including everything I did in the organization – seeking the approval of this remote father figure. It was a father figure that contained many elements of the consciousness of anti-christ, and the real El Morya contains no elements of anti-christ in his Being. I could never win the approval of this father image based on anti-christ because the consciousness of anti-christ will never approve anything, my beloved.

You can never satisfy the consciousness of anti-christ. Nothing is ever enough or good enough, therefore you will be constantly running like a donkey with the carrot dangling in front of its nose. It is pushing the carrot as it is running, and it will never catch up. Neither will *you* ever catch up with whatever external image you have that has become your frame of reference, your perception filter, the one through which you seek approval. You think that when this image approves you, then God will approve you as well. The real El Morya has no elements of the consciousness of anti-christ, therefore he approves you already for he sees only the Christ in your being. I should perhaps rephrase this, for El Morya, of course, sees everything. He sees the elements of anti-christ only as a temporary unreality, and he sees through them and beyond them to the Christ that is the deeper reality. Even though he may be stern and direct in challenging the elements of anti-christ, he does so only to free you so that you too can see the Christ in you that he sees at a deeper level. Had I only been able to grasp that while in embodiment!

The central challenge on the spiritual path

After going through my period of regret and remorse, I saw that, again, everything was outplayed exactly as it needed to be outplayed. Those who had the same elements of the anti-christ consciousness that I did needed to encounter it in me as the leader figure in order to get the test of whether they would continue to project that leadership image. This was the leadership image that humankind needed to transcend in the Age of Pisces, the image they had projected onto Jesus and God as the angry judgmental God in the sky. Those who had those elements of anti-christ in their beings received their test through me. Those who did not have or who were willing to question that image, they saw beyond it, they recognized that El Morya was not quite as strict and stern as portrayed by me. He also had a pink side. Many experienced this, and for those who did not, it was because they were not willing to see beyond their own image of the remote God.

What I am seeking to convey to you here is: Yes, we all make mistakes while we are in embodiment, but in order to ascend we have to shift our view of our mistakes. We may have to go through a period of regret and remorse where we say: "Oh, if only I could have done that differently." When we see deeper, when we see with the eyes of Christ, we learn to see that it was not good, it was not bad; it was not a mistake it simply was what it was. It is what it is, and now that it is in the past the challenge is: "Will we transcend it or will we continue to carry it with us?"

This is the central challenge you face on the spiritual path, this is the central challenge you face in the ascension process where you have fulfilled the outer requirements, but now you need to work on the inner, psychological requirements. As the saying goes: "You cannot take it with you." You can take things with you when you re-embody because you carry them with you in your soul vehicle, but you cannot take it with you into the ascended state. You can take nothing into the ascended state, *nothing,* my beloved. You will say, perhaps: "Well, how can you then claim to be an ascended master and talk about what happened in your last lifetime?" But you are not quite understanding.

Everything you do sends a signal to your I AM Presence. Your I AM Presence looks at it and it stores its perception of the situation in your causal body. After you have ascended, you can, if you like, access any record, like you can access the Akashic records of what you did in any lifetime on earth. What I am talking about is that while you are in embodiment, you perceive a situation through the state of consciousness that makes up your soul vehicle. You react through what is in your four lower bodies, and this creates a record in those four lower bodies that is separate from the record in your causal body.

In order to ascend, there is nothing from your lower bodies that you can take with you into the ascended realm. No action, no possession, no feeling, no thoughtform, no sense of identity, not even the human memory that is stored in the lower levels of the etheric body. Even the memory, the human memory, that sees a situation through the human mind must be left behind for you to ascend. You can take *nothing* with you. The sooner you realize this, my beloved, the sooner you can begin to look at your four lower bodies and let go, let go of *this,* let go of *that.*

How many of you, in your life, have gone through a period where you either moved to some other place or felt the need to get rid of your material things? This is a symbol for what you can do in the emotional, the mental and the identity realms. Get rid of all the old stuff that you are dragging with you. Look at it, let it go and then experience how much more free you feel, as many of you have already experienced. Then use that as an encouragement to say: "Well, if I felt freer by letting go of *this* stuff, how much more free would I feel if let go of some more stuff? How much more free would I feel if I let go of all of it?"

A higher level of service

There is a certain level of service that you can give in your divine plan, based on your current state of consciousness. If you could step up to the Buddhic detachment where you have let go of so much, then you can step up to a much higher level of service. This is what I wish for all of you, and thus I would remind you of a sentence given by Saint Germain in one of the Shakespearean plays: "To thine own self be true." Take the teachings that have been released through this messenger about perception filters, about the ego and the epic mindset. Look at yourself and realize that you have created an image, perhaps several, that are standing out there in the periphery of your aura. They are, so to speak, the interface between you and the world. You react to the world through those images and you respond to the world through those images. You give out through them and you take in through them. What does this mean? It means that you are essentially living your life "out there" in and through that image.

You are attempting to live up to that image with all of your mental activity, all of your thoughts, feelings, the way you look at yourself. You are attempting to live up to this image, but where did Jesus say the kingdom of God is found? Not out there on the periphery but within, within the secret chamber of your heart, within your heart chakra and the other chakras when they are purified and you connect to the core of the chakras.

My beloved, do not live other people's lives, do not live the life of society, do not live the life of an ideal you have created. Do not live your life "out there;" strive to live it "in here." To thine own self be true!

I, by being this formidable messenger figure, caused many people to reinforce these remote images they had and actually live their lives even more out there than they did before they found the organization. They reinforced their remote images by using me personally, my example, my teachings, even the teachings of the ascended masters.

They built on to these images, and some people are still living their entire lives and consciousness through those images out there, instead of doing what was the hope of the ascended masters of finally realizing the unreality of the image. You realize that no image on earth can portray the ascended masters, and then you shatter the images, go beyond them and say: "I will use the teachings and the example of the ascended masters to do what they did: live my own life, not the life of someone else, not the life of the fallen beings."

There are still people, wonderful people dear to my heart, who are following the teachings and the example I set, who are part of the organization I created and they feel they have to continue to do this out of loyalty to me. They are in reality loyal to the images that they created in their own minds. Surely, they used me – my example, my teachings, even the sense of being my personal chela – to build those images. In many cases, I encouraged this or at least I was instrumental, I played the role. But I did not create those images, and in order to ascend I had to transcend all of the images I had in my own mind of who I was, what it means to be a messenger, how I was a messenger, how I ran the organization. I had to transcend it all.

Misguided loyalty to Guru Ma

There are two things that I wish to convey here in the off chance that someone might actually acknowledge this teaching as being valid. First of all, the people who came to the organization did not build an image of who I was even then. They built an image that was a combination of the way I expressed myself and their own state of consciousness. I know you feel that you are my personal chelas, I know you feel you love me, you respect me, you have vowed to give me your obedience. I know you feel you have to be loyal to me, but the reality is that even while I was in embodiment you did not see me, as I did not see El Morya.

You saw me through your own images and instead of fulfilling my highest mission of setting you free from the human consciousness, I actually became an instrument for you reinforcing the human consciousness. How can that be being loyal to me even as I was back then?

The next thing that I want to convey is that regardless of how I was when I was in embodiment, I have transcended *all of it!* The Guru Ma that was in physical embodiment – that was a messenger for the ascended masters, that was the leader of a spiritual organization – *is no more,* for I have let her go! I have consumed the records, the energies, I have transcended it all, I have let it go. I have looked at it all and I have said: "I do not want this no more, for I want to be *more.*"

How can you be loyal to what was there when I now am an ascended master who has transcended it all? If you want to be loyal to me, be loyal to me as I AM today. Then make an effort to look beyond your images, the images in your own mind, the images I had in my mind at the time. Lock in to the flame that I AM, not as an unascended being but as an ascended master. I AM infinitely more than I was while in embodiment, and I can assure you that I am also much more beautiful than my physical form. I was, quite frankly, never really happy with my looks in that embodiment, but now I have transcended it completely. I have taken on an appearance that is of a transcendent beauty that you might be able to catch a glimpse of with your inner eye if you are willing.

I am grateful for the opportunity to speak these things in the physical to a group of people who, although they did not know me, nevertheless love me. Perhaps *because* you did not know me, you love me more easily.

I have had my say, and Lanello wants to butt in and say that he would also have liked to speak when he heard his music played, but that he could never get the last word with me while we were in embodiment together so why should that have changed now? Indeed, there is some truth to it for in this day and age it is necessary that the female element, and this means in many cases also those embodied in a female body, come more to the fore. That is why many men who are spiritually attuned might feel that it is more difficult to get the last word with their wives, but you might also come to recognize that this is to a certain degree the sign of the times. I was, which I may discourse on at some future time, a female leader in a Piscean state of consciousness and that was a whole other adventure in itself. I will find opportunity to give you my impressions of that also, at some future time.

For now, my gratitude for the students here at this conference. My gratitude for the many students around the world, whether they knew me or not, who have found the teachings, have appreciated the teachings, have appreciated the work and the example – for better or worse – that Mark and I set. Our gratitude and our joy *to all of you!*

25 | LOVE MATTERS MORE

NOTE: *This dictation was given on November 9, 2015, during the radio show Divine Love Talk, hosted by Dr. Parthenia Grant. The occasion was that Moira Prophet and Tatiana Prophet were being interviewed about this book and their relationship with their mother.*

So, I am, indeed, the Ascended Master Guru Ma. And I am extremely happy to be here and to be able to speak this in the presence of my two beautiful daughters, Moira and Tatiana. I did not know, when I was still in the denseness of the body, just how beautiful you are. You can only fully see this from the ascended realm. Of course, I did not see how beautiful *you* are because I did not see how beautiful *I* am. For again, none of us can see the beauty of our Divine beings while we are still in such a dense body.

I want you to know that an ascended master does not give a dictation on command. There is nothing on earth that can force us. But, we do, of course, respond to human beings or we would not be ascended masters associated with earth. And love can magnetize us. There is no force in love, but there is beauty.

And so, I come, not to say any specific words to you or to those of my students who have accepted my book. I come only to share the love. The love that we had for each other before we came into embodiment together. The love that was so often overshadowed by the temporary concerns we had while we were in those very often hectic and difficult situations. Often, as you and I both know, the hecticness, the stress was created by me. Very often. Too often, one might say. But, as an ascended master those words fade away.

What, my beloved, is love? So many words have been associated with it. There is really only one thing that matters. Love is beyond anything in the material world. It is that which connects us to what is beyond. Ultimately, it is what connects us to the fact that we are beyond the material world. And so, when we are in the flow of love, in the presence of love, we gain a different perspective on everything on earth.

It is not that I expect you, all of you – my students, my children – to look at what happened while we were in physical embodiment together and suddenly say that it didn't matter. I know very well from my own experience that while you are still in the body, the things that happen in the material world do matter. I hope you can all see and sense through the book and through my Presence that when you reconnect to love and when you know that you are beyond this world, then it is not that the things that happened do not matter anymore, but it is so that *love matters more*.

Suddenly, you begin to look at what has happened to you as if it happened to you; but it did not change you, control you, own you. When you realize that what happened to you does not own you, *you* can begin to own *it*. You can begin to accept that what happened to you was a result – partly – of choices you made and partly by choices other people made. When you own *that,* you can give it away. Then, you are set free to once again flow with love and know that *love matters more*.

26 | RECOGNIZING ASCENDED MASTERS

NOTE: *This dictation was given on November 16, 2015, during the radio show Divine Love Talk, hosted by Dr. Parthenia Grant. The occasion was that Dr. Richard Bartlett was being interviewed about this book and his relationship with Elizabeth Clare Prophet.*

I am the ascended master, Guru Ma. I am once again drawn by the love of my friend, Richard, my two daughters, those of my students who have recognized me and those of my students who have not recognized me. This is what I wish to address today: How do you recognize an ascended master?

What does it mean to have spiritual discernment? Do you know, my beloved, why I entitled this book, *Don't Drink Your Own Kool-Aid?* Well, it was, of course, because I so often was accused of being the woman-equivalent of Jim Jones, who was making all of you, all of my students, drink the Kool-Aid. It was also because you cannot recognize an ascended master if you are drinking your own Kool-Aid.

Do you realize, as I am sure you do, that we have had a number of organizations sponsored by the ascended masters. I, myself, recognized several of the previous dispensations and organizations. Do you know that so few students of one ascended master organization have moved on to the next messenger and the next organization?

Why is that? It is because, as I talk about at length in the book, you start forming an image, based on the teachings of the organization you are following, of what ascended masters are like. You start forming an image of what *you* are supposed to be like as an ascended master student. What you do not realize is that there are two aspects of an ascended master message, dictation, teaching. There is the master and then there is the outer form of the teaching.

Why did you recognize an ascended master teaching? Surely, very few of you were brought up in ascended master teachings. You were brought up in traditional religions so you had to go against the mainstream to recognize an ascended master teaching. You did this because you were open to considering something new. You also did it because beyond the outer words given by that ascended master teaching, you were able to tune in to, to resonate with, the vibration that was higher than anything you had experienced in these mainstream religions.

There are two aspects of discernment. One is openness and that means that if you do not have openness you cannot exercise discernment. Of course, you cannot be open to just anything, or you would easily be fooled by false teachings. My point is that if you use one teaching to set up outer criteria for what the ascended masters should say or should not say – how they should talk through a certain messenger and how they should not talk – then you are drinking you own Kool-Aid and you are shutting off your openness.

When you are not open to reading vibration, you cannot read vibration. You cannot accurately read vibration through a filter of a set of outer criteria for what we of the ascended masters should or should not say and how we should or should not express ourselves.

Why do you think we call it progressive revelation? Why do you think we sponsor new organizations and new messengers? It is because the message is progressive. When we have a given organization, such as the Summit Lighthouse, we were not meant to say exactly the same or say it the same way as previous organizations. Then, the teaching would not have been progressive.

Likewise, today, I cannot say exactly the same things as I did when I was in embodiment because it would only validate your image of me. I cannot help you move on unless you are willing to look beyond the image and stop drinking your own Kool-Aid. I may have been the trigger for you developing and creating that Kool-Aid. This is true. But, *I* did not create it. It was created in *your* mind. And that is where you need to overcome it, my beloved children and students.

27 | TO MY STUDENTS—PAST, PRESENT AND FUTURE

NOTE: *This dictation was given on December 6, 2015 as the second edition of this book was being prepared for publication.*

I am the Ascended Master Guru Ma. I wish to make some comments here, based on the fact that my two beautiful daughters and my beautiful friend have decided to write forewords to this book. The significance of this is that I am now allowed to take this release to a higher level. This is also brought about by the fact that a critical mass of the students who knew me while I was in embodiment have also accepted this book, or at least used it to increase their attunement with me.

Do you understand, my beloved, that whether you believe this book is dictated by the real Ascended Master Guru Ma or whether you do not believe this, you can still use the book to increase your attunement with the real Ascended Master Guru Ma? This may seem like a contradiction or a paradox, but there is no one who will make it to the higher stages of the path of the ascension without being able to deal with paradox. There are innumerable paradoxes presented by the dark forces for the purpose of keeping your minds trapped in a closed loop from which there seems to be no escape.

The purpose of paradox

Do you not see, when you look back at my physical life and the organization that I was the leader of for so many years, that both my life and the organization presented certain paradoxes, certain contradictions? In fact, you may say that my entire life presented one big paradox. Have you never considered that this was exactly the same paradox presented by Jesus when he was in physical embodiment? You may not have considered this because you do not remember – those of you who were in embodiment with Jesus – what it was like to have a living master in embodiment.

You see, my beloved, Jesus – however perfect you may think he is, based on the idolatry of official Christianity – was still in a physical body. He had human characteristics. When he had walked a whole day on the dusty roads, his body smelled as bad as those of his disciples. He did not walk around always with clean clothes, neatly trimmed hair and a halo around his head, as you see in so many pictures of him. He could at times be moody and grumpy, burdened by the energies for which he was holding the balance for the planet.

The disciples of Jesus faced the same paradox as the disciples of any master in embodiment who has had a certain measure of spiritual mastery, a certain gift of the Holy Spirit streaming through them. The paradox is to bridge the gap between what you observe as a human being with human qualities and human limitations and then locking in to the greater light that does not come from the person, is not produced by the person but is nevertheless streaming through that person—for the person is the open door.

I was the one who barked at you

While I was still in embodiment, I once told you, my students, about how it was for me, often being the one who had to be tough on you, present you with a message that your ego did not like, give you a discipline, give you a spiritual spanking, so to speak. I said to you that many of you had an idolatrous image of El Morya as the perfect master. But I was the one who barked, I was the one who was right there, having to confront you with your momentums or whatever it might have been.

I was the one who received the negative energy from you whereas you never dared to direct it at El Morya because you did not see the real El Morya, you saw an idolatrous image of him. For me, those of you who had gotten offended – or rather whose egos had gotten offended by me – could so easily find some human limitation, some human quality that you could then use, that your egos could use, as an excuse for not heeding what I said to you.

So many times I have been the one who had to confront a student with his or her momentum. Then I saw how, suddenly, the idolatry that the student had of me was shattered. Suddenly, the light in the students' eyes changed and they shifted in their minds from the blind idolatry of thinking I would always live up to their image of me. Suddenly, they realized that I am not always going to be whatever they expected me to be, such as gentle and kind. I will sometimes be tough, I will be direct, I will confront you with your ego momentums, I will challenge what we called the Dweller on the Threshold.

An excuse for not heeding the guru

When that happened, so many of you then made this very subtle shift. You would now start looking at me and look for some human quality, some human flaw – whether real or perceived

– and you would use it as an excuse for not heeding the guru. Suddenly, the guru had fallen from being the idol on the pedestal to being the ant beneath your feet. And you did not think you had to heed the ant. Now, you had an excuse, and many of you managed to somehow create this double state in your minds. With your conscious minds you were fully convinced that you were still my loyal and obedient students, you were still following me. Yet there was a certain aspect of my instruction to you, a certain challenge of your ego momentum, that another part of your mind was convinced could not be right and therefore you did not have to heed it.

The challenge of having a living guru

How many of you are willing to look back at your personal interactions with me – those of you who *had* personal interactions with me – and acknowledge the very tendency I am describing? Are you willing to acknowledge how you used a human imperfection to refuse to look at yourself? How you used a human imperfection of the guru to refuse to heed the guru's direction? This, my beloved, is the central challenge you face when you have a guru in physical embodiment, as opposed to a guru who is either ascended or who died before you came into that movement.

Look at previous ascended master organizations, look at the organization created by Yogananda. Look how, when the guru is no longer in embodiment, they have created this idolatrous image of how perfect the guru was. You see, my beloved, this is all well and good. You can make progress in an organization like this, but the real advantage of having a guru in physical embodiment is that this guru can give you the supreme test of chelaship, and it is the test I have just outlined. Will you use a human imperfection of the embodied guru to refuse to heed the guru's exposure of your own ego?

Are you hiding from the guru?

This I say because, since this book was published, I have watched every one of my students – or those who consider themselves my former students – who have heard about this book. I have watched your reactions. Do you really think that I cannot see you? Many of you do because you think that when the guru is no longer in embodiment, it is much easier to hide from the guru.

It *is* in the sense that I cannot physically call you into my office or call you on the phone and tell you what your dweller is doing. Therefore, you can believe that if you cannot hear me, then your dweller is probably not doing anything it shouldn't be doing. You come to believe that I am not seeing what you are doing. Then, when you hear about a book supposedly dictated by the Ascended Master Guru Ma, you think that I do not observe how you react to this. But I *do* observe. Not with judgment, not with criticism, but I observe with love. Love is not blind; ascended, divine love is not blind, my beloved.

Excuses for rejecting this book

I see exactly how many excuses have been used by those who call themselves my students to reject this book, often without even looking at it, without holding it in their hands, without reading a word in it. How amazing it is to see – again – this division in the mind. With your conscious mind you are convinced that you are my loyal and faithful student, but another part of your mind convinces you that you do not even have to investigate whether I have actually dictated a book. You think you can know and reject the book without looking at it.

How would you have come to be my follower if you had rejected me in physical embodiment, and the teachings of the ascended masters, without looking at it? So how can you claim to still be my follower without being willing to look at my book, to read it with the heart – and not with the analytical mind – and to tune in to my vibration? So that I might show you – not *tell* you – but give you an experience in your heart of my Presence.

I know well that many of my students – or should I say, *some* of my students – have an ability to tune in to my Presence and they do not need this book. I can assure you that by reading it, you would still be able to tune in to my Presence in a stronger, more profound way than you can now. There are only very, very few people who are so attuned to me that you could not benefit from the book. There is also a group of students who have sporadic contact and attunement with me but who could greatly benefit from using the book to increase your attunement.

Transcending your image of Guru Ma

The simple fact is, my beloved, that the underlying message in this book, and the main reason I dictated this book, is that so many of my students are limited by the image of me that you created while I was in embodiment, after I left embodiment or after I was no longer functioning as a messenger. This is the underlying message in the book, and the outcome or the consequence of that message is, of course, that I want you to transcend your image of me based on how I was in embodiment. Why? Because, as I say in the book, in order to qualify for my ascension, I had to transcend the images of myself that I had while I was unascended.

This is the same for everyone. Do you not understand that it is your image of yourself as an unascended person that keeps you tied to the body? You will not ascend until you let go of the image that you are an unascended person, an unascended being. *That* is when you can ascend. In order to let go of that last image of yourself as an unascended being, you have to let go of all of the other images of your identity that are based on conditions on earth.

Did you not get this by reading my book? It is the most profound message that I want to give you as a newly ascended master because it is something that I did not fully get while I was still conscious and functioning in my busy daily schedule. I want you to have it so that you can look beyond even the image of myself that I had while I was in embodiment and tune in to my Presence as an ascended master. I have no interest whatsoever in seeing you being loyal to a mental image of me. I have every interest in having you tune in to me in my ascended state, for that is how I can help you grow!

Many of my students cannot make their ascension

A considerable majority of those who came in contact with me while I was in embodiment cannot make their ascension as long as you hold on to the image of me that you created while I was in embodiment. You are so close to qualifying for your ascension, but you cannot take that last step until you free yourself from your image of me and the image of yourself—that you do not even realize that you have built based on my example and teachings. It is not that there is anything wrong, dark or false about this image but as I said, all of the self-images based on earth must be let go. As long as you hold on to my image, I cannot help you from the ascended state. *Do you not see this?*

What did I say when I was in physical embodiment? This messenger was sitting in King Arthur's Court when he heard me say this from the stage and he almost jumped out of his chair. I said: "I am not going to leave until the last one of you has ascended." He realized very clearly that this was making my ascension contingent upon the free-will choices of other human beings, which you cannot do. I, of course, responded to the fear that many of you had at the time where it was beginning to be rumored that I had some mysterious illness. I was trying to reassure you that it was my desire to stay with you as long as I possibly could. This was before I had come to the realization that there was no stopping my illness and that I had to go through this, for me rather humiliating and disconcerting, experience of losing my mind and memory.

Leaving my students behind

When I came to that acceptance at inner levels, I also realized that I faced a choice. In order for myself to ascend, I had to let go of the sense of loyalty to my students. Do you understand that it was a misconception on my part that I could stay in physical embodiment until all of my students had qualified for their ascension? It was a misconception because when you are the guru, you must remain ahead of the students. That means there comes a point, when you have been an embodied guru, where in order to help your students ascend, you must ascend yourself.

This is what Jesus also demonstrated at the beginning of the Piscean age, and I realized that this is what I had to demonstrate at the end of the Piscean age. Jesus was the example at the beginning and I am – potentially, for those who will accept it – the example at the end of the Piscean dispensation. This is potentially significant if enough people come to accept it. There is a significance here that I may expound upon at a later time, but for now I wish to leave it open for you to ponder what this might mean.

I realized that I could not fulfill this vow of mine. I had to surrender it and I had to ascend. Only by ascending could I fully help you who are my students. That is why I have brought forth this book in order to explain to you that I cannot help you from the ascended state if you hold on to the unascended image of me. I cannot give you the help you need in order to qualify for your ascensions unless you are willing to let go and tune in to me as an ascended master. In order to tune in to me you must be willing to surrender your unascended image of me. You must be willing to go into this no-man's land of having no image of me until your mind becomes empty so that you can experience my living Presence as an ascended master.

Experiencing the ascended Guru Ma

I am not talking about you analyzing, understanding, conceptualizing with the mind what I am like as an ascended master. I am not talking about you trying to form an image of what I am like as an ascended maser and projecting it upon me. I am talking about you opening your mind and heart, emptying it of your previous images so that you might experience my Presence as an ascended master. It is not a conceptualization of me as an ascended master that will help you ascend; it is only the direct experience of my Presence that will help you ascend. *Do you not get this?*

The significance of this cannot be overstated. There are many of those who call themselves my students who will not ascend unless you experience my Presence as an ascended master. Otherwise, you cannot accept that the path I taught can lead you to your ascension. Therefore, you will stand there on the threshold, but your dweller will keep whispering in your ear why you cannot take that last step.

I know this because when I was standing at the threshold of my ascension, my dweller was whispering in my ear why I could not take the last step—and so it has been for everyone who has ever ascended. You will not fully leave the ego or the dweller behind until you take that last step into the ascended realm. What would keep you in a physical body? Nothing but that last aspect of the ego or the dweller can keep you in this dense realm once you begin to tune in to and experience the bliss of the ascended realm.

The clever arguments

Now, my beloved, I have listened to your arguments for why this book cannot be true and why it cannot be genuine. They are very clever, very ingenious, very imaginative, some even amusing. I will not comment on any of them. I will not give you any reason or argumentation for why this book is genuine.

I have heard some of you comment on this messenger and why he cannot be a genuine messenger, and again you have used many reasons, many arguments. Again, I will not comment on any of them. If you desire to hold on to your arguments for rejecting my book and the outstretched hand that it is, then I will simply stand by and say: "Until another time when you are ready. *Then* I am still here for you." I will hope that you are ready to accept my hand before your time runs out in this embodiment.

Do you see, my beloved, that I have no intent other than helping you win your ascension? I do not even have the intent to use this messenger and this book to comment on the organization that I spent so much time and effort to build. Do you not see that this messenger has no intention of becoming a leader of a past organization or starting his own organization? He has no intention of personal gain or recognition.

Why has he been the open door for this book? Well, partly because those who are able have an obligation to let the ascended masters bring forth what we want to bring forth. But also, of course, because he was a part of my organization. Although he had little personal interaction with me, he did indeed tune in to my Presence. Because he benefited greatly from being affiliated with my organization, my teachings and myself, he had—not a debt but maybe a debt of honor that he wished to fulfill.

Cosmic cycles and this book

Cosmic wheels turned in such a way that the book was brought forth when it was, which was exactly according to certain cycles. Even this second edition is also brought forth according to other cycles that few people understand with their conscious minds. *I* understand them, *Lanello* understands them and we are happy to see – *very* happy to see – that this release from our hearts can now be accelerated to the next level.

How many of you truly understand the message in Jesus' parable about the talents? How many of you understand that we of the ascended masters are allowed to give an initial offering, but then we can only give more when there are enough people in embodiment who take what we have given and multiply it in their own beings?

You see how long it took before there was a readiness for me to give this book. You see that for me to give more, or Lanello to give more teachings – either through this messenger or another – a critical mass of people will need to take what is given and multiply it in their hearts. That is why I started out by presenting you with the paradox that whether you believe this book is from the Ascended Master Guru Ma or whether you do not believe it, you can still use the book to increase your attunement with the real Ascended Master Guru Ma—whomever you may think this is.

Beware that if you read this book through the filter of your dweller and ego, then this book will not help you increase your attunement with me. Thus, it will in a certain sense be your judgment for refusing to follow the guru beyond the clever arguments of your ego-dweller. Do you not realize, at least in glimpses, how clever the dweller can be in presenting you with a seemingly watertight argument for rejecting the guru? So many of you, so many of those who came into contact with me, my organization or my teachings, have not fully grasped this. You have not fully grasped either that the goal of the ascended masters has never been to create an organization and to give a teaching that is an end in itself.

The key to your ascension

The goal of the path given by the ascended masters has always been one thing only and it is that you win your ascension. How do you win your ascension? Some of you have come to believe various illusions about it. One is that the masters will do it for you. Another is that you can do it entirely by your own efforts. The truth is a combination of the two.

You cannot win your ascension without tuning in to the Presence of some ascended master. *It cannot be done!* There is no being who has ever qualified for the ascension without tuning in to an ascended master and receiving a gift of light – acceleration – from that master. Likewise, there is no one who has ever qualified for the ascension without multiplying the talents they have been given from the master.

My goal as an ascended master is not that you are loyal to an outer organization or teaching. Neither is it my goal to get you to abandon an outer organization or teaching. My goal is to give you the opportunity to tune in to my Presence as the ascended master I am today, for this is how I can help you win your ascension.

Now, it may be that whether you knew about me while I was in physical embodiment or whether you have found this book without being affiliated with my organization that you cannot fully tune in to me as an ascended master. There is, of course, nothing wrong with this. Then, I encourage to find another ascended master with whom you can have greater attunement and then by all means go after that attunement. It is by no means my goal with this book to say that you *should,* if you have read it, tune in to *my* Presence. You should tune in to whichever master is closest to your heart and expands your heart. My goal with this book is to present those who do feel an attunement with me with the opportunity to accelerate that attunement to a higher level.

Has Guru Ma ascended?

Therefore, I say: The real question to ask yourself, is not: "Is this book from the ascended master Guru Ma or is it not?" The real question to ask yourself is: "Do I believe Guru Ma is now an ascended master?" If the answer is "No," then obviously I cannot help you and you must seek another guru. If the answer is "Yes," then the existence of this book and the validity of it is not the issue. The issue is: "What can help you tune in to the ascended master Guru Ma?"

If the book can help you: "Good!" If not, find other ways. Use the teachings I have brought forth while I was in embodiment. There are so many tools and teachings, and if they can help you, by all means use them.

The infinite field of daisies

I will give you one last tool, a very simple tool. Because it is simple, it is also potentially very effective—if you can approach it with the childlike mind. You may know that while I was in embodiment my favorite flower was the daisy. Some of you will even recall a picture taken of me in my younger days while I was sitting in a meditative posture in a field of daisies. Well, I wish you, if you knew of that picture, to put it out of your mind.

Instead, I wish to give you another image. It is the image of a field of daisies. Bright green grass, like the first tender grass of spring. Sprinkled on this field: daisies. Dozens, hundreds, thousands, millions. The sun is shining on the field from a low enough angle to create this golden light that is almost ethereal.

I wish you – whenever you have time, whenever you desire to tune in to my Presence – to sit in a quiet room in a meditative posture and visualize this field of daisies. Do not focus on a particular flower but allow your inner eye to be drawn towards the distance, towards the horizon. Then see how the field stretches to infinity, and in *that* infinity *I* AM. *There* you can tune in to my Presence if you will, for I will always be there waiting for you.

I am an ascended master and I have unlimited time. You are in embodiment; you do *not* have unlimited time. But you do have the ability to choose. I cannot choose for you, and therefore I can only wait for you to open yourself to my Presence.

I have now done everything I wished to do, and everything I am allowed to do, at this particular point in the eternal cycles of being. I am the Ascended Master Guru Ma. I know who I am. If you do not know who *I* am, it is because you do not fully know who *you* are. Thus, you might ponder that question!

28 | INVOKING THE PRESENCE OF GURU MA

NOTE: *An invocation is a tool given by the ascended masters. It is designed to help us invoke the spiritual light from one or more masters, directing it into dissolving limitations in our personal lives or on a planetary scale. This invocation is given by Guru Ma in order to help us increase our attunement with her. You give an invocation by reading it aloud. For further instructions on how to use an invocation, see www.transcendencetoolbox.com.*

In the name of the I AM THAT I AM, Jesus Christ, I call to the Ascended Master Guru Ma to manifest your Presence in my life and help me transcend my personal limitations so that I can bring the gift that I came here to give. I especially ask for your help and intercession with . . . [Make personal calls]

Part 1

1. Guru Ma, help me see myself as you see me from the ascended realm, without criticism or judgment but with the love that is not blind.

> O Guru Ma, with you I see,
> that my life is not all for me,
> it is my new reality,
> that I am here to set all free.
>
> **O Guru Ma, your Presence near
> the call of God I always hear,
> your love consumes my every fear,
> you and Lanello always here.**

2. Guru Ma, I want your love, even the tough love that exposes my illusions and the games played by my ego.

> O Guru Ma, I have the will,
> for Summit of Ascension's Hill,
> desires of ego falling still,
> as love for God my mind does fill.
>
> **O Guru Ma, your Presence near
> the call of God I always hear,
> your love consumes my every fear,
> you and Lanello always here.**

3. Guru Ma, help me resolve the paradoxes presented by the dark forces for the purpose of keeping my mind trapped in a closed loop from which there seems to be no escape.

O Guru Ma, your wisdom's sphere,
my path in life becoming clear,
my ego cannot interfere,
my inner voice I always hear.

**O Guru Ma, your Presence near
the call of God I always hear,
your love consumes my every fear,
you and Lanello always here.**

4. Guru Ma, help me resolve the paradox presented by your physical life and your organization and teachings.

O Guru Ma, we still the mind,
you show me love of every kind,
serenity I surely find,
I see beyond the daily grind.

**O Guru Ma, your Presence near
the call of God I always hear,
your love consumes my every fear,
you and Lanello always here.**

5. Guru Ma, help me bridge the gap between what I observe as a human being with human qualities and limitations and then locking in to the greater light that comes through that person.

O Guru Ma, intentions pure,
I'm going home with you for sure,
the world has lost its last allure,
in your heart I am now secure.

**O Guru Ma, your Presence near
the call of God I always hear,
your love consumes my every fear,
you and Lanello always here.**

6. Guru Ma, I want to overcome all idolatry of you or any other spiritual teacher, including the ascended masters.

O Guru Ma, your healing light,
pierces my soul's darkest night,
your mandala a healing sight,
as I ascend to lofty height.

**O Guru Ma, your Presence near
the call of God I always hear,
your love consumes my every fear,
you and Lanello always here.**

7. Guru Ma, I am willing to have you expose to me my personal limitations, momentums, habits and limitations, all the stuff that my ego does not want me to see.

O Guru Ma, such peace within,
it truly makes my atoms spin,
beyond the consciousness of sin,
the veil of matter now so thin.

**O Guru Ma, your Presence near
the call of God I always hear,
your love consumes my every fear,
you and Lanello always here.**

8. Guru Ma, help me see through my ego's attempts to use a supposed human limitation to reject the message of the spiritual teacher that might be disguised as an ant.

> O Guru Ma, I'm free at last,
> transmuted, burdens of the past,
> as daisies grow on vistas vast,
> this is the life of everlast.

> **O Guru Ma, your Presence near**
> **the call of God I always hear,**
> **your love consumes my every fear,**
> **you and Lanello always here.**

9. Guru Ma, I am willing to have you be tough, be direct, confront me with my ego momentums and challenge my Dweller on the Threshold.

> O Guru Ma, it is a treat,
> to visit your Divine Retreat,
> on Titicaca's waters sweet,
> you and Lanello do me greet.

> **O Guru Ma, your Presence near**
> **the call of God I always hear,**
> **your love consumes my every fear,**
> **you and Lanello always here.**

Part 2

1. Guru Ma, help me overcome the dual state of consciously thinking I am following a true spiritual teacher while subconsciously rejecting certain parts of the teacher's message.

> O Guru Ma, with you I see,
> that my life is not all for me,
> it is my new reality,
> that I am here to set all free.
>
> **O Guru Ma, your Presence near**
> **the call of God I always hear,**
> **your love consumes my every fear,**
> **you and Lanello always here.**

2. Guru Ma, help me overcome the tendency to use the human imperfections of other people to refuse to look at myself or follow the guru's directions.

> O Guru Ma, I have the will,
> for Summit of Ascension's Hill,
> desires of ego falling still,
> as love for God my mind does fill.
>
> **O Guru Ma, your Presence near**
> **the call of God I always hear,**
> **your love consumes my every fear,**
> **you and Lanello always here.**

3. Guru Ma, help me pass the supreme test of chelaship and never use a human imperfection of the guru to refuse to heed the guru's exposure of my ego.

> O Guru Ma, your wisdom's sphere,
> my path in life becoming clear,
> my ego cannot interfere,
> my inner voice I always hear.

> O Guru Ma, your Presence near
> the call of God I always hear,
> your love consumes my every fear,
> you and Lanello always here.

4. Guru Ma, help me accept that my ascended teachers can always see what I am doing and that you only look at me with love.

> O Guru Ma, we still the mind,
> you show me love of every kind,
> serenity I surely find,
> I see beyond the daily grind.

> O Guru Ma, your Presence near
> the call of God I always hear,
> your love consumes my every fear,
> you and Lanello always here.

5. Guru Ma, help me stop hiding from the guru so I can welcome the guru in any form, even a form my ego wants to reject.

> O Guru Ma, intentions pure,
> I'm going home with you for sure,
> the world has lost its last allure,
> in your heart I am now secure.

> O Guru Ma, your Presence near
> the call of God I always hear,
> your love consumes my every fear,
> you and Lanello always here.

6. Guru Ma, help me overcome the trap of thinking I can reject a spiritual teaching or direction without looking at it and sensing its vibration with my heart.

O Guru Ma, your healing light,
pierces my soul's darkest night,
your mandala a healing sight,
as I ascend to lofty height.

**O Guru Ma, your Presence near
the call of God I always hear,
your love consumes my every fear,
you and Lanello always here.**

7. Guru Ma, I am willing to have the direct experience of your Presence so that I can increase my attunement with you.

O Guru Ma, such peace within,
it truly makes my atoms spin,
beyond the consciousness of sin,
the veil of matter now so thin.

**O Guru Ma, your Presence near
the call of God I always hear,
your love consumes my every fear,
you and Lanello always here.**

8. Guru Ma, I am willing to transcend any image of you created while you were in embodiment, either by myself or other people.

O Guru Ma, I'm free at last,
transmuted, burdens of the past,
as daisies grow on vistas vast,
this is the life of everlast.

**O Guru Ma, your Presence near
the call of God I always hear,
your love consumes my every fear,
you and Lanello always here.**

9. Guru Ma, I am willing to transcend any image of you and myself that holds me back from qualifying for my ascension.

O Guru Ma, it is a treat,
to visit your Divine Retreat,
on Titicaca's waters sweet,
you and Lanello do me greet.

**O Guru Ma, your Presence near
the call of God I always hear,
your love consumes my every fear,
you and Lanello always here.**

Part 3

1. Guru Ma, help me let go of all self-images that are based on conditions on earth and support the image of myself as an unascended person.

O Guru Ma, with you I see,
that my life is not all for me,
it is my new reality,
that I am here to set all free.

> **O Guru Ma, your Presence near
> the call of God I always hear,
> your love consumes my every fear,
> you and Lanello always here.**

2. Guru Ma, help me free myself from any image of myself that I do not see and that is keeping me from my ascension.

> O Guru Ma, I have the will,
> for Summit of Ascension's Hill,
> desires of ego falling still,
> as love for God my mind does fill.

> **O Guru Ma, your Presence near
> the call of God I always hear,
> your love consumes my every fear,
> you and Lanello always here.**

3. Guru Ma, I want to stay attuned to you in your ascended state so that I can follow along with your growth.

> O Guru Ma, your wisdom's sphere,
> my path in life becoming clear,
> my ego cannot interfere,
> my inner voice I always hear.

> **O Guru Ma, your Presence near
> the call of God I always hear,
> your love consumes my every fear,
> you and Lanello always here.**

4. Guru Ma, help me discover what it means that you were the example of the embodied guru at the end of the Piscean age.

O Guru Ma, we still the mind,
you show me love of every kind,
serenity I surely find,
I see beyond the daily grind.

**O Guru Ma, your Presence near
the call of God I always hear,
your love consumes my every fear,
you and Lanello always here.**

5. Guru Ma, I am surrendering any image I have of you, and I want you to give me the help I need in order to qualify for my ascension.

O Guru Ma, intentions pure,
I'm going home with you for sure,
the world has lost its last allure,
in your heart I am now secure.

**O Guru Ma, your Presence near
the call of God I always hear,
your love consumes my every fear,
you and Lanello always here.**

6. Guru Ma, I am willing to empty my mind of all images and experience your living Presence as an ascended master.

O Guru Ma, your healing light,
pierces my soul's darkest night,
your mandala a healing sight,
as I ascend to lofty height.

> O Guru Ma, your Presence near
> the call of God I always hear,
> your love consumes my every fear,
> you and Lanello always here.

7. Guru Ma, I give up all tendency to intellectualize about how you are as an ascended master or to project any image upon you.

> O Guru Ma, such peace within,
> it truly makes my atoms spin,
> beyond the consciousness of sin,
> the veil of matter now so thin.

> **O Guru Ma, your Presence near**
> **the call of God I always hear,**
> **your love consumes my every fear,**
> **you and Lanello always here.**

8. Guru Ma, I am opening my mind and heart, emptying it of my previous images so that I can have a direct experience of your Presence as an ascended master.

> O Guru Ma, I'm free at last,
> transmuted, burdens of the past,
> as daisies grow on vistas vast,
> this is the life of everlast.

> **O Guru Ma, your Presence near**
> **the call of God I always hear,**
> **your love consumes my every fear,**
> **you and Lanello always here.**

9. Guru Ma, help me have the direct experience of you as an ascended master so that I can fully accept that the path you taught leads to the ascension.

> O Guru Ma, it is a treat,
> to visit your Divine Retreat,
> on Titicaca's waters sweet,
> you and Lanello do me greet.
>
> **O Guru Ma, your Presence near**
> **the call of God I always hear,**
> **your love consumes my every fear,**
> **you and Lanello always here.**

Part 4

1. Guru Ma, help me see when my dweller is whispering in my ear all of the reasons why I cannot take the last step into the ascended state.

> O Guru Ma, with you I see,
> that my life is not all for me,
> it is my new reality,
> that I am here to set all free.
>
> **O Guru Ma, your Presence near**
> **the call of God I always hear,**
> **your love consumes my every fear,**
> **you and Lanello always here.**

2. Guru Ma, help me see through any cleaver arguments, whether thought up by myself or other people, for why your book cannot be genuine, why you could not have been a genuine guru or why you could not have ascended.

> O Guru Ma, I have the will,
> for Summit of Ascension's Hill,
> desires of ego falling still,
> as love for God my mind does fill.
>
> **O Guru Ma, your Presence near**
> **the call of God I always hear,**
> **your love consumes my every fear,**
> **you and Lanello always here.**

3. Guru Ma, help me tune in to the cosmic cycles behind the release of your book and the future work you and Lanello intend to do for humankind.

> O Guru Ma, your wisdom's sphere,
> my path in life becoming clear,
> my ego cannot interfere,
> my inner voice I always hear.
>
> **O Guru Ma, your Presence near**
> **the call of God I always hear,**
> **your love consumes my every fear,**
> **you and Lanello always here.**

4. Guru Ma, help me fully internalize the lesson of how I can multiply everything I have received from the ascended masters.

O Guru Ma, we still the mind,
you show me love of every kind,
serenity I surely find,
I see beyond the daily grind.

**O Guru Ma, your Presence near
the call of God I always hear,
your love consumes my every fear,
you and Lanello always here.**

5. Guru Ma, help me fully multiply everything I have received from you and Lanello so I can help open the way for the work you intend to do in the future.

O Guru Ma, intentions pure,
I'm going home with you for sure,
the world has lost its last allure,
in your heart I am now secure.

**O Guru Ma, your Presence near
the call of God I always hear,
your love consumes my every fear,
you and Lanello always here.**

6. Guru Ma, help me fully grasp how clever my dweller can be in presenting me with a seemingly watertight argument for rejecting the guru.

O Guru Ma, your healing light,
pierces my soul's darkest night,
your mandala a healing sight,
as I ascend to lofty height.

> O Guru Ma, your Presence near
> the call of God I always hear,
> your love consumes my every fear,
> you and Lanello always here.

7. Guru Ma, help me fully grasp that I cannot win my ascension without tuning in to the Presence of an ascended master and then multiplying what I receive from that master.

> O Guru Ma, such peace within,
> it truly makes my atoms spin,
> beyond the consciousness of sin,
> the veil of matter now so thin.

> **O Guru Ma, your Presence near**
> **the call of God I always hear,**
> **your love consumes my every fear,**
> **you and Lanello always here.**

8. Guru Ma, help me discover which ascended master is my personal master and thus the key to my ascension.

> O Guru Ma, I'm free at last,
> transmuted, burdens of the past,
> as daisies grow on vistas vast,
> this is the life of everlast.

> **O Guru Ma, your Presence near**
> **the call of God I always hear,**
> **your love consumes my every fear,**
> **you and Lanello always here.**

9. Guru Ma, help me accelerate my attunement with you to a higher level. Help me know myself so that I might truly know you.

> O Guru Ma, it is a treat,
> to visit your Divine Retreat,
> on Titicaca's waters sweet,
> you and Lanello do me greet.
>
> **O Guru Ma, your Presence near**
> **the call of God I always hear,**
> **your love consumes my every fear,**
> **you and Lanello always here.**

Sealing:

In the name of the Divine Mother, I fully accept that the power of these calls is used to set free the Ma-ter light, so it can outpicture the perfect vision of Christ for my own life, for all people and for the planet. In the name I AM THAT I AM, it is done! Amen.

29 | DECREE TO GURU MA

NOTE: *A decree is a tool given by the ascended masters. It is designed to help us invoke the spiritual light from a particular master. This decree is given by Guru Ma in order to help us increase our attunement with her. You give a decree by reading it aloud. A decree can be given fast and in a rhythmic way that is very efficient for invoking light. For further instructions on how to give decrees, see www.transcendencetoolbox.com.*

In the name of the I AM THAT I AM, Jesus Christ, I call to the Ascended Master Guru Ma to manifest your Presence in my life and help me transcend my personal limitations so that I can bring the gift that I came to earth to release. I especially ask for your help and intercession with . . . [Make personal calls]

1. O Guru Ma, with you I see,
that my life is not all for me,
it is my new reality,
that I am here to set all free.

Refrain:

**O Guru Ma, your Presence near
the call of God I always hear,
your love consumes my every fear,
you and Lanello always here.**

2. O Guru Ma, I have the will,
for Summit of Ascension's Hill,
desires of ego falling still,
as love for God my mind does fill.

**O Guru Ma, your Presence near
the call of God I always hear,
your love consumes my every fear,
you and Lanello always here.**

3. O Guru Ma, your wisdom's sphere,
my path in life becoming clear,
my ego cannot interfere,
my inner voice I always hear.

**O Guru Ma, your Presence near
the call of God I always hear,
your love consumes my every fear,
you and Lanello always here.**

4. O Guru Ma, we still the mind,
you show me love of every kind,
serenity I surely find,
I see beyond the daily grind.

**O Guru Ma, your Presence near
the call of God I always hear,
your love consumes my every fear,
you and Lanello always here.**

5. O Guru Ma, intentions pure,
I'm going home with you for sure,
the world has lost its last allure,
in your heart I am now secure.

**O Guru Ma, your Presence near
the call of God I always hear,
your love consumes my every fear,
you and Lanello always here.**

6. O Guru Ma, your healing light,
pierces my soul's darkest night,
your mandala a healing sight,
as I ascend to lofty height.

**O Guru Ma, your Presence near
the call of God I always hear,
your love consumes my every fear,
you and Lanello always here.**

7. O Guru Ma, such peace within,
it truly makes my atoms spin,
beyond the consciousness of sin,
the veil of matter now so thin.

**O Guru Ma, your Presence near
the call of God I always hear,
your love consumes my every fear,
you and Lanello always here.**

8. O Guru Ma, I'm free at last,
transmuted, burdens of the past,
as daisies grow on vistas vast,
this is the life of everlast.

**O Guru Ma, your Presence near
the call of God I always hear,
your love consumes my every fear,
you and Lanello always here.**

9. O Guru Ma, it is a treat,
to visit your Divine Retreat,
on Titicaca's waters sweet,
you and Lanello do me greet.

**O Guru Ma, your Presence near
the call of God I always hear,
your love consumes my every fear,
you and Lanello always here.**

Sealing:

In the name of the Divine Mother, I fully accept that the power of these calls is used to set free the Ma-ter light, so it can outpicture the perfect vision of Christ for my own life, for all people and for the planet. In the name I AM THAT I AM, it is done! Amen.

GLOSSARY

Akasha, Akashic records
An energy of a higher vibration than anything else in the material realm. It serves as a recording device, recording everything that has ever happened in the material world. People with developed faculties can read the Akashic records. In the future, it will be possible to read them with technological devices.

Angel
A self-aware being that is not created to take physical embodiment. Angels serve in a variety of capacities, the most commonly known for us is as messengers who deliver a message from the spiritual realm to human beings. Another important function is angels who protect us against lower energies or dark forces.

Anti-christ
The consciousness of separation and duality. This consciousness forms a filter that distorts perception in such a way that it seems plausible that we are separate beings, separated from God, from each other and from the material universe. The more firmly beings are trapped in this

consciousness, the more real the illusion of separation seems to them. They will be acting as if they truly are separate beings, meaning they will believe that what they do to others will not affect themselves. This is the origin of man's inhumanity to man and the origin of evil. Human beings can be trapped in this consciousness, but so can non-material beings, forming the dark forces.

Archangel, Archeia

Angels are organized into bands, and each band is led by an archangel. Each archangel has a feminine complement, called an archeia. There is such a pair for each of the seven rays, but there are also other bands of angels.

Ascended Master

Normally refers to a being who was embodied as a human being on earth and who, often after many embodiments, qualified for the process of the ascension. The term can also be used more broadly to refer to all beings in the spiritual realm, even those who have not taken embodiment in the material world.

Ascension

A process whereby a being evolves to the self-awareness represented by the full Christ consciousness. In this state of consciousness, one can see through all of the lies created by the illusion of separation and duality. One sees the underlying reality that nothing can be separated from the Creator and that all self-aware beings are extensions of the Creator. One therefore seeks to raise all life, instead of seeking to raise oneself as a separate being. After a being ascends, it resides permanently in the spiritual realm and does not have to reembody.

Astral Plane
Everything is made from energy, and energy is a continuum of vibrations. There are certain divisions of this energy continuum, for example the material universe is made from vibrations within a certain spectrum. The material universe has four divisions: the etheric (identity) level, the mental level, the emotional level and the physical level.

The emotional level itself has further divisions, and the lowest of these are created when people engage in negative emotions, such as fear, anger and hatred. The astral plane is a division within the emotional realm, and it resembles the visions of hell that people have had throughout the ages.

Aquarian Age
There is a precession of astrological cycles, lasting approximately 2,150 years each. The previous age was the Age of Pisces, for which Jesus was the spiritual master. For the Aquarian age, the ascended master Saint Germain is the master. According to Saint Germain, the Aquarian age was officially inaugurated on March 22, 2010.

Aura
An energy field surrounding the human body. There are levels of the aura, corresponding to the levels of the material realm. You have an identity body, a mental body and an emotional body beyond the physical body.

Carnal mind
Sometimes used by ascended masters to refer to the entire lower consciousness, including the ego. Can also be used more specifically to refer to that part of the subconscious mind that is

designed to take care of the functions of the physical body. This includes certain basic instincts, such as protection, food and propagation. The carnal mind will seek to satisfy these needs without any regard for long-term interests and thus needs to be under the control of your conscious mind.

Causal Body
An energy "body" surrounding your I AM Presence. It stores all of the attainment gained and the lessons learned from all of your embodiments. When you raise your consciousness sufficiently, you can make use of this attainment for fulfilling your divine plan.

Catch-22
Described by the popular saying "you can't get there from here." It is a seemingly impossible situation that you cannot get out of. The ascended masters use this to refer to the mechanisms created through the illusion of separation and duality. The mind of anti-christ creates innumerable catch-22s in order to stop or slow down our spiritual growth. They are always based on an illusion, which means you can transcend them by changing your perspective. Note that a catch-22 often appears as a problem that you have to solve. The problem has no solution so the real solution is to walk away from the struggle.

Chakra
A focal point within your aura. There are seven major chakras, corresponding to each of the seven spiritual rays. If your chakras are pure, high-frequency energy from your I AM Presence can stream through them, and this gives you maximum creative powers. If your chakras are polluted, the stream of higher energies is reduced. Instead, the chakras can become open doors for lower energies to enter your aura. Severely polluted chakras can open you to energies from the astral plane.

Chela, chelaship
A Sanskrit word that is often translated as "slave." This refers to Indian spiritual tradition, where a person makes him- or herself the virtual slave of a spiritual teacher, or guru, who will thereby expose the student's ego. Used by the ascended masters to refer to a sincere student, who is willing to submit to the disciplines of the spiritual path, designed to expose the ego.

Chohan
For each of the seven spiritual rays, there is an ascended master who serves as the leader or main teacher. This spiritual office is called the "Chohan."

Christ
In its broadest sense, this refers to the basic consciousness out of which everything in the world of form is created. The purpose is to maintain the oneness between the Creator and its creation. This is especially relevant for beings with free will who have the option to descend into the illusion of separation, thereby believing they are separated from their source. The Christ consciousness ensures that no matter how far you descend into separation, you always have the option to return to oneness with the Creator. Because the Christ consciousness is within everything that is created, you can never go to a place where you are unreachable for Christ.

In a more specific sense, Christ refers to a being who has overcome the illusion of separation and has attained the Christ consciousness. There are degrees of Christ consciousness.

Christ Self
A mediator sent by ascended masters to assist beings who have become trapped in separation and duality. Most people know their Christ selves as intuition or the "still, small voice within." The Christ self does not actually tell you what choices to make.

It seeks to give you a frame of reference for making better choices. The Christ self will not necessarily give you an ultimate or absolute truth. It will give you an insight that is a bit higher than your present state of consciousness.

Christ discernment
The ability to see through the innumerable illusions created through the consciousness of separation and duality. Also the ability to see the underlying oneness behind all visible phenomena.

Christhood
When a being has attained the Christ consciousness, that being is said to have put on Christhood.

Conscious You
The core of your lower being. It is the Conscious You that descends from the spiritual realm as an extension of your I AM Presence. It is the conscious you that is the seat of your free will. You make choices based on the perception you have. It is possible for the Conscious You to have pure perception, which means it serves as an open door for the I AM Presence. When beings go into separation, the Conscious You projects itself into an outer self or role, and it now perceives everything through the filter of that separate self. It will often make choices as if it really were a separate being.

The Conscious You is and will always remain pure awareness. This means that while the Conscious You can project itself into any role it chooses, it can never lose the ability to extricate itself from that role and attain the Christ consciousness in which it can say with Jesus: "I and my father (my I AM Presence) are one."

Creator
The being who created the particular world of form in which we exist. There are other worlds of forms created by other Creators. A Creator must create a world of form out of its own Being, meaning the Creator experiences everything that happens in a given world.

Dark forces
Beings who have become trapped in the illusion of separation and duality. Many such beings reside in the astral plane. Everything in the material universe is sustained by a stream of energy from a higher realm. When you begin to deliberately harm other self-aware beings, you are cut off from receiving energy from a higher realm. You can sustain an existence only by stealing energy from beings in the material realm. This means that dark forces can continue to exist only by stealing energy from humans, and they do this by getting us to misqualify energy through lower emotions and selfish acts.

Dark forces can take over the minds of human beings (if people let them), and most of the warfare and crime seen on earth is caused by dark forces. They do this by agitating people to violate others, and the pain caused releases energy that the dark forces can use to sustain themselves.

Decree
A spiritual technique for invoking high-frequency energy from the spiritual realm and directing it into specific conditions on the personal or planetary level. A decree is a worded expression, usually in rhyme, that is spoken aloud with great power and authority.

Divine Plan
A plan for what you want to accomplish in this embodiment. This includes the spiritual gift you want to bring to earth, experiences you want to have, lessons you want to learn and karma you want to balance. Often, this means there are certain people you want to meet and with whom you want to engage in various types of relationships.

Duality, duality consciousness
When the Conscious You sees with pure perception, it sees the underlying reality that all life is one and came from the same source. The duality consciousness obscures this oneness, and it makes it seem like matter is separated from spirit, humans are separated from God and people are separated from each other.

Duality also implies a negative polarity between two opposites that work against each other, one seeking to annihilate the other. Duality always involves two opposing sides, and there is usually a value judgment attached to them, making one good and the other evil.

Duality is always an illusion because nothing can change or destroy the oneness of all life. Duality can exist only as an illusion in the minds of self-aware beings. As long as you are blinded by duality, you cannot attain Christ consciousness and thus cannot ascend.

Ego
An element in the psyche that is created when the Conscious You descends into the illusion of separation and duality. The Conscious You is pure awareness so it cannot act as a separate being. It can step into a separate sense of self, and when it perceives the world through the perception filter of that self, it can believe that it really is a separate being. What makes this distorted perception seem real is the ego.

Emotional body
An aspect of your aura/mind that houses your emotional energies.

Etheric body
An aspect of your aura/mind that houses your sense of identity.

Fall, Fall of Man
In its broadest sense, the term refers to the process whereby a self-aware being descends into the consciousness of separation. Before the fall, you will see yourself as a being who is not isolated but is connected to something greater than yourself. After the fall, you will be convinced that you are a separate being who has been abandoned or punished by God.

After the fall, you will find it difficult to take responsibility for your own growth. Because the fall was caused by your own choices, it can only be undone through your own choices. When you think you are a separate being, you think you can do whatever you want without considering the consequences for others. This causes you to engage in an ongoing struggle against other people, which can lead to a state of mind where you think you have to fight against other people, the matter universe or even God.

This state of mind becomes a catch-22 because as long as you will not accept that you have created your own situation as a result of your own choices, you cannot change those choices. Instead, you are seeking to create a change in your situation by forcing other people, the matter world or even God to come under your control. You are seeking to change the splinter in the eyes of others while ignoring the beam in your own eye.

Fallen beings or fallen angels
In its broadest sense, refers to all beings who are blinded by the duality consciousness. The masters often use this more specifically to refer to a group of beings who fell in a previous sphere. These beings had attained considerable attainment before they fell, which means they often feel superior to the beings who started their existence in this world. They are also more sophisticated in terms of being able to manipulate others and more aggressive in seeking to control others.

In world history, fallen beings have often become powerful but abusive leaders, and obvious examples are Hitler, Stalin and Mao. Many fallen beings hold important positions without visibly abusing their power and thus have a huge influence in society. Their main characteristic is that they are absolutely sure that they are right because they feel they are superior to most people on earth. There are also fallen beings who are not in physical embodiment, but who reside in the astral plane or the mental realm.

Fallen consciousness
The consciousness of the fallen beings. In its broadest sense, the illusion of separation and duality. It can also refer more specifically to the consciousness of feeling superior to others, wanting to have special privileges or wanting others to follow you.

The main characteristic of the fallen consciousness is the belief that the ends can justify the means. This often causes people to believe they are engaged in an epic struggle and that it is their duty to use all means available to eradicate what they have defined as evil. The underlying belief is that you have the right to define what is good and evil, because you have a godlike status.

Glossary

Four levels of the material realm
Everything is made from energy. The entire world of form is made from energies of various vibrational qualities. There is a continuum of vibrations, ranging from the highest level, the level below the Creator, to the lowest. In between, one can define several divisions, compartments or octaves of vibrations. For example, one major division is between the spiritual realm and the material realm.

There are several divisions in the spiritual realm. In the material realm there are four divisions. They are, from higher to lower vibrations:

- the etheric or identity level

- the mental level

- the emotional level

- the physical level

Four lower bodies, four levels of the mind
Corresponding to the four levels of the material universe, the masters sometimes say that we humans have four lower bodies: the identity body, the mental body, the emotional body and the physical body.

The masters also talk about four levels of the mind:

- the identity mind houses our deepest sense of identity (who we are and what we can do)

- the mental mind houses our thoughts (how we can do things)

- the emotional mind houses our feelings (why we want to/have to do something)

- the physical mind relates to the needs of the body.

Free will

The masters teach that it is extremely important to understand free will, especially in relation to the duality consciousness. Free will is the basic law that guides the function of the material realm. For example, the earth was created in a much higher state than what we see today. There was originally no lack of resources, no imbalances in nature and no diseases.

These limiting conditions have been created because a majority of human beings used their free will to descend into duality. Nature outpictures as material conditions what is in the consciousness of a majority of the people. Human beings were created to have dominion over the earth, and the Ma-ter Light can only take on the images we hold in our identity, mental, emotional and physical minds.

The important point about free will is that we have the right to, at any time, transcend our previous choices. God and the ascended masters will never seek to stop us from transcending previous choices. It is only the ego and the dark forces who will seek to make us believe we are bound by past choices.

Guru

A Sanskrit word for teacher or master.

Garden of Eden

The deeper symbolism behind the Biblical concept of the Garden of Eden is that it represents a schoolroom in which self-aware beings are being prepared to take embodiment on earth. The "God" mentioned in the Bible was the Ascended

Master Lord Maitreya, who was the "headmaster" of the mystery school.

Students were given graded lessons, and only more advanced students were meant to take the lesson represented by the duality consciousness. A number of beings in the mystery school had fallen in a previous sphere. These beings are symbolized by the Serpent, and they deceived some students into taking the initiation of duality before they were prepared by the teacher. This initiation is symbolized by the "fruit of the knowledge of good and evil," which makes beings think they are like gods and can define what is good and evil without the Christ consciousness.

The symbolism is that the fallen beings have deceived most people on earth into believing in the dualistic lies. This is what causes all conflict and struggle on earth. The only solution is that a critical mass of people follow the true path of initiation and attain Christ consciousness. The real purpose of the ascended masters is to help us do this.

Great White Brotherhood
Another name for all ascended beings. The term "white" does not refer to race, but to the fact that ascended masters radiate a white light.

I AM Presence
Your higher or spiritual self. The Conscious You is an extension of your I AM Presence. Your highest potential is to achieve identification with the Presence so you serve as an open door for it to express itself in the material world. Your spiritual identity and individuality is anchored in your I AM Presence, which means it could never be destroyed no matter what happens to you on earth.

Judgment

There is a group of ascended masters, called the Great Karmic Board, who oversee the overall planetary growth. One of their tasks is to determine which lifestreams are allowed to embody on earth and for how long. When a being falls into duality, it is assigned a certain time to turn around and start the path back to God. If a being violates the free will of other beings, this time can be shortened. The being is then judged by its own actions. The ascended masters also teach that it is lawful for people in embodiment to call forth the judgment of fallen beings. If such beings will not change, then the Karmic Board can authorize their removal from embodiment.

The concept of judgment is not the same as the kind of value-laden judgment exercised by beings trapped in the duality consciousness. Such beings judge based on their own state of consciousness, often labeling as evil anything they do not understand or agree with. This is what Jesus called judging after appearances.

Initiation

A gradual process whereby you raise your consciousness towards the Christ consciousness. This can be an individual process, where you are guided from within, but it usually involves you following an outer teaching or even a guru or organization.

Karma

Everything is energy. Whatever we do – even what we think and feel – is done by using energy. We receive this energy as a gift from the I AM Presence. The energy we receive is pure, but we will qualify it according to the contents of the four levels of our minds. We are responsible for our use of energy, and misqualified energy becomes stored in both our auras and in the Akashic records as karma. In order for us to ascend, we must balance all energy by raising it to its original vibration.

The masters have also given a deeper understanding of karma in which karma is the images we hold in the four levels of our minds. Because we see everything through the filter of these energies, we are constantly qualifying energy. We have the option to, at any time, examine our mental images and transcend limiting images—which is truly the path to Christhood where we accept our divine identity.

This gives us two ways to balance karma. We can invoke spiritual energy through decrees and invocations and requalify the energy from our present level of consciousness. This is possible, but it is a slow process because we are constantly making more karma. The faster way is to work on transcending the mental images so we stop making new karma. Once we achieve this, we can then balance all remaining karma much faster because our higher state of consciousness allows us to invoke more energy.

Lifestream
A term used for an individual self-aware being. It is often used instead of "soul," as a lifestream refers to parts of our beings that are beyond the soul, including the I AM Presence and the lineage of spiritual beings leading all the way to the Creator.

Light
Usually refers to spiritual light, meaning energy that vibrates at higher levels than the energy that makes up the material realm.

Living Christ
A person who has attained some level of Christ consciousness while still in embodiment.

Mass consciousness
Every human being has an aura, a personal energy field. The entire planet also has an aura, and within it we find a combination

of the individual energy fields of all people embodying on earth. There are certain divisions within this collective or mass consciousness, but all people are affected by the greater whole to some degree. There is a stage on the spiritual path where our main task is to pull ourselves above the magnetic pull of the mass consciousness so we can express our individuality.

Ma-ter Light,
The cosmic base energy out of which everything that has form is created. It has no form in itself, but has the capacity to take on any form. It also has a certain basic form of consciousness, which among other characteristics has a built-in striving for its source, the Creator.

The Ma-ter light has been stepped down in vibration to create succeeding spheres. We live in the seventh of these spheres, and the six previous ones have all ascended, becoming part of the spiritual realm.

Messenger
A person who has been trained to receive teachings and dictations from the ascended realm through the agency of the Holy Spirit.

Mystery School
An environment designed to present self-aware beings with initiations aimed at raising their consciousness. It is usually overseen by an ascended master of high attainment.

Path
The masters teach that the ultimate goal of life on earth is to manifest the Christ consciousness, which allows us to permanently ascend to the spiritual realm and become ascended masters. We are originally created at a much lower state of consciousness, and thus we follow a gradual path that raises our

consciousness to the ultimate level. There are 144 different levels of consciousness that are possible for people on earth. You can ascend only after reaching the 144th level.

Rays, or spiritual rays
Everything is made from energy. Even Einstein's famous equation, $E=mc^2$, says that matter is created from a very high form of energy that is reduced in vibration by a factor (the speed of light squared). The masters teach that while Einstein's theory is basically correct, there are seven of these reduction factors. The material universe is made from seven types of spiritual energies that are combined to form all phenomena in the material realm. These types of energy are called rays or spiritual rays. There is a total of 15 rays used to build the entire world of form.

Retreats
Many ascended masters have a spiritual retreat that exists in the etheric or identity realm. We can make a call to go to such retreats in our finer bodies while our physical bodies sleep at night. A retreat is usually located over a physical location on earth, yet because the retreat is in the etheric realm, it cannot be detected through physical means. A retreat focuses certain spiritual energies that are released to earth. It can also be a focus for giving specific teachings to people who are ready.

Sanat Kumara
An ascended master of high attainment. In a previous age, so many people on earth had descended so far into the duality consciousness that the Karmic Board and other cosmic councils had determined that the earth was no longer a viable platform for growth and thus would be allowed to self-destruct. Sanat Kumara then came with 144,000 lifestreams from Venus in order to hold the spiritual balance until enough people on earth had been raised in consciousness to where they could

hold the balance for the planet. Many of the 144,000 lifestreams that came with Sanat Kumara are still in embodiment and they are often very spiritual people with a great desire to help other people or improve the world. There can come a point where such people will hold back their own ascensions unless they let go of the desire to help or change others.

Serpent

A symbol for a certain state of consciousness that induces doubt into our minds. The specific purpose is to create a division in our beings so we start to distrust our divine direction, our intuition, our own inner knowing and our spiritual teachers. Can also refer to a specific group of fallen beings.

Serpentine lie, plot

The primary serpentine lie is that the Christ consciousness either does not exist or is not attainable for us. Instead, the ultimate reality is the duality consciousness, in which we set ourselves up as gods who believe we have the right and the capacity to define good and evil by ourselves. This inevitably causes a relative definition of good and evil, because good is seen as that which confirms our existing beliefs and desires whereas anything that challenges them is labeled as evil.

The serpentine plot is to either get us so paralyzed by doubt that we blindly follow the fallen beings, or to get us so blinded by spiritual pride that we really do believe we are always right. In the latter case, we are also following the leadership of the fallen consciousness, which is in complete opposition to the Christ. We now seek to raise the ego to a godlike status, instead of seeking the Christ consciousness as a means to raising all life. One aspect of the serpentine plot is to get us to believe that even God can be fit into a dualistic world view. God is portrayed as the opposite of evil or the devil.

We are tempted to believe that in order to further God's cause, it is acceptable to do evil, including killing other people. History has many examples of how people have been deceived into fighting these epic battles against a self-defined evil. In order to win this final victory for good, it is necessary and justified to commit this ultimate act of destroying the enemy. In reality, such struggles only serve to misqualify more energy that feeds the dark forces and thus give them power to deceive people into continuing the endless struggle. The only way out is the Christ consciousness that sees the oneness of all life.

Sin
In ascended master terminology the same as karma, meaning misqualified energy that we need to balance before we can ascend.

Spiritual Rays
Everything is made from energy. Even Einstein's famous equation, $E=mc^2$, says that matter is created from a very high form of energy that is reduced in vibration by a factor (the speed of light squared). The masters teach that while Einstein's theory is basically correct, there are seven of these reduction factors. The material universe is made from seven types of spiritual energies that are combined to form all phenomena in the material realm. These types of energy are called rays or spiritual rays. There is a total of 15 rays used to build the entire world of form.

Soul
The ascended masters sometimes use this word as it is commonly used, namely as that part of our beings that reincarnates. However, the masters also give a deeper understanding, namely that it is the Conscious You that originally descended into embodiment. The soul is a vehicle that the Conscious You has

created in order to express itself in this world, and it is often highly affected by the duality consciousness.

Jesus' crucifixion is a symbol for the fact that the Conscious You is crucified (paralyzed) by its own creation. The soul cannot be raised up or perfected. The soul is made from limiting beliefs and misqualified energies. As the energies are requalified and as the Conscious You transcends the limiting beliefs, the soul gradually dies until the Conscious You gives up the Ghost of the final illusion of separation. The Conscious You can then claim its true identity as an extension of the I AM Presence and can ascend.

Spheres
The world of form was created by the Creator defining a spherical boundary and withdrawing its being into a singularity in the center of a void. The Creator then created a sphere in the void by using the Ma-ter light. The Creator defined structures in that sphere and projected self-aware extensions of itself into it. As these extensions grew in awareness, they raised the vibration of their sphere until it ascended and formed the first sphere in the spiritual realm. The Creator then created a second sphere, and the ascended masters from the first sphere then defined structures and sent extensions of their own beings into the second sphere.

This process of one sphere ascending and a new sphere being created has continued so that we now exist in the seventh such sphere. In the first three spheres, all beings ascended without going into the consciousness of separation and duality. In the fourth sphere, some beings refused to ascend and they became the first fallen beings. As the fourth sphere ascended, these fallen beings could not ascend, and thus they "fell" into the sixth sphere. Because the newly created sphere had a generally lower vibration, the fallen beings could still exist there.

Unascended being

A being that has not yet qualified for the ascension and thus cannot abide in the spiritual realm. This does not only refer to human beings in embodiment. There are unascended beings in all four realms of the material world. For example, many souls who have ties to the astral plane can descend there between embodiments or can become permanently stuck there, not being able to reembody. We human beings can make calls for the cutting free of all unascended beings, so they can move on to the next station on their path.

Violet flame

A spiritual energy that is especially efficient for transmuting karma or misqualified energy. Saint Germain received a cosmic dispensation to reveal the violet flame in the 1930s. Since then, ascended master students have been invoking it through decrees, invocations and affirmations.

The violet flame can be misused. Misqualified energy is caused by a limiting belief. The energy gradually accumulates in your aura, making you feel burdened. You can invoke the violet flame without changing the limiting belief, which will make you feel better in the short run. However, if you do not change the belief, you will continue to misqualify energy. If you continue to use the violet flame to transmute the energy, you are misusing Saint Germain's dispensation because you are not attaining long-term spiritual growth.

www.ingramcontent.com/pod-product-compliance
Lightning Source LLC
Chambersburg PA
CBHW030516230426
43665CB00010B/637